Management for Professionals

The Springer series *Management for Professionals* comprises high-level business and management books for executives. The authors are experienced business professionals and renowned professors who combine scientific background, best practice, and entrepreneurial vision to provide powerful insights into how to achieve business excellence.

More information about this series at http://www.springer.com/series/10101

Thomas Pyzdek

The Lean Healthcare Handbook

A Complete Guide to Creating Healthcare Workplaces

Second Edition

 Springer

Thomas Pyzdek
The Pyzdek Institute
Tucson, AZ, USA

ISSN 2192-8096   ISSN 2192-810X   (electronic)
Management for Professionals
ISBN 978-3-030-69903-1   ISBN 978-3-030-69901-7   (eBook)
https://doi.org/10.1007/978-3-030-69901-7

The first edition originally published as The Lean Healthcare Handbook: A Complete Guide to creating healthcare workplaces that maximize flow and minimize waste in 2018 by Atlantis Publishing.

This Springer imprint is published by the registered company Springer Nature Switzerland AG.
The registered company address is: Gewerbestrasse 11, 6330 Cham, Switzerland

Introduction

There is a better way to lead healthcare organizations: one that makes much more sense than the traditional methods taught in business schools. The Lean way of designing work involves all levels of the organization, from the leaders who create a culture of continuous improvement to the person actually doing the work. This book covers the following topics:

- The origins and drivers of Lean
- What is value?
- Waste and value
- Value streams, flow, push and pull systems
- Why it is important to move towards perfection
- Improving physical and logical work flow using spaghetti diagrams
- Mapping value streams
- Principles of work design
- Workplace organization and housekeeping
- Changing quickly from producing one product or service to producing another, or from treating one type of patient to treating another
- Continuous improvement and Kaizen
- Leveraging results

By using the approach described in this book you will be able to produce the same amount of value while using far fewer resources, which benefits all of your stakeholders and the environment as well. Or, you can produce much more with the resources you now have. This improved productivity can, in turn, be used to expand capacity, capture new markets and increase profitability.

I have seen many value streams that contain as much as 95% non-value added work, otherwise known as waste. A surprising number of value streams are actually 100% waste! That is, they are duplicating the work of another value stream in the firm while adding no additional value. For example, a financial company had two groups in two different locations performing the same audit on the same paperwork. As you undertake your Lean journey be prepared to be astounded at the amount of improvement you will see.

Contents

List of Figures

Part I

Lean Tools and Techniques

Introduction to Lean and Muda (Waste)

1

In this chapter, we provide a 10,000-foot overview of Lean healthcare. In subsequent chapters, we explore each topic in much greater depth. The purpose of the overview is to help you understand the big picture of what Lean healthcare is and where it came from.

The central challenge of leadership is to balance and align the interests of various stakeholders over both the short- and long-term. Lean is a method that helps leaders align customer satisfaction and employee satisfaction and personal fulfillment. As such it is much more than a set of technical tools. It is an invaluable way for leaders to operationalize their top-level vision, mission, and goals for all stakeholders. This is why many healthcare organizations are embracing Lean as their primary operating system.

Lean's origins date back to the post-WW II era in Japan. It was developed by Taiichi Ohno, a Toyota production executive, in response to a number of problems that plagued the Japanese industry. In fact, what we now refer to as "Lean" is based on the Toyota Production System. The main problem facing Toyota was that the domestic Japanese market did not need large numbers of identical cars or trucks. Smaller quantities and a lot of variety were, quite literally, the order of the day. Mass production techniques, which were developed by Henry Ford to economically produce long runs of nearly identical products, were ill-suited to the situation faced by Toyota. Today the conditions faced by Toyota in the late 1940s are common and Lean is being adopted by businesses all over the world as a way to improve efficiency and to serve customers better. Healthcare organizations, of course, deal with people who are all different. So Lean is perfect for healthcare.

1.1   What Is Lean?

A major focus of Lean is the ability to rapidly and automatically reconfigure organizations in response to changing needs of the market. Flexibility is the key. This flexibility is possible only if waste is systematically targeted and eliminated. In Lean, we address three broad categories of inefficiency:

1. Muda (waste)
2. Mura (unevenness)
3. Muri (overburden)

Waste comes from a variety of sources. It takes training to see waste in an operation. You will learn how to see waste as you go through this course. By the way, the word Lean was not used by Toyota. It was coined by American researchers who studied the Toyota approach in the 1990s.

Value Stream

So, what is the value stream anyway? The Lean Enterprise Institute defines a value stream as all activities, both value added and non-value added, required to bring a product from the raw material into the hands of the customer, a customer requirement from order to delivery, and a design from concept to launch. These are endpoints of processes. A value stream consists of product and service flows and information flows. Information initiates activity in the value stream and shows the status of the value stream. Value stream improvement usually begins at the door-to-door level within a facility, and then expands outward to eventually encompass the full value stream, including supplier and customer value streams. In healthcare, an example of this would be pre-treatment and post-discharge instructions to the patient and follow-up.

Thinking Lean

Lean is all about eliminating waste in value streams. To accomplish this, you must identify waste. Identifying waste is easier if you have more detailed knowledge about what kind of waste to look for. Then you can address the more manageable waste categories, rather than tackling all types of waste at one time. In Lean we are talking about process waste, not medical waste.

To be Lean we must eliminate waste of all kinds. This is easier to do if you know something about what kinds of waste exist.

This exercise will help you develop skill in identifying waste by telling you about useful waste categories. Here are some types of waste to look for:

1. *Over Processing.* Unnecessary processing waste includes things like asking the patient for the same information multiple times or giving the patient information that they do not need or cannot use.
2. *Transport.* Transportation waste involves moving patients for tests or procedures as well as the movement of specimens, medications, equipment, and so on. Although transportation sometimes cannot be avoided, it does not add value and should be minimized.
3. *Over producing.* Overproducing means producing too much of something, or producing something before it is needed. With Lean, we try to make what is needed at the time that it is needed.
4. *Waiting.* Waiting wastes the most precious thing of all, time. Waiting is endemic in healthcare. Patients wait to get into the exam room, then wait for the physician, then for the discharge process, then for the meds they need. There is no end to the amount of waiting.
5. *Inventory.* Inventory is having more than the absolute minimum needed to do the job. For example, ordering more supplies than are needed in the short term. Inventory is related to overproducing. However, overproducing creates the inventory in-house (Work-In-Process, or WIP, inventory) while inventory also includes supplies you purchase.
6. *Unnecessary Motion.* Unnecessary movement of employees such as looking for a needed form or piece of equipment is also waste. You must learn to look for processes that have people and things moving much more than they need to.
7. *Errors and Mistakes.* Mistakes and errors are serious problems in healthcare. The Leapfrog Group estimates that up to 440,000 Americans die annually from preventable hospital errors and mistakes.
8. *Unneeded Goods and Services.* In healthcare unneeded goods and services include things such as unnecessary tests or procedures. Not only does unnecessary medical testing not reduce one's risk for illness or death, it can create a "potential for harm," according to The Society of General Internal Medicine. In healthcare eliminating unnecessary tests and procedures is sometimes a challenge because there is money to be made by doing them. However, it is clearly unethical to do things to patients simply for the money!
9. *Wasted Human Potential.* The people attracted to the healthcare profession represent the best and the brightest and they have a great deal to offer. Perhaps the saddest waste is when people employed in healthcare are not utilized to the fullest. Their contributions are restricted, their ideas are ignored, and their skills are underutilized. Lean is all about maximizing the contributions of everyone in the organization.

Keep in mind that this is not a comprehensive list of waste, there is no such thing. Learn to ask if what is being done adds value for the patient and if it does not, think about ways to reduce or eliminate it. Lean is a journey of continuous improvement.

How to "Think Lean"

To "think Lean" is to declare war on Muda. To win the war on Muda you must learn to think Lean. Thinking Lean is to focus on Muda's opposite: value. Defining value means answering some questions.

- *What Is Customer Value*? What do customers want? What would customers willing to pay for? The answers to these questions define customer value. In healthcare, the customer is usually the patient. There are other stakeholders (e.g., payers) but ultimately it is the patient who receives care.
- *Processes*. By what processes are these values created? Processes add value by taking action on inputs and producing outputs that have greater value.
- *Activities*. How does each activity in the process help meet the wants and needs of the customer?
- *Value flow*. How can we make the value creation processes flow more efficiently?
- *Just in Time*. How can we be sure that we are producing only what is needed, when it is needed?
- *Perfection*. How can we become more perfect at creating value? Perfection is the ultimate goal of Lean Healthcare.

Summary of Thinking Lean
Thinking Lean involves answering five categories of questions:

1. Value
2. The value stream
3. Flow
4. Pull and
5. Perfection

These are the core principles of Lean.

Value

Value is what customers want or need, and are willing and able to pay for. This is not always easy to determine, especially in healthcare, but it must be done. For existing products and services use focus groups, surveys, and other methods described in this book. Most importantly, do not rely on internal sources! The definition of value must begin with the provider and customer jointly analyzing value and challenging old beliefs. Talk to customers rather than guessing about what they want. But go beyond this and study customers to see what they need that you can help them with. True innovation involves learning about customer needs that they do not even know they have! For example, not long ago it was believed by hospital workers that their responsibility began when patients came in the door of the hospital and ended when they left. It is now widely accepted that proper treatment requires work both before entering and after leaving the hospital.

Here is an example. A hospital wanted to improve the satisfaction of its in-patients. Surveys and one on one conversations were held to learn what patients wanted, and the hospital staff worked hard on the things that they learned. Later the hospital was surprised to learn that patients were expressing unhappiness with the hospital on social media. The reason? No one called them to follow-up after they went home. The hospital thought that the relevant patient experience ended upon discharge, but the patients thought otherwise. If the hospital nurse was asked to define value, chances are she would not think beyond her own workplace. In Lean training, you learn how to translate the "voice of the customer" (VOC) into useful internal requirements.

With your definition of value in hand, you now Evaluate which activities add value and which activities are Muda. The results are usually surprising. In many cases, most activities are not value added. Processes that are as high as 90% Muda are not uncommon.

Example

A Lean team working on improving the emergency department process conducted a test. Rather than meeting in a conference room, the team "met" in the ED on a busy evening; In Lean we call this "Going to the Gemba" (or "Going to the Genba").[1] In Japanese, it means the actual place or, specifically, shop floor and refers to the location where the actual work is performed. Each team member observed patients one at a time and logged their observations, along with time stamps. Later the team members each reported their results in a more traditional meeting in a conference room. The time patients were actually with a doctor or nurse, value added time, was only a tiny fraction of the time spent from entering the ED to leaving it. Most of the time was spent on waiting, filling out forms, trying to figure out what to do next, and other activities patients viewed as not what they came to the ED for in the first place.

Value Added and Non-value Added

Let us elaborate on the concepts of value added and non-value added. Non-value-added activities consume resources but do not create anything a customer wants and would willingly pay for. Value added activities are the opposite of this; they are activities that produce something the customer wants and would pay for willingly. Of course, patients cannot always know what types of tests or treatments they need. In part, it is up to the provider to honestly determine if an activity is value added or not. To the extent possible, they should do this by helping patients understand the purpose and risks of the care they are about to receive.

---

[1] In practice some people spell it one way, some the other way. For consistency, we will use Gemba in this book. You can find out more at bit.ly/2ddHJgO.

The A3 Report

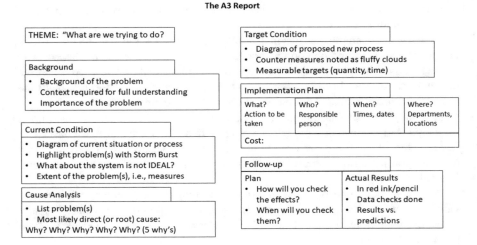

THEME: "What are we trying to do?"

Background
- Background of the problem
- Context required for full understanding
- Importance of the problem

Current Condition
- Diagram of current situation or process
- Highlight problem(s) with Storm Burst
- What about the system is not IDEAL?
- Extent of the problem(s), i.e., measures

Cause Analysis
- List problem(s)
- Most likely direct (or root) cause:
Why? Why? Why? Why? Why? (5 why's)

Target Condition
- Diagram of proposed new process
- Counter measures noted as fluffy clouds
- Measurable targets (quantity, time)

Implementation Plan

What? Action to be taken	Who? Responsible person	When? Times, dates	Where? Departments, locations

Cost:

Follow-up

Plan	Actual Results

• How will you check
  the effects?
• When will you check
  them?
	• In red ink/pencil
	• Data checks done
	• Results vs.
	  predictions

Fig. 1.1 Value stream mapping as A3 thinking

Value Stream Maps

Value stream maps are shown as pictures on a single sheet of paper no larger than 11-in. by 17-in. In the part of the world that uses the metric system, this size of paper is known as A3 and learning how to clearly present a complete idea or picture on one large sheet of paper is known as A3 thinking. The purpose of value stream mapping is to define value from the customer's viewpoint. When creating value stream maps, you begin with a map of the current state, then you apply the Lean toolkit to identify Muda in the current value stream and to design a process with much less Muda. At a later stage in the project, you map the Leaner future state process. If it is not possible to make all of the needed changes immediately, you develop a transition plan. Then the plan is implemented and the new Lean process validated. Value stream mapping is just one of several different types of flowcharting techniques that are taught in the Lean Healthcare Advisor training course offered by The Pyzdek Institute (Fig. 1.1).

Figure 1.2 is an example of a current state value stream map for an Emergency Department. All value stream maps are somewhat unique, but all share a common underlying design. This value stream map shows the activities that occur from the time a patient is *en route* to the ED until they are discharged or admitted to the hospital. Special symbols and lines are used to show things like transportation operations, inventory or waiting, information flows, processes and process data, and other information. The maps include a timeline showing the time spent on value added and non-value-added activities. When finished, the value stream map provides a comprehensive picture of the entire value stream.

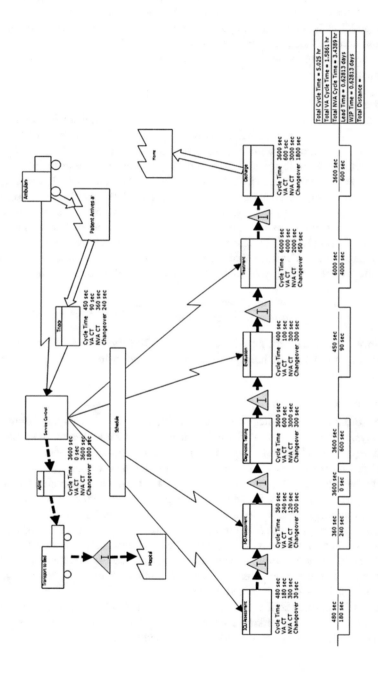

Fig. 1.2 Value stream map of an emergency department process before applying Lean

Value stream mapping and mapping symbols are covered in detail in Lean Healthcare Advisor training and in this book. For now you should just understand that it is possible to create a one-page drawing that conveys a vast amount of information about a value stream in an easily understood way. This makes it much easier to understand the value stream, see the waste, and know what to do to make improvements.

Takt Time

In Lean we pace all activity in the entire value stream to match the customer demand. A Lean concept called takt time helps us do this. Takt time is calculated by dividing the available work time in a short period of time, such as one workday, by the customer required volume for that time period. We want the value to flow to the customer as the customer needs it. Takt time is the key to value flow. If we produce too fast or too slowly, it is wasteful. When you calculate takt time you exclude non-working time, such as breaks. Takt time is used to create short-term work schedules for such purposes as staffing, scheduling machines, ordering materials, and so on. Equation (1.1) is a simple example of calculating takt time for a labor and delivery department of a hospital that delivers an average of 6000 babies/year. Since babies come whenever they want to, the takt time is based on a full 24-h day.

$$\text{takt} = \frac{\text{Available work time}}{\text{Customer required volume}} = \frac{24\text{ h}}{6000/_{365}} = 1.46\text{ h} \qquad (1.1)$$

Of course, babies will not pop out every 1.46 h like clockwork. You will learn about several tools that will help you deal with variation in demand as you read this book.

Spaghetti Diagrams

One source of Lean improvement is reducing wasted movement. Spaghetti diagrams map the physical movement of work through a process or value stream. In traditional "batch-and-queue" organizations, where work or customers wait for service, there is a lot of wasted movement as work units travel through the process. If you draw a line showing the way a part or person moves through a batch-and-queue value stream, it looks like a plate of spaghetti. Some people use push pins and colored yarn or string to make it even more dramatic looking. In any case, a spaghetti diagram is a drawing of the path a person or item takes through a physical process. The Lean route will look a lot different than the non-Lean route. The difference between the Lean route and the spaghetti route is Muda, or wasted movement (see Figs. 1.3 and 1.4). Note that different colors are often used to show the motion of different people, which might not be easy to see in black and white.

Figure 1.4 is the spaghetti diagram after Leaning out the process. In this book, you will learn methods for making changes like these. For now, just remember that unnecessary motion is waste that needs to be studied and eliminated.

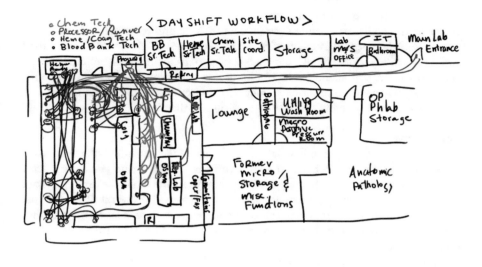

Findings: Heavy traffic and bottleneck in specimen progressing area. Technical workbenches spaced far apart when techs need to cover multiple areas, which results in overall excessive movemebt staff.

Fig. 1.3 Spaghetti diagram before Lean

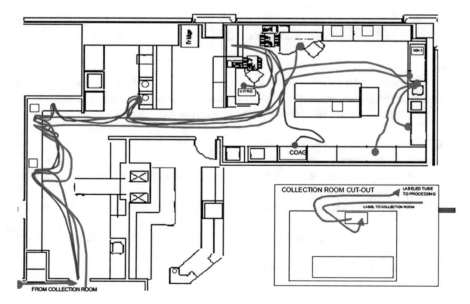

Fig. 1.4 Spaghetti diagram after Lean

Creative Thinking Is Important

When setting goals for a future state process, it is helpful to stretch the mind. One way to become inspired is to identify the absolute best in class performance for a particular activity. For example, the quickie lube joints' claim to exceptional value is that they can get you in and out in 15 min or less, much quicker than the old corner service station which often took a couple of hours or more. Sounds impressive, right? However, a pit crew can service a car in less than 7 s!

Value Flow

The key to value flow is to break the mental bonds of the batch-and-queue mindset. Batch and queue is everywhere. At your favorite restaurant where you are handed a little gadget to alert you when your table is ready. At the airport where you move from one line to another and another and show the same ID several times. At your physician's office where it is made clear to you that your time is less important than the doctor's time. On the phone where you find yourself on hold waiting for a tech support agent.

Lean work processes are designed to create flow. Flow focuses on the object of value. The product, design, service, order, etc. that is being created for the customer. In the case of healthcare, the object of value is often the patient. The focus is not on the department, the supplier, the hospital, or any other facet of the enterprise or its operation. All work practices are carefully evaluated and rethought to eliminate stoppages of any kind so the object of value proceeds smoothly and continuously to the customer.

Flow requires that the whole value stream be considered simultaneously. Processes within the value stream are designed and arranged to maximize flow. Creating these maps is discussed later in this book (See Value Stream maps below.)

5S

Flow is easier to achieve if the workplace is properly designed and maintained. Lean begins with a safe and well-organized workplace. In Lean we use 5S to help organize the workplace. Here are brief descriptions of each of the five S's:

SORT. Clearly distinguish what is necessary to do the job from what is not. Eliminate the unnecessary.

SET IN order. Put needed items in their correct place to allow for easy accessibility and retrieval.

SHINE. Keep the workplace clean and clear of clutter. This promotes safety as well as efficiency.

STANDARDIZED cleanup. Develop an approach to maintaining a clean and orderly work environment.

SUSTAIN. Make a habit of maintaining your workplace.

Later we discuss each of the 5S's in greater depth.

Constraint (Bottleneck) Management

In Lean a constraint is any step in the process that cannot produce at a rate equal to or greater than takt time.[2] Constraints, or bottlenecks, require special attention. A constraint is that step or part of the process that limits the throughput of the entire value stream. As such, constraints determine how much output the value stream can produce. When a constraint is not producing, the *value stream* is not producing. Every effort needs to be focused on assuring that:

- The constraint has sufficient resources to keep running
- Every unit supplied to the constraint is of acceptable quality
- Every unit produced by the constraint is of acceptable quality
- The constraint is operated in as efficient a manner as is possible

Level Loading

Level loading is the process of generating a schedule that is level, stable, smooth, and responsive to market demand. The goal of level loading is to make the same quantity of an item every day. An example in healthcare would be for a physician practice to see the same numbers of given categories of patients every day, such as walk-ins, routine physicals, and so on. Level loading is driven by Takt time. Very briefly, a level-loaded schedule can be obtained as follows:

- For each "flow object" such as a patient or a prescription, list patient identification information, relevant numbers, and other data, daily quantity needed, and the Takt time. A healthcare example would list things like types of patient visits or types of emergency department cases typically seen.
- Then sort the list by the quantity needed and Takt time. This is your level-loaded schedule.

Of course, this does not always work as simply in healthcare as it does in other businesses! For example, consider the labor and delivery department or the emergency department. Sometimes additional steps must be taken to deal with variability beyond our control. Level loading and these exceptions are discussed in Lean Healthcare Advisor training and later in this book.

Push and Pull Systems

Traditional batch-and-queue systems, like mass production systems or physician practices where patients are scheduled weeks into the future, are *push* systems. Push systems can be summarized as "Make a lot of stuff as cheaply as possible and hope people will buy it." Or, perform a large number of nearly identical procedures. Push systems minimize the number of setups and changeovers and use dedicated

---

[2]This definition is different than the definition of bottleneck used in the theory of constraints.

equipment, specially designed equipment to produce nearly identical units. Push systems depend on stable long-term environments with highly predictable demand, conditions which seldom exist in the real world.

Pull systems can be summarized as "don't make anything until it is needed, then make it fast." A pull system controls the flow and quantity produced by replacing items when they are consumed. A well-organized emergency department is an example of a pull system. Pull systems require level loading and flexible processes.

Pull System Example (Supermarkets)

When I was in high school in the 1960s I worked in a supermarket that used a pull system. Customers would buy merchandise constantly and I would patrol the aisles, note what was in short supply, then put more on the shelf. Many of the items, such as bread and dairy products, were perishable so we put a limited quantity out, and the store's supplies were replenished daily or even multiple times each day. The storage area of a modern supermarket is very small compared to the retail floor area. Supermarkets were one inspiration behind the Toyota executive Taiichi Ohno's production system at Toyota, and we use both the supermarket concept and the supermarket term in Lean.

Flexible Processes

Flexible processes are lightweight and maneuverable tools and equipment located and positioned to improve safety, ergonomics, quality, and productivity. They are the opposite of the big, heavy, permanently positioned counterparts traditionally used in mass production. A flexible workplace can be quickly reconfigured to serve different needs of different patients. Flexible processes are related to level loading and pull. A completely flexible process would allow the workplace to be instantly reconfigured to service a need as soon as a patient with the need arrived.[3] This ideal cannot be perfectly achieved, but it can be approximated over some small-time interval, such as a day.

Batch Size Reduction

Batch size refers to the amount of an item that is ordered or issued as a standard quantity to the healthcare process. In mass production, such as routinely prescribed medications, procedures, or treatments, larger batches are common because they have some advantages such as quantity discounts, fewer orders needing to be placed, lower transportation costs per unit, etc. However, experience has shown that these things are often outweighed by the disadvantages. Larger batch sizes lead to larger quality problems due to delayed feedback when quality problems occur, excessive inventory, obsolete inventory, delays when quality problems are discovered, etc. The

---

[3] A computer is an ideal flexible process. Click and it is an invoicing system. Click again and it is a patient check-in system. The trick is to integrate this hyper-flexible device with other systems and processes!

ideal batch size for flow is one. In practice, the costs and benefits must be balanced to achieve an optimum batch size.

Some services are also batched. For example, patients queued in hospital emergency waiting rooms and many other areas. Batched services waste the most precious resource of all, the customer's time.

Summary of Value Flow

In an ideal flow situation a customer orders a product or service, the organization schedules the resources to fill the order, processes are instantly configured to create the product or service ordered, and the order is produced and delivered to the customer exactly when needed.

Lean is the total collection of activities directed at moving from the current state to this ideal.

Perfection

Lean is, at its core, the pursuit of perfection. One way to do this is to eliminate errors. Errors are the ultimate Muda. The ultimate waste. Errors in healthcare kill hundreds of thousands of people every year and cost billions of dollars. According to a study conducted by Johns Hopkins, in the USA medical errors are the third leading cause of death.[4] There is an unfortunate tendency to blame people for errors, but over 90% of the time it is the system, not the people, responsible for errors. We will look at some Lean tools and techniques to help identify and eliminate errors by finding the root causes and by designing systems that do not create errors in the first place. Later in this book, we will explore additional tools for reducing errors.

Years ago, there was a popular concept in the area of quality known as the "Acceptable Quality Level," or AQL. AQL was a term used to define the long-term defect rate for a process that was acceptable. Thankfully, most enlightened organizations no longer consider *any* process error rate above zero to be acceptable for the long-term. Historically, the AQL concept resulted in limiting the amount of improvement activity. When quality was "good enough" to meet the AQL, improvement tended to stop. I saw this when, in the 1970s, I worked as the responsible quality engineer for fabrication for a defense contractor that produced guided missiles. Nearly every fabrication process was producing *at* the AQL; no better, no worse. The message here is simple: concepts like acceptable quality level are powerful drivers of behavior. That is why Lean leaders accept nothing less than perfection as their quality standard.

As you may know, I wrote the *Six Sigma Handbook*, and Six Sigma quality is still not quite perfection. It is still much better than most healthcare organizations though, about three errors per million opportunities. For example, Medicaid billing error

---

[4]http://bit.ly/2nBxHbt.

rates in 2016 were 100,500 errors per million opportunities.[5] I tell people that once they have achieved Six Sigma performance, they will want to keep moving toward perfection. For healthcare that is a long journey indeed.

One of the objections to a goal of perfection is that it is not realistic or that it is too expensive. But it can be shown mathematically that often perfection *is* the optimum level of performance, even considering the costs involved. More importantly, however, is the power of perfection to motivate people. People are a lot more likely to get behind a goal of perfection than a goal of "good enough."

Kaizen

There is a saying that the biggest room of all is the room for improvement. Kaizen is a philosophy of continuous improvement, a belief that all aspects of life should be constantly improved. In Japan, where the concept originated, Kaizen applies to all aspects of life, not just to the workplace. In the rest of the world, the term Kaizen is applied mainly to work.

The Kaizen approach focuses attention on making ongoing improvements that involve everyone. Its domain is that of small improvements from ongoing efforts. Over time these small improvements can produce changes every bit as dramatic as the "big project" approach. Kaizen does not concern itself with changing fundamental systems. Rather, it works to optimize existing systems. If you want to design a new process or product from scratch you would use Design for Six Sigma, or the Lean 3P process.

As always, Kaizen is discussed in greater detail later in this book.

Deploying Lean at the Value Stream Level

Here is a seven step overview of the process for deploying Lean at the value stream level. Specific tools and techniques for accomplishing these tasks are discussed later in the book.

1. *First, identify the value.* Use all known means to determine what existing and potential customers really want.
2. *Next, map the value stream.* Identify how work flows to create the value. Determine how information flows to support this process. Identify non-value-added activities and set goals for reducing Muda.
3. *Distribute the work evenly.* Balance the process workload.
4. *Standardize the process.* Identify the core process and eliminate steps needed because of unpredictability by minimizing variation, errors, and defects.
5. *Eliminate "just in case" activities and resources.* Schedule Just In Time deliveries instead of carrying inventory just in case there is a problem. Stop

---

[5]http://go.cms.gov/2nByFUV.

ordering extra items to deal with uncertainty. Stop hiring temps or per diem workers to deal with unexpected problems.

6. *Nurture supplier relationships.* Bring the supply chain into the design of work processes. Integrate their delivery and information systems with yours.

7. *Create "autonomation."* Autonomation is a word invented by Toyota executive Taiichi Ohno to describe a production system that mimics the human autonomic nervous system. It automatically adjusts to external and internal conditions. For example, when we get too hot, our body automatically reacts to cool us down by causing us to perspire; we do not have to think about it. Similarly, healthcare systems should react to customer demands, increasing capacity when demand goes up or decreasing capacity when demand goes down. They should automatically react to internal situations such as excessive inventory buildup by producing or purchasing more or less or on a different schedule. Importantly, they should react to defects by stopping the line. In healthcare, the equivalent is stopping when a threat to patient safety is found.

Elements of Lean Production

Lean Production is based on the Toyota Production System (TPS). It usually includes the elements shown in Fig. 1.5.

When properly implemented, a Lean Production system can dramatically improve productivity compared with traditional batch-and-queue production systems, in some cases by 95%. Healthcare productivity can be improved by as much or more.

Six Sigma

You may have heard about another approach to improvement known as Six Sigma. Although there is overlap between Lean and Six Sigma, this book's focus is Lean. However, you should know a little bit about Six Sigma since it is a complementary approach and you are likely to hear about it.

Six Sigma is more statistically technical than Lean and it includes a number of analytical tools to track down hard-to-find causes of variation and errors. Since both Six Sigma and Lean address the problem of Muda, there is overlap. The two approaches complement one another and both approaches are often integrated into an approach called Lean Six Sigma.[6] Table 1.1 Lean and Six Sigma Synergy, shows how the different elements of Lean and Six Sigma blend to form a synergistic approach to continuous improvement.

There are times when you can deploy Lean without using Six Sigma at all.

- Use Lean by itself if you know that the Lean approach will address the causes of Muda, then you will not need the advanced problem-solving skill set of Six Sigma Black Belts or Green Belts.

---

[6]Lean Six Sigma training is offered by The Pyzdek Institute. Visit www.pyzdekinstitute.com for details.

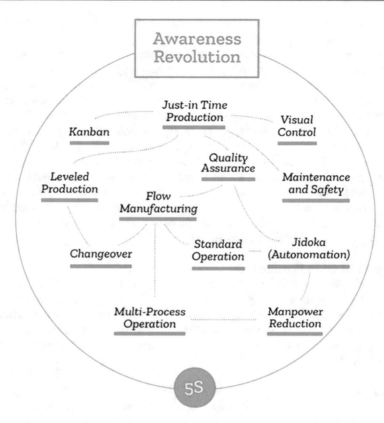

Fig. 1.5 Elements of Lean production

- Use Six Sigma when Lean by itself does not produce the expected results.
- Finally, use Six Sigma if you just do not know what is causing variability, quality, and productivity problems. The Six Sigma framework and toolkit will help you find the root causes.

Six Sigma Infrastructure and "Belts"

Another difference between Lean and Lean Six Sigma is that Lean Six Sigma has a hierarchy of experts known as "Belts." Lean Six Sigma belts are named after the martial arts belts, with the colors (white, yellow, green, and black) representing increasing levels of expertise. Lean has no such formal hierarchy.[7] Lean relies less on the use of teams and projects to make improvements, and more on workers themselves finding ways to improve their own work. Most of the advanced technical

---

[7]Lean "Senseis" are an exception to this lack of hierarchy. Senseis are experienced masters of Lean whose primary role is to teach others how to successfully adopt Lean.

Table 1.1 Lean and Six Sigma Synergy

Lean	Six Sigma contribution
Established methodology for improvement	Policy deployment; Hoshin-Kanri
Focus on customer value stream	Customer requirements measurement; cross-functional process management
Workplace-based implementation	Process control
Kaizen events	Project management; Plan-Do-Study-Act
Understanding current conditions	Knowledge discovery; understand special/common cause variation
Collect product and production data	Data collection and analysis tools
Document current layout and flow	Process mapping and flowcharting
Time the process	Data collection tools; statistical process control (SPC)
Calculate production capacity and takt time	Data collection tools; statistical process control (SPC)
Create standard work	Process control planning
Evaluate options	Cause-and-effect; failure mode and effects analysis (FMEA)
Plan new workplace layouts (3P)	Team skills; project management; simulation
Test to verify improvement effectiveness	Statistical tools for valid comparison; SPC
Reduce cycle times, product defects, errors, changeover time, equipment failures, etc.	7 Quality Tools; 7 Management Tools; quality control; design of experiments

tools taught to Lean Six Sigma belts are not used in Lean. However, many of the less advanced tools are shared with both Lean and Lean Six Sigma.

Product Family Matrices

2

This chapter will introduce you to what product families are and how to use information about product families to leverage your success by applying process improvements to several other related products or services.[1]

Sub-optimizing occurs when a process or system is designed in a way that is optimized for one thing, but less than optimal overall. We try to avoid this trap in Lean by designing solutions that apply to families of products, rather than just to a single product. One tool that helps us avoid suboptimization is the product family matrix (PFM).

2.1   What Is a Product Family

A product family is a group of products that use similar downstream work processes, have similar work content, and/or use similar equipment. A product family matrix is a tool used to help identify product families. The rows of the matrix represent products, i.e., the things we create or the services that we provide. The columns are processes or processing steps used to create these things. The cells of the matrix tell us about the relationship between the product and the process. If the process in the column is not used for the product in the row, the cell is blank. If the process is used by the product, the cell will contain the letter X, a checkmark, or some other mark that indicates that the row and column are related. If the product sometimes uses the process, and sometimes uses an alternate process, the cell will contain the letter A.

Product family matrices are important tools in helping define Lean projects. By using PFMs you can set the scope of your project in a way that it improves the value stream for many products, rather than only one or only a few products. PFMs make it

---

[1]For the remainder of this book and for simplicity we will simply say products unless it would be confusing to do so.

T. Pyzdek, *The Lean Healthcare Handbook*, Management for Professionals,
https://doi.org/10.1007/978-3-030-69901-7_2

		Process						
		Vital Signs/Physical Characteristics	Blood Work	EKG	Pregnancy Test	IV Therapy	Antiembolic Prophylaxis	Product Family
	Age	ALL	50+	50+	10 -51	10+	All	
	Ortho	✓	✓	✓	✓	✓	✓	1
	General	✓	✓	✓	✓	✓	✓	1
	Gynecology	✓	✓	✓	✓	✓	✓	1
	Neurology	✓	✓	✓	✓	✓	✓	1
Product	**Ent (Ear - Nose - Throat)**	✓	✓	✓	✓	✓		2
	Ophthalmology	✓	✓	✓	✓	✓		2
	Plastics	✓	✓	✓	✓	✓	✓	1
	Vascular	✓	✓	✓	✓	✓		2
	Pediatrics	✓	✓	✓	✓	✓		2

Fig. 2.1 Product family matrix—surgical/out-patient treatment

easier to leverage what you learn during the project. The lessons learned can be shared among an entire family of related products.

Example of a PFM

Figure 2.1 is an example of a product family matrix for Surgical/Out-Patient Treatment. It is really just a simple table. The products in the rows are surgical and out-patient treatment process such as Ortho, general, gynecology, and so on. The processes in the columns are vital signs, blood work, EKG, et cetera. For this particular operation (pardon the pun) there are no alternative processes, so no "A" appears in the matrix. Patient flow moves roughly sequentially through the processes from left to right, although there can also be parallel processing where multiple processes occur simultaneously. There are two product families in the matrix. Family 1 includes the products ortho, general, gynecology, neurology, and plastics and is shown here by light gray shading and the number 1 in the Product Family column. Family 2 includes the products ENT, ophthalmology, vascular, and pediatrics. Any Lean improvement effort conducted for one of the products in a given product family should consider how improvements could be applied to the other products in the family.

2.2   Creating Product Family Matrices

Emergency Department Example

The concept of Lean product families applies in many other healthcare processes as well. Consider a hospital emergency department. Instead of products in the rows, you can use types of patients. For example, patients entering the emergency department with different problems that require different handling.

- Broken bones
- Cuts and lacerations
- Gunshot wounds
- Chest pain
- Conscious or unconscious
- Poison
- Animal bites
- Et cetera

The columns would be the different processes in the hospital. For example,

- Triage
- EKG
- Crash cart
- Radiology
- Patient transportation
- Admit to hospital
- Discharge to home
- Lab tests
- Et cetera

A patient product family would be those patients who use similar processes, such as patients with broken bones in the extremities.

Services Example

The same idea applies to back office processes of all types. An insurance company would look at different types of claims, their processes would relate to how the claims are processed, and product families would be those claims that use similar processes.
Rows: Different Types of Claims

- Small claims (e.g., windshield cracks), claims involving injuries, large claims, commercial versus non-commercial clients, incomplete claims.

Columns: Insurance Company Processes

- Legal department review, escalation, simple payment approval, referral to agent.

  A claim product family would claim that use similar processes

- E.g., claims involving injuries, large claims.

2.3   What Makes a PFM Unique?

Product family matrices are the only Lean tool to help you choose product families so you can avoid sub-optimizing value streams. By using product family matrices you also simplify value stream mapping, which you will learn about later in this book.

2.4   Creating and Using a PFM

1. To create a product family matrix begin by making a table that shows products or parts in the rows and processes or process steps in the columns. Mark each cell with an X, an A, or a checkmark if the product in the row uses the process step in the column.
2. Sort the matrix by eye if possible.
   (a) If the matrix is too complicated, use a computer spreadsheet or word processor to sort the rows according to the columns.
3. Search the matrix by looking for products that use all or nearly all the same process steps. Paths do not have to be identical, for example, a product may go through alternative process steps. Or differences may only involve non-critical items such as different labels, packaging, storage containers, or other non-essential processing.
4. Once you have the product family matrix, use it when you scope your project and when you use other tools, such as the value stream map.

Spaghetti Diagrams

3

This chapter will introduce you to a tool that will help you and your team identify wasted movement. This tool is called a Spaghetti Diagram because before the value stream is made Lean, the diagram resembles a tangled plate of spaghetti!

3.1   What Is a Spaghetti Diagram?

A spaghetti diagram is a visual tool that shows the physical movement of a "work object" such as a product, an employee, or a patient through the processes in a value stream. In healthcare, the movement of patients is the primary concern. Spaghetti diagrams are also useful for validating products in a product family. Products or patients in the same product family should move along similar paths.

By looking at the Spaghetti Diagram your team will be able to identify non-value added movement that can be eliminated. Often spaghetti diagrams show the movement of unexpected complexity, illustrating for the first time why congestion and work-in-process inventory occur. The Spaghetti Diagram provides a visual tool that your team can use to work toward agreement on just what the physical flow of work actually is, and what it should be. It also helps the whole team understand the physical movement involved in the complete value stream, often for the first time.

3.2   Creating Spaghetti Diagrams

Here are the steps to follow in creating a spaghetti diagram:

© The Author(s), under exclusive license to Springer Nature Switzerland AG 2021   25
T. Pyzdek, *The Lean Healthcare Handbook*, Management for Professionals,
https://doi.org/10.1007/978-3-030-69901-7_3

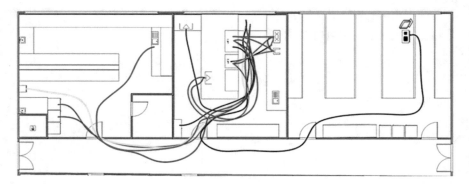

Fig. 3.1 Example of Spaghetti diagram before Lean

1. Begin building the Spaghetti Diagram by identifying the value stream start and end points.[1]
2. Once you have chosen the value stream, find a graphical or pictorial layout of the whole value stream. This may be a map that shows an area as large as the world, or it may be as small as a facility diagram of a part of a building.
3. Now break the team into groups, one for each product in a product family. If the product is a patient or some other physical object, then go to where the work is done, the Gemba, and watch the actual flow of products or patients.
4. Then have team members pretend to be the work object being studied and actually physically walk the spaghetti diagram route (if possible.) Be sure to stay in the aisles, as the work object would.
5. Draw a line on the map or diagram to show where each team member traveled. To show all of the different work objects you can use different colored pens or different colored pieces of string or yarn for different work objects. Do not draw lines through walls or over equipment or other barriers.

Figure 3.1 is an illustration of a spaghetti diagram before Lean is applied. This spaghetti diagram looks at the movement of people in a small lab. There are six people, each represented by a different colored line. There are a few trips to the room on the left, and one trip to the computer workstation on the right. This suggests that the small room at the center-top would be a good candidate to start looking for reducing wasted movement. The person represented by the blue line entered the room, visited one station, then left. The person represented by the magenta line moves the most, followed by the person represented by the green line. In addition to the paths of motion themselves, we also need to know how often a given path is used.

---

[1]You may recall from Chap. 1 that a value stream consists of all activities, both value added and non-value added, required to bring a product from raw material into the hands of the customer, a customer requirement from order to delivery, and a design from concept to launch. These are end points of processes. A value stream consists of product and service flows and information flows. Information initiates activity in the value stream and shows the status of the value stream.

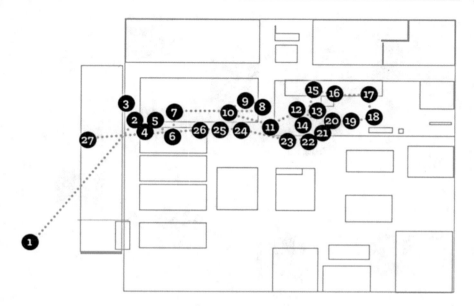

Fig. 3.2 Spaghetti Diagram with Numbered Stops

Additional study is needed to determine how to identify if any of this movement is waste. You will learn about tools for reducing this waste later in this course.

Figure 3.2 is another example of a Spaghetti Diagram. In this example, the team member numbered the stops taken by the work object as it moved through the value stream. This is useful when the path backtracks on itself, which is otherwise difficult to show. By the way, I think this Spaghetti Diagram is hard to read because the area where the work occurs is small compared to the entire area shown. I would recommend that the team zoom in on the area of the diagram where the action takes place to make it more readable and useful.

Figure 3.3 shows what a generic spaghetti diagram might look like for several products. Each product is identified using a different color or type of line, and processes in the value stream are identified by the boxes. The lines should be compared to the product family matrix to see if the spaghetti diagram validates the product families. Members of the same product family should follow identical or nearly identical paths.

3.3   Summary

Spaghetti diagrams are Lean tools that can be used to identify wasted motion. They also serve the purpose of validating products in a product family.

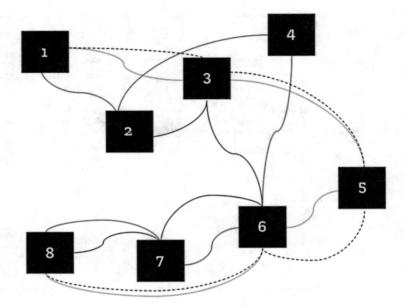

Fig. 3.3 Using Spaghetti Diagram to Help Validate Product Families

Value Stream Maps

4

Value streams are the whole set of activities, resources, and information required to provide a product or service to a customer. In this lesson you will learn about production flow value stream maps, which cover the flow of value from the customer back to the suppliers. We will begin by creating a value stream map (VSM) of an existing process. VSMs help the team see how value flows to the customer, and where waste exists. Current state value streams are nearly always Push systems. This lesson also elaborates on the differences between push and pull systems.

4.1 Push Systems and Pull Systems

Before discussing VSMs we need to understand what type of value stream is being mapped. There are two systems used by most organizations: *push systems* and *pull systems*. Push systems, or mass production systems, begin with long term forecasts of demand. The forecast is used to create schedules that drive systems like materials requirements planning (MRP.) Accounting systems such as traditional costing system and newer systems such as activity-based costing (ABC) or resource consumption accounting (RCA) measure the performance of supervisors and administrators based on how well they produce to the schedule or how they utilize equipment of other resources. These systems were developed for manufacturing, but many healthcare organizations such as hospitals and clinics also use them. This results in large quantities of goods being produced and offered for sale, or accumulated in work-in-process or finished goods inventories. In healthcare one result is, ironically, both overstaffing and understaffing, crowded waiting for rooms, long patient wait times, unnecessary patient tests, and other problems. Because of problems with the uncertainties of forecasting future demand, and the front-to-back nature of push systems, they typically contain huge amounts of waste. However, with the widely used accounting systems typical in healthcare, the waste is not visible to leadership. In fact, these accounting systems often reward people for creating the waste by using flawed key process indicators (KPIs) and performance

© The Author(s), under exclusive license to Springer Nature Switzerland AG 2021   29
T. Pyzdek, *The Lean Healthcare Handbook*, Management for Professionals,
https://doi.org/10.1007/978-3-030-69901-7_4

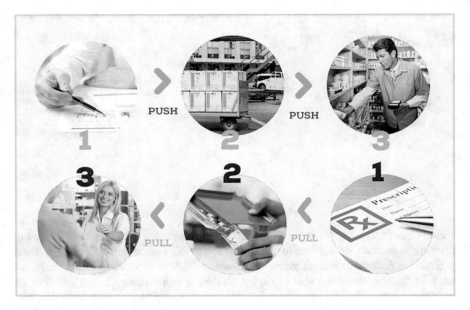

Fig. 4.1 Illustration of push versus pull pharmacy value streams

metrics. This makes it very difficult to measure things like return on investment for specific Lean Healthcare investments, and many visionary organizations simply abandon the exercise and look at very broad indicators such as total revenue and bottom-line results.

An alternative way to schedule work is the pull system. Pull systems begin with customer demand. Production is triggered when customers purchase something. Purchases are monitored continuously by people, often manually rather than with computers. When inventory gets low replenishment requests are automatically generated by the system. Production in upstream processes are triggered in response to customer demand signals and small batches are produced to meet the demand. Inventory and lead time are minimized with pull systems (Fig. 4.1).

4.2   Why Value Stream Maps Are Important

By looking at the whole value stream, rather than at separate processes in the value stream, you help avoid the trap of suboptimization, which occurs when you improve part of a value stream but leave the overall flow unaffected. VSMs help you see waste, but they do more than that. They also help you identify the *sources* of waste. VSMs provide a picture that helps you build a shared vision of how value is created with the rest of your team. This facilitates discussions about improvement and it helps people understand how their decisions affect value flow. By showing the interrelationships among different processes VSMs help you avoid tackling obvious problem processes and process steps that are easy to see, but that may not do much to improve the overall flow. Too often Lean Healthcare initiatives fail to consider the door-to-door value stream. This leads to "improvements" of processes that already have excess capacity and that do not improve throughput and therefore deliver nothing to the bottom line. The value stream perspective helps you avoid this trap.

4.3   Value Stream Symbols

Figure 4.2 value stream map symbols shows some value stream mapping symbols. You can find more symbols and templates on the internet or in the Pyzdek Institute's Lean Healthcare Advisor course, but these are the symbols most often used. Bear in mind that you should not need too many symbols to make a useful value stream map, especially with the push systems that you will find when initially doing Lean Healthcare projects. It is all about creating a clear picture of the value stream

4.4   Example: Emergency Department VSM

Figure 1.2 (repeated) is an example of a VSM for an emergency department value stream. The patients arrive by ambulance and other means on an ongoing basis. The team creating the map start when the patient arrives and work their way back through

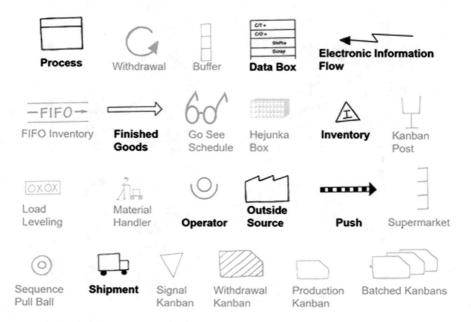

Fig. 4.2 Value stream map symbols

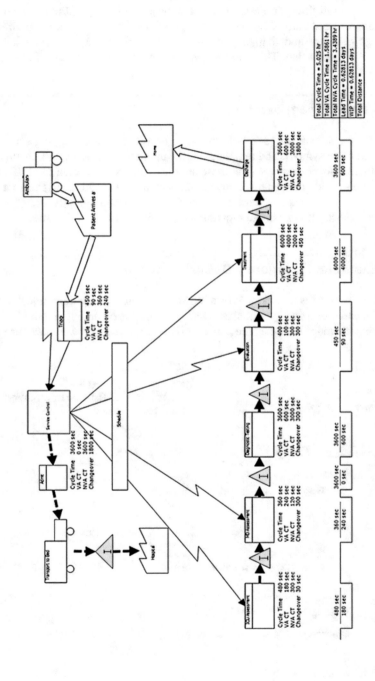

Fig. 1.2 (repeated) Value stream map of an emergency department process before applying Lean

the value stream to the point where the patient leaves the ED value stream. Since it is a current state VSM of the value stream before Lean has been applied, there is a lot of inventory, which is denoted by this symbol △.[1] Inventory in this value stream means patients are waiting for treatment, test results, paperwork, etc. to be processed or for other things. In this case, the thick black dashed arrow indicates that the hospital is using a push system rather than a pull system. Processes, such as the MD Assessment process in the bottom row of process boxes, are denoted with boxes and simple symbols and numbers can be added to denote how many people are involved in providing the service. Data boxes provide details about the processes in the value stream. The map goes all the way back to the final disposition of the patient, either discharge to home, shown by the ⌂ symbol at the middle-right of the figure with the word "Home" inside, or to the hospital bed, shown on the middle-left by the same symbol with the word "Hospital" inside. Electronic information flows are shown with lightning bolt lines and arrows, while manual information flows are shown with straight arrows.

Note that with this push system every process step is scheduled individually; i.e., there are lightning bolts pointing to each process in the value stream. As you will see, this is different than the way a pull system is scheduled.

Finally, at the bottom a timeline shows how much time is value-added and how much is waiting. Time a patient spends waiting or receiving a non-value-added service such as filling out forms is shown as a step up in the timeline, the time a patient spends receiving treatment is shown as a step down. Boxes at the end of the timeline show the total time spent in the ED process, and time spent on various types of activity, including value-added (VA) and non-value-added (NVA) time. Distance traveled can also be shown in the data box. All-in-all the value stream map provides a good high-level view of the way value is created for patients of the ED process.

For this example VSM we only used the symbols shown in bold in Fig. 4.2. Most of the other symbols are only needed for Lean pull systems, which are discussed later. Again, it is best not to overdo the number of symbols used.

4.5   What Makes VSMs Unique

VSMs show the flow of value from suppliers to customers. With VSMs you can see waste and, often, the sources of the waste. The level of detail shown is not too detailed and not too high-level. This often provides the guidance you need to make decisions and take action. VSMs show information flow and link this to material flow. VSMs show you where waiting occurs or where inventory accumulates and the timeline shows you how waiting and inventory impacts lead time. Actual process data, collected during the go to the Gemba phase of the VSM creation process, gives

---

[1]The hand-drawn inventory symbol is shown deliberately. When creating VSMs it is advisable to avoid using computer programs at first. It is much easier to do them by hand until it is time to make a formal presentation.

you a quick quantification of key process metrics much more quickly than you could get combing computer databases. Lean process concepts are integrated by VSMs, showing how they relate to one another to improve flow and reduce waste. Unlike most other process mapping tools, VSMs are drawn based on actually going to the work area and seeing the work, the processes, and the waste. This makes them much more meaningful to most people than maps created in a conference room.

4.6   How Value Stream Maps Are Used

VSMs often show that immediate improvements are possible. These improvements do not always require a full-blown Lean Healthcare project, many can be done right away. We call these "Just-Do" projects. VSMs are also useful for identifying where *future* improvements can be made. Of course, implementing pull systems will improve flow and this should usually be done right away. The Lean Healthcare skill set is not always necessary to do this either; it is often a "Just-Do" project too. When we cover pull systems and work cell design later you will see what this involves in the context of Lean Healthcare, but you can often make these improvements without using special Lean Healthcare tools and techniques at all. Kaizen events are "quick-and-dirty" versions of full-blown Lean Healthcare projects, usually done in 2–5 days. "Kaizen" means "continuous improvement" and this philosophy applies even beyond Lean Healthcare. VSMs by their very nature help you create a shared vision of the value stream as it is and as it should be. The language and images used to create value stream maps help everyone communicate better when discussing improvements.

4.7   Creating the Value Stream Map Phase I

Go to the Gemba

The current state VSM is created in two separate phases. During the first phase, the team will make a quick walk through of the entire value stream, from the end to the start. Be sure that you have discussed this with the value stream owner and that everyone in the work area knows that the team is coming and what the team is doing there. Tell them that you are there to look at the value stream, not the people. When creating the VSM use pencils or sticky notes so you can make changes easily. Stick to the standard symbols and do not use any more symbols than are needed. Get real data, do not rely on people's opinions, computer reports, or process documentation. Follow the smallest unit of production possible. The VSM shows how a single unit that you have defined acquires value.

Identify the Customer and Their Needs

You need to ask several questions regarding the customer. Who is the customer for this value stream? What is a value to this customer, i.e., what is the customer willing to pay for? How many items in this product family are required by the customer? What is the mix of each type of item? For products that are not people, ask what sized package is convenient for the customer? What delivery size? When does the customer get deliveries? Are there demand cycles, such as seasonal variation?

Delivery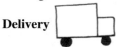

The goal is to eventually achieve just-in-time delivery, in other words, the correct amount at the time it is needed. But it is unlikely that this is the current state. Determine how deliveries are made to customers. For example, standard delivery services, special courier, etc. Do patients arrive by regular ambulance? Helicopter ambulance? Walk-ins? Determine how often these deliveries are made.

Processes

Now identify the processes in the value stream. A process is an operation where the flow object, such as the patient, the purchase order, the insurance claim, et cetera is flowing without significant waiting time. Draw the process boxes from left-to-right in the order they are executed. Show parallel process tracks and branches. As an example of a parallel track, a procedure may be processed for payment approval at the same time it is being performed on a patient. An example of a branch might be a procedure performed due to a complication.

Supplier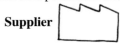

The information you need for suppliers is similar to that which you obtained for customers. When are deliveries received from suppliers? What are the delivery modes? The batch sizes? What other important information do you have about suppliers?

Preliminary Sketch of the Value Stream
Now put it all together in a sketch showing the value stream's suppliers, processes, and customers. This is your 10,000-foot view of the value stream. If you draw this in pencil you can erase and modify it as the team discusses it. Sticky notes also make it easy to change things. See Fig. 4.3.

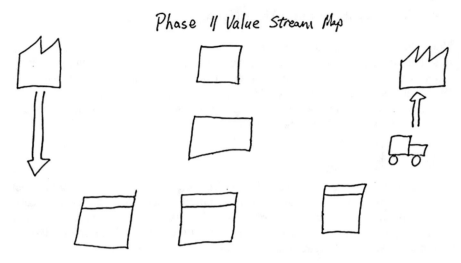

Fig. 4.3 Preliminary sketch of a value stream

4.8   Creating the Value Stream Map Phase II

Now you are ready to complete the current state VSM by adding data and showing information flows. You will want to get a Goldilocks amount of data, not too much (which would take too long and delay your project) and not so little that you do not see the opportunities for improving lead time and flow.

Process Data

For each process, add a data box showing key information such as cycle time, processing time, changeover time, scrap rates, available time, et cetera. You can collect a sample of these by timing the operation (Fig. 4.4).

Workers

In the process, box draw the operator symbol and write down how many people are doing the work using full-time-equivalent workers. This may be a fractional number if some of the people are not assigned to work within the process full time (Fig. 4.5).

Fig. 4.4 Data box symbol

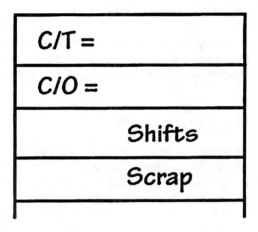

Fig. 4.5 Worker/operator symbol

Fig. 4.6 Inventory symbol

Inventory

Next record how much inventory is on hand or how many people are waiting within the entire value stream. There are several types of inventory, consult the lexicon for definitions. However, all inventory is waste because it is waiting. Inventory causes lead times to be longer and interrupts product flow. Show the inventory levels on the value stream maps where they occur in the value stream. For example, if there is an accumulation of patients between MD assessment and diagnostic testing, draw the inventory symbol there on the value stream map, along with the quantity of inventory (Fig. 4.6).

Electronic Information

Now draw in the information flows of an electronic nature. These are such things as forecasts, MRP, automated inventory replenishment orders to suppliers, prescriptions sent electronically to the pharmacy, and so on (Fig. 4.7).

Manual Information

No system operates entirely on electronic information, at least not yet. Show the information that flows manually to the value stream. Examples include priority lists to supervisors, work schedule changes due to material shortages or worker absences, and so on.

Note that the definition of manual information is that it is not automatically generated by an electronic system. The information does not need to be hand-written or hand-carried, it can be *transmitted* electronically. However, the key is that a *person* creates the information on a real-time basis rather than a machine doing so (Fig. 4.8).

Material Data

Under each inventory symbol, draw the push arrow to show that the value stream is using push scheduling rather than pull scheduling (Fig. 4.9).

Timeline

Now, draw a timeline at the bottom of the value stream map. This tells you how long one unit, such as 1 patient, takes to move through the value stream and separates the time into non-value added time and processing time, which is value-added time.

Fig. 4.7 Electronic
information symbol

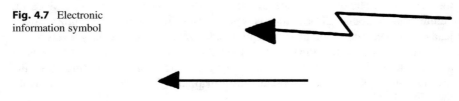

Fig. 4.8 Manual information symbol

Fig. 4.9 Push symbol

Fig. 4.10   Timeline symbol

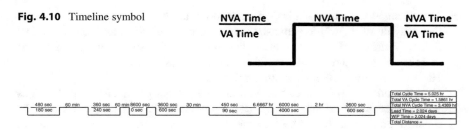

Fig. 4.11   Example of completed timeline

To calculate the timeline, begin by determining the available time in a day and the average customer demand per day. Use a representative period such as a month to calculate the average. You may want to create different timelines for different periods, such as for ED times that are normally slow and ED times on days or shifts that are normally busy. Next measure the processing time for each process in the value stream. Show this on the lower part of the timeline for each process.

Determine the lead time that a unit spends in inventory by dividing the observed inventory quantity by the daily customer demand. Show this on the upper part of the timeline for each inventory accumulation (Fig. 4.10).

Value-Added and Non-Value-Added Time

Now add up all of the lead times and process times and record the results in a box at the end of the timeline. See Fig. 4.11 for an example of a timeline with value added and non-value-added data.

Step-by-Step Process for Creating Value Stream Maps

1. One-page, size A3 or 11"×17". Draw by hand at first.
   VSMs are initially drawn on a single large sheet of paper, preferably by hand so that you do not get bogged down learning to use a computer program. Use a *pencil*, not an ink pen, and keep a large eraser handy!
2. Decide where the value stream starts and stops.
   Like spaghetti diagrams, you begin by identifying the start and end points, only here you are looking at a value stream instead of a workplace.
3. Identify the value stream owner.
   During this exercise, you will go to the Gemba and your value stream will likely cross-organizational boundaries so you will need permission from more than one leader to visit their areas. This can become an insurmountable barrier if you do not have the support of an individual who has responsibility for the entire value stream. Find this person and get them to help you ahead of time.
4. Get a layout diagram of the whole value stream.

5. Form a small team for each important product family.

Get a layout of the whole value stream and form a team for each chosen product family. Write down key details about the product family, such as the patients to be included, expected demand quantities and schedules, and so on.

6. Have the team walk the value stream together.[2]

Creation of a VSM requires that you and your team physically visit the place where value is created. It is usually best if you start at the end, the place where the finished product is being sent to customers, then work your way backward through the value stream. Walk the value stream and try to develop an integrated and shared view of the value stream. You should not split up the team to map separate parts of the value stream. Nor should you take partial maps created by others and put them together.

7. Record actual observations and data.

As you move through the value stream record what you see, rather than relying on computer reports. Write down the quantities of inventory or number of patients waiting at the different locations, time samples of the work as it is being done.

8. Draw the value stream map.

Once done with the Gemba walk and data recording you can have the team draw the value stream map, and it is best to do this by hand at first.

9. Discuss and revise.

Discuss and revise the VSM until the team reaches a consensus on its accuracy.

---

[2]Another useful approach is the "Ohno Circle." Here you draw a circle in the work area and someone sits or stands inside the circle and quietly observes the work for an extended period of time.

Lean Value Stream Design

5

5.1 Overview

The steps that you will take to create a Lean value stream are

1. Select a product family
2. Identify the value stream owner
3. Map the current value stream
4. Determine the rate of production required to meet customer demand, "takt time"
5. Develop continuous flow wherever possible
6. Use Supermarkets and Kanbans to control production where continuous flow does not extend upstream
7. Send the customer schedule to only one production process, the "pacemaker process"
8. Level the production mix
9. Level the production volume
10. Develop the ability to make every part every day (or faster) upstream of the pacemaker process

Some of these steps were described in earlier chapters. This chapter will describe the remaining steps.

5.2 Continuous Flow

The goal of Lean is to develop a value stream where value flows continuously to customers with no waste. This means no waiting, no inventory, no defects, errors, or mistakes, no unnecessary motion; none of the types of waste discussed earlier. Ideally, a patient would say "I am having this problem" and that would trigger the emergency department or other value stream to produce the care required to return the patient to health. I.e., the personnel with the required training would appear, the needed supplies would be delivered to each process in the value stream at exactly the right time, all work would be done perfectly, and the patient would be moved a minimal distance until she was finally returned to health and released with complete and accurate discharge instructions.

Henry Ford's assembly line is an example of a value stream that could have been an ideal Lean value stream. (It was not because Ford cars were identical and made to long-term forecasts, but that is another story.) What if every Model T that came off of the assembly line was driven away by the customer who had ordered the car? If the production line value stream was triggered by the customer's order, we would have something very close to the ideal of continuous flow.

Continuous flow is possible when the product can be produced and moved to the next process one-unit-at-a-time, without delay and without errors or scrap. A work cell is a place in a value stream is where continuous flow exists.[1] Many benefits result from continuous flow, such as lower costs, instant signals of quality problems, no work-in-process inventory, etc.

When the flow is not continuous it will create the opposite results. In other words, discontinuous flow will result in higher costs, delayed signals of quality problems, work-in-process inventory accumulations, etc.

5.3   Reasons for Discontinuous Flow

Discontinuous flow has many possible causes. Batch production or work scheduling of separate processes using long-term forecasts is a primary cause. Other causes include

- Long physical distances between processes and process steps.
- Quality problems due to either sporadic special causes of variation or chronic problems caused by process or product design flaws.
- Poor machine or equipment maintenance.
- Unpredictable customer demand.
- Acts of God causing unpredictable interruptions to supplies.
- Long changeover times.
- Long setup times.
- Supplier issues: unreliable deliveries, long lead times, business failures, multiple suppliers for the same item, quality problems, etc.

Some of these causes can be addressed immediately by the design of the value stream, which is the subject of this chapter. This will involve making the value stream as close as possible to continuous flow at the outset. The remaining causes are addressed long-term by Kaizen events, which are short-duration projects that make quick improvements. Lean is used to tackle especially stubborn problems identified

---

[1]Design of work cells is discussed in a later chapter.

by leadership or during Kaizen events. The importance of an organizational culture that promotes the ideal of zero waste cannot be overemphasized.

5.4   Steps Toward Continuous Flow

Takt Time[2]

To achieve our ideal of continuous flow we need to know how many items our customers want and when they want them. This demand rate is known as *takt time*. As discussed earlier takt time is calculated using Eq. (1.1).

$$\text{Takt time} = \frac{\text{Available time per day}}{\text{Customer demand per day}} \tag{1.1}$$

This value is used to synchronize the entire value stream. For example, if a disability claims office works from 9 am–5 pm with 1 h for lunch and two 10-min breaks then it has 400 min of time available to work each day. If it receives an average of 50 claims/day, then the *takt time is* **400/50 = 8 min/claim**. Therefore, the office should complete an average of one claim every 8 min. If it completes more claims than this, then it is probably overstaffed (wasted resources.) If it completes fewer then customers will have to wait too long to receive payment of their claims (wait time waste.)

If a physician's practice saw patients in the same 9-to-5 schedule with the same 1-h lunch and two 10-min breaks, then it would need to know the average number of patients seen per day. If the answer was 50 patients/day, then the office should process one patient every 8 min. Faster production would result in workers with slack time. Slower production would mean patients would wait to be seen. Takt time is shown in data boxes for processes on value stream maps (VSM.)

5.5   Supermarkets and Kanbans

When continuous flow is not possible you will use "supermarkets" and "Kanbans." You may recall that in Lean the term supermarkets refers to small, controlled amounts of inventory that are used to schedule production at upstream processes. Kanbans are cards (or other devices such as computer programs, but for simplicity we will use the term "cards" for all Kanbans) used to control the production and movement of materials and parts. There are several types of Kanbans as shown in Table 5.1.

---

[2]Takt Time was also introduced earlier in an example (see Eq. (1.1)).

Table 5.1 Types of Kanbans

Symbol	Type of Kanban	Comment
	Withdrawal Kanban.	Kanban that instructs the material handler to get parts from the supermarket to the process that needs them.
	Production Kanban	Kanbans that tells a process how many of an item to produce and gives it permission to do so.
	Batched Kanbans	A group of Kanbans to be picked up at one time
	Signal Kanban	Signals when a reorder point is reached and another batch needs to be produced. Used when the supplying process produces in batches and requires a changeover to produce the required item.
	Kanban post	The place where Kanban cards are collected for pickup

5.6   Pacemaker Process

Takt time is used to schedule the "pacemaker process" in the value stream. This process is used to trigger production by other processes in the value stream. Because of its importance, care should be taken when selecting the pacemaker process. The pacemaker process should be the continuous flow process that is the furthest downstream in the value stream. Since we want pacemaker processes to schedule the entire value stream, there should not be any supermarkets downstream from the pacemaker process. Figure 5.1 shows a simple example of a pacemaker process for a value stream.

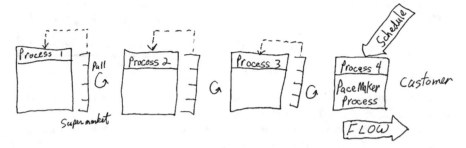

Fig. 5.1 Pacemaker process

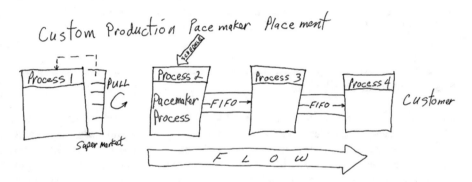

Fig. 5.2 Pacemaker placement for custom production

If value streams are producing customized, made-to-order items, then the pacemaker process may need to be further upstream. However, the "no supermarkets downstream" rule still applies. Figure 5.2 shows an example of this situation.

5.7   Production Mix

The production mix is set at the pacemaker process. The basic idea is to produce a mix of products that, over a relatively short time interval, matches the mix of products demanded by customers. The ideal flow process is single-item flow, so the ideal product mix would be build-to-order. However, for a variety of reasons, this ideal is seldom possible.[3] The primary purpose of creating an even production mix is to eliminate the need for batching. When the pacemaker process produces in batches, the resources it consumes are also used in batches. This creates batching in all

---

[3]Services are an exception. Produce-to-order is relatively common in the services sector. It would be pointless to treat an emergency patient before they experience the emergency!

Fig. 5.3 Load leveling
symbol

upstream processes that feed the pacemaker process, and upstream inventories tend to grow larger as you move further upstream.

A level production mix also makes it easier to respond to different customer requirements with a short lead time and little inventory. The downside is that at assembly there will be a larger number of changeovers and the need to keep components for different assemblies near at hand. The symbol for leveling is shown in Fig. 5.3. On the value stream map the icon is shown in the information flow, see Fig. 5.4.

5.8   Production Volume

After leveling the production mix, the next step is to level the production volume. This is achieved at the pacemaker process by releasing and withdrawing small and consistent amounts of product in pace with takt time. By doing this we keep the entire value stream responsive to the demands of the customer. Batch-and-queue systems, in contrast, produce according to schedules at each separate process in the value stream, causing all of the problems discussed earlier. In addition to the chronic problems, the situation is even worse when customer demand changes suddenly and the company is left with large inventories and no demand for them. This has led to catastrophes that have spelled the end of more than one company.

Consistent, level production rates are a primary goal of Lean. It is only possible when quality is high because poor quality disrupts production flow and is usually compensated for by maintaining large stocks of "just in case" inventory. When small amounts of production are released, say an hour's worth or less, poor quality will bring things to a halt. This is actually a good thing because it is likely that the cause of the quality problem is still identifiable. The time delay created by inventories is a huge barrier to quality improvement because the cause of quality problems has long since vanished, only to reappear again and again in the future. With large inventories, the causes of quality problems are merely items of academic interest rather than something that can be realistically addressed in real time.

Of course, production is removed from the pacemaker process at the same rate that production orders are issued. This "paced withdrawal" keeps the pacemaker process free from inventory buildup.

The consistent increment of work is referred to as the **pitch**. The pitch increment is calculated by considering both takt time and the quantity held by a container (pack size.) The formula used is:

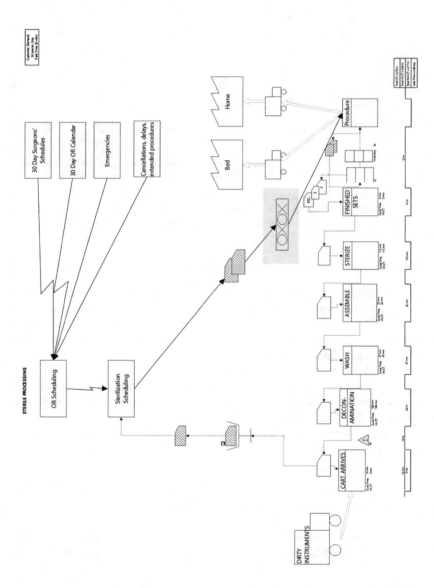

Fig. 5.4 Example of using load leveling icon

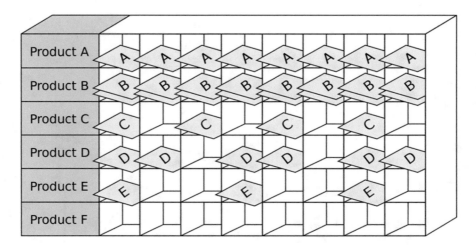

Fig. 5.5 Load-leveling box (Heijunka box) (http://en.wikipedia.org/wiki/Heijunka_box. In this illustration, each time period builds an A and two Bs along with a mix of Cs, Ds, and Es. What is clear from the box, from the simple repeating patterns of Kanbans in each row, is that the production is smooth for each of these products.)

$$\text{Pitch} = \text{Takt time} \times \text{Pack size} = \text{Time it takes to produce a full container} \quad (5.1)$$

For example, if your takt time is 1 min and the container size is 10 units then pitch = 10 min (1-min × 10 units = 10 min) This is called the "takt image." In practice we would, every 10 min, tell the pacemaker process to make 10 units and take away one finished pitch quantity from the process. The pitch quantity is the unit by which the production is scheduled for a given product family. Just as we do not batch parts, with Lean we also do not batch production schedules.

The pitch time is the time frame used to monitor value stream performance. This is in stark contrast to the usual management time frame, which is often days, weeks, or even months. Just as the delay created by inventories makes it almost impossible to solve quality problems, the delay created by long management time frames does the same with production problems.

5.9   Load-Leveling Box (Heijunka[4] Box)

One mechanism used to accomplish load leveling is the load-leveling box, Fig. 5.5. Think of a load-leveling box as a physical manifestation of a data table where each row in the table represents one product in the product family (for example, one type of insurance claim) each column represents a pitch time period, and each cell in the

---

[4]According to a Japanese colleague the correct spelling is Heijyunka. For the sake of standardization, I will use the popular spelling heijunka in this book.

Table 5.2 Table explaining Heijunka box

Pitch time → Product ↓	9:00	9:10	9:20	9:30	9:40	9:50
A	Kanban			Kanban		
B		Kanban			Kanban	
C			Kanban			Kanban

table is a place where Kanbans are stored, see Table 5.2. The bins in the box each hold one or more Kanbans. By staggering the Kanbans in the load-leveling box at the pitch interval we automatically create a consistently level production mix.

There is no separate icon for leveling the production pace, we use the same symbol as for leveling the production mix (See Fig. 5.3). Actually, it is not only the icon that is the same, leveling the mix and the pace of production are two sides of the same coin since we must level both simultaneously to have Lean production.

5.10 Every Part Every Day

If items (surgical procedures, parts, insurance claims, prescriptions, services, transactions, etc.) are produced repeatedly, we would like to have a system where upstream processes could create the quantity of each item needed by customers immediately. As a step towards this goal, we begin with a target of producing every item needed, in the quantity needed, at least every day. Once this is accomplished we can begin the continuous improvement journey and reduce the "EPE" interval from a day to an hour or eventually a pitch interval.

The primary factor that determines the ability of an upstream process to produce multiple items is the time it takes to changeover from one item to another. As this time decreases, the number of different items that can be produced in a day increases. In fact, changeover time can be used to determine batch sizes. Calculate the number of hours you have available in a workday, then subtract the number of hours required to produce the daily requirement. The time leftover is the time available for changeovers.[5]

---

[5]Actually, this is also done for batch-and-queue processes. But before Lean has been applied the changeover times are frequently so long that huge batch sizes are required to amortize the changeover costs.

5.11   Surgical Procedures Scheduling Case Study[6]

A hospital that we will call Southwest Medical Center, or SMC, performs various surgical procedures and needs to schedule the operating rooms, medical supplies such as clothing, gloves, etc., surgical instruments, staff and recovery rooms needed to perform these procedures. This case study will focus on providing the surgical instrument sets. Scheduling the other required people and materials is similar.

Demand Forecasting

Forecasts are made for 1 week ahead, based on surgeons' schedules for the next 30 days and on historical data regarding the frequencies of emergencies, flu season, holiday schedules, etc. Historically, weekly schedules have been 70% accurate. While this is not bad for healthcare, it is necessary to update schedules each day for the volume expected on a given day or on the next day. While emergencies are unpredictable, their statistical likelihood within a given time interval can be estimated with a relatively high degree of confidence.

In healthcare, it is much less of a problem to have too many supplies on hand than to not have enough, so the amount of inventory carried tends to err on the high side of the forecast. Of course, the more accurate the match between the forecasted demand and the actual demand, the better. Healthcare professionals are often surprised to learn how predictable their apparently chaotic environment can be! However, the demand for any given procedure still varies, as does the time required to complete any procedure. The surgical procedures value stream needs to have a supermarket to smooth out the variation due to these uncertainties. The supplies needed are based on the forecast for the procedures scheduled for today and tomorrow, plus the small buffer. With a batch-and-queue approach the inventory levels would be much higher. Weeks or months of some types of inventory are not uncommon for traditional healthcare systems, along with the associated waste from obsolescence, expired product, wait times, etc.

Surgical Procedures

The weekly demand for common procedures conducted at SMC are shown in Table 5.3. Takt time will be based on this demand. The overall demand is for an average of 23 procedures/day, but 24 procedures will be scheduled after the averages are rounded to whole numbers. If the operating rooms can begin procedures starting at 7 am and can schedule them to start up to and including 6 pm (without downtime

---

[6]We are aware that this case study simplifies a much more complex situation. However, our purpose is to teach basic Lean principles and the principles illustrated by this case study can also be modified to apply to a wide variety of real-world situations.

Table 5.3 Surgical procedures at SMC

Procedure	Avg/Wk	Avg/day	Scheduled	Avg Time
C-Section	25	5.0	5	60
Joint replacement	14	2.8	3	120
Circumcision	19	3.8	4	30
Broken bone repair	13	2.6	2	60
Angioplasty and atherectomy	10	2.0	2	120
Stent procedure	9	1.8	2	120
Hysterectomy	10	2.0	2	120
Gallbladder removal	9	1.8	2	60
Coronary artery bypass graft	8	1.6	2	210

Table 5.4 Heijunka "Box" (Schedule) (number are OR room numbers)

Procedure	7 am	8 am	9 am	10 am	11 am	12 pm	1 pm	2 pm	3 pm	4 pm	5 pm	6 pm
C-Section	1		1	5		5			4			
Joint replacement		4			1			3				
Circumcision		5		3		2			5			
Broken bone repair							1		1			
Angioplasty and atherectomy				4						2		
Stent procedure	2							2				
Hysterectomy			2								3	
Gallbladder removal						3						4
CABG	3					4						

scheduled for breaks or lunches) then there will be 12 h (720 min) of clock time available for procedures. Assume that any OR can be used for any procedure, and assume that there are 5 ORs available. Be sure that the schedule allows for the average time a procedure is expected to take.

Heijunka

This information is used to create the Heijunka (level) schedule shown in Table 5.4. This Heijunka schedule is for a typical workday during a typical workweek.[7] Every procedure is performed every day at least once (in this case, at least twice) so the

---

[7]Schedules for evenings, weekends, holiday periods etc. will use the same approach shown here, but a different demand forecast. We will not consider these schedules here.

Table 5.5 Schedule by Operating Room

Operating Room	7 am	8 am	9 am	10 am	11 am	12 pm	1 pm	2 pm	3 pm	4 pm	5 pm	6 pm
1	x	■	x	■	x	■	x	■	x			
2	x	■	x		■	x	■	x	■	x		
3	x		■	x	???	x		x	■		x	
4		x	■	x	■	x			■			x
5		x		■	x	■	x	■	x			

Lean goal of "Every Part [Procedure] Every Day" is accomplished. If you count the number of procedures of any given type, you will see that this leveled schedule accurately reflects the weekly demand shown in Table 5.3. However, it is only a starting point. Once determined it can be adjusted to reflect daily changes in demand and to deal with scheduling conflicts as you will see below.

Changeovers

The key constraint to determining how much flexibility this value stream has is changeover time, for example, the time required to prepare an OR for the next procedure. Or it might be some other process in the value stream, such as instrument sterilization. If the different procedures must take place in ORs that require special immovable equipment or rooms, the Heijunka schedule must be modified to reflect these constraints.

It takes 30–60 min from the end of a procedure until an OR is ready for the next procedure; we will use a fixed 60-min changeover time during this case study for scheduling purposes. Assume that there are two central services (CS) teams available for changing over ORs. For the purposes of calculating available time in a given day, we only need to count changeovers between procedures on the same day. Changeovers after the last procedure of the day for any given OR can be processed without impacting the availability of the room on that day.

The constraint of two CS crews creates a problem with the schedule shown in Table 5.4. This is easier to see if we show the schedule by OR number (Table 5.5). The problem is that OR 3 has two surgeries scheduled too close together to allow sufficient time for a changeover because there is no CS crew available.[8] However, we could move the gallbladder procedure scheduled for OR 3 at noon to either OR 1 or OR 5 at either 5 pm or 6 pm, or to OR2 at 6 pm.[9] Schedule conflicts such as this make it wise to examine schedules early enough to make required changes.

---

[8] My English teacher would be proud that the previous sentence uses all three forms of the word "to"!

[9] Once the new OR is determined we would, of course, need to schedule a changeover prior to the procedure.

OR number	Changeovers
1	5
2	4
3	3
4	3
5	3

Table 5.6 Changeovers between procedures

The changeover count might change[10] depending on where we decide to move the conflicted gallbladder procedure. If we move the procedure to OR 1 at 5 pm or 6 pm and revise Table 5.5 we get the changeover count shown in Table 5.6. Note that the changeover count only includes changeovers that impact today's schedule. *All ORs are cleaned prior to the start of the next day's procedures.*

Adjusting the Schedule

It may be possible to level-load slow days by moving up procedures scheduled for later in the week or even more than a week out. We can also try to level-load days made busy because of emergencies, surgeries taking longer than expected, or other factors by rescheduling surgeries scheduled for later the same day, but this has the effect of causing employee and patient dissatisfaction, which needs to be taken into account. In contrast to unexpected events that occur on the same day, some cases are scheduled several days or even weeks in advance and it is often possible to move these cases up in the schedule to make the workload more level.

Takt Time

Takt time for the surgical procedure value stream is calculated by first determining the available work time per day. Assuming that ORs are available for 60 min after 6 pm (the latest time a procedure can be scheduled to begin on a normal weekday) and assuming that ORs are not shut down for breaks or lunches, then takt time for the OR process is found by Eq. (5.2).

$$\text{Takt} = 12\text{ h} \times 60\text{ min} \div 24\text{ Procedures} = 30\text{ min /Procedure} \qquad (5.2)$$

Thus, the surgical procedure value stream needs to complete, on average, one procedure every half-hour to meet demand. The Heijunka schedule shows that this system is capable of handling somewhat more procedures than this, but as mentioned a bit of "overcapacity" is often needed in healthcare to handle emergencies and other sources of variation. Dealing with variation requires some slack in the system. Lean continuous improvement methods should be used to help keep the slack time to the minimum required to meet all customer needs. A common mistake in Lean is to obsess on removing slack to the point of causing other problems elsewhere.

---

[10]I say *might change* because if the procedure were moved to another day the changeover count would not change.

Flexibility

A Lean system must be flexible and responsive to changing demand. Let us say that the schedule is interrupted by an increase in the C-section demand of an additional 3 C-sections in a given day. The supermarket or buffer would have sufficient supplies for this increased demand. Assuming all other required resources are available, such as surgeons and other members of C-section teams, the Heijunka schedule would be modified to accommodate the new C-sections. For example, the current Heijunka schedule has only 1 procedure scheduled at 4 pm, 5 pm, and 6 pm and only 2 at 8 am, 9 am, 10 am, and 2 pm and 3 pm. Every other hour there are three procedures scheduled. The hours with fewer procedures would be candidates for the additional C-section procedures.[11] Better still would be if the schedule for a work-week could accommodate the additional demand at a more level rate of 1 per day. This may be possible, for example, by rescheduling non-urgent joint replacement procedures. Knowing the Heijunka schedule makes these decisions much easier to evaluate.

5.12   Future State Value Stream Map Case Study

The principles presented above serve as guidelines for creating a Lean value stream. The tools and icons will be used to draw a picture of the new value stream you plan to build. In Lean we are usually not asked to create a brand-new value stream from scratch. Instead we start with the current value stream and apply Lean principles to evaluate and improve it. Figure 5.6 shows a current state value stream map for an instrument sterilization value stream for the hypothetical Southwest Medical Center (SMC.) We will use this example to illustrate the process of creating a future state value stream map.

Current State

In the current state which uses batch and queue the instrument sterilization schedule is determined for 1 week ahead, based on 30-day forecast and the instruments required for finished sets inventory level. A finished goods inventory level of 1 week's worth of supplies is kept just in case demand forecasts are inaccurate. Each of the instrument sterilization process steps is scheduled separately. Dirty instruments that were used for the previous day's procedures are queued up and waiting when the sterilization department opens for business in the morning.[12] Instruments sets are broken up and individual instruments (e.g., forceps, clamps, scalpels, etc.) are counted and put into separate baskets for processing. Instrument

---

[11]Do not forget the CS team constraint when rescheduling!

[12]After point-of-use prep of course.

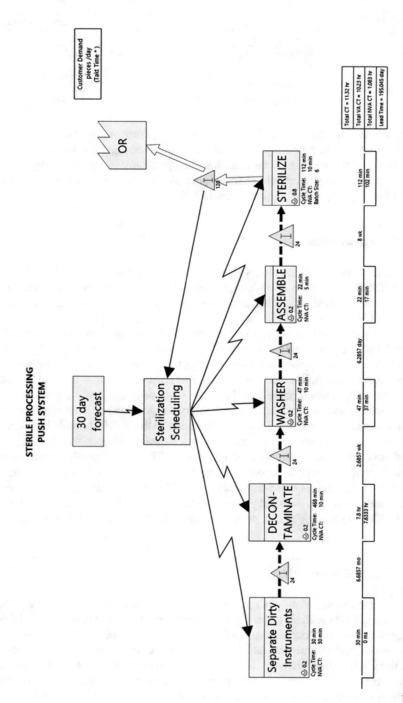

Fig. 5.6 Current state value stream map

Table 5.7 Sterilization
process times

Process step	Cycle time (Min)
Dirty instrument cart arrives	10
Decontamination	156
Washer	47
Assemble set	22
Sterilizer (capacity = 6)	112 × 4

sets needed for the forecasted OR procedures in the upcoming work week are assembled and sent to inventory. As procedures are conducted the instrument sets needed by the ORs are withdrawn from finished goods inventory on a daily basis. Finished sets inventory levels are checked periodically by hand and the results are used to manually adjust the sterilization schedule.

Process Information

The times required for each process step in the value stream shown in Fig. 5.6 are given in Table 5.7. Cycle times are per load. The sterilizer processes can only process 6 sets in a load. The other processes can process the instruments used in a normal day (24 sets) at once.

On average there will be enough instruments of work-in-process inventory (WIP) to create 24 sets, equal to the average number of procedures scheduled per day. WIP is shown by inventory symbols between each process step where work-in-process inventory exists. Depending on the number of unscheduled procedures and normal variation in daily demand, there may be a few more or a few fewer instruments in WIP. The sterilization process builds to inventory, not to demand. After sterilization, the newly cleaned and sterilized sets will be added to the finished goods inventory. Instruments not required for the next day's forecasted procedures are put into separate inventories for each type of instrument. There are literally hundreds of different instruments kept in inventory. The finished goods inventory is 120 sets, enough for the demand for one 5-day work week. ORs draw the sets needed from this finished goods inventory. Finished goods inventory is shown by the Inventory symbol above the Sterilize process box on the lower right-side section of the VSM in Fig. 5.6.

5.13   Future State Plan

Obviously, the current state push system is a far cry from continuous flow. The current state is a classic Push system. Value stream processes do not respond quickly to changes in customer demand, there is a lot of inventory both in process and in finished goods, and instruments and sets of instruments spend days or weeks sitting in inventory before they are used. If a problem is encountered with an instrument in the OR, it is nearly impossible to determine what caused the problem and it is very likely that many other instruments in inventory will have the same problem. In short, there is lots of room for improvement.

Takt Time

The first step toward improvement is to calculate takt time. The average customer demand is 24 surgical instrument sets per day and the OR suite operates for 12 h/day. The ORs do not stop for rest breaks or lunch breaks. Takt time is calculated as follows:

Available work time (min): 720 min/day.
Customer demand: 24 instrument procedures/day.
Takt time: 720/24 = 30 min/procedure.

In other words, SMC needs to complete 1 procedure every 30 min to meet customer demand within available work time. SMC might decide to produce at a faster rate than takt, but takt is determined by customer demand and cannot be changed by SMC. Takt time is shown in data boxes on the future state value stream map.

Where Should Finished Sets Go?

We have started with the customer's rate of demand, now we will work our way upstream. The next question we address is whether the completed instrument sets should be sent directly to the operating rooms, or whether we need supermarkets and, perhaps, buffer stock. If we are able to build sterilized instrument sets for immediate delivery to the ORs the value stream map would look like Fig. 5.7. This is known as continuous flow.

There are a number of problems preventing us from achieving continuous flow. For one, demand varies quite a bit. For another, the timing of procedures does not match with the time required for the cleaning and sterilization process. Thus, in this case, we will need supermarkets to help us smooth the impact of varying demand on the value stream. Also, because healthcare tends to error on the side of caution, we will keep an extra few sets of buffer stock on hand.

SMC will use the customer's weekly forecast to determine the capacity they will need in the upcoming scheduling period (1 day, in this case) and they will adjust staffing and supplies produced accordingly. The weekly forecast will be based on the 30-day surgeons' schedules and other factors. Actual production on any given workday will be based on Kanbans coming upstream from the finished sets supermarket. The future state value stream map shows the configuration in Fig. 5.8.

Fig. 5.7 Continuous flow

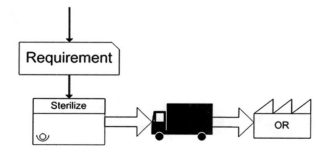

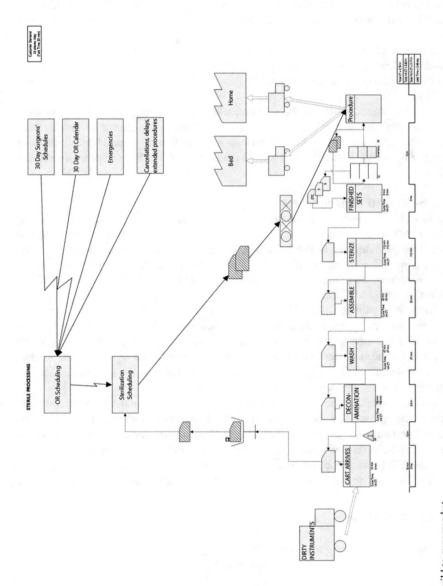

Fig. 5.8 Build to supermarket

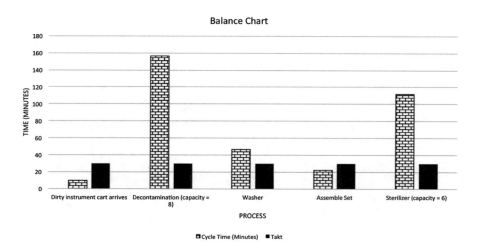

Fig. 5.9   Takt time versus cycle time

Sterile sets are packed for each different procedure. (Some sets are even packaged with instruments requested by a particular surgeon.) Each set of instruments in the staging area has one production Kanban on it. 1 set is called the "Kanban size." We will use the set as the Kanban size. As the OR staff removes sets from the sterilization supermarket or buffer stock it removes the Kanbans from the sets and sends them back to the sterilization department via the Heijunka box. This tells the sterilization department that the sets have been used and need to be replenished.

Continuous Flow

The operator balance chart for this value stream is shown in Fig. 5.9. Not all processes can produce faster than takt. The total processing time through all of the steps is 11 h 23 min, due to the fact that the decontamination and sterilizer processes can only process smaller batches. Thus, the value stream will need to work more than a single shift. However, our VSM is incomplete and it does not show how many people are required or their required training, transportation time between the process steps, or other important data. Ways to address these omissions will be covered in the upcoming chapter on standardized work design.

Kaizen and Continuous Improvement

Kaizen and Lean and other continuous improvement methods can be used to improve this value stream. If we identify areas where improvements are needed, they are shown using "Kaizen Bursts" at the appropriate places on the VSM. See Fig. 5.10 for an example of how Kaizen burst projects are indicated on a VSM.

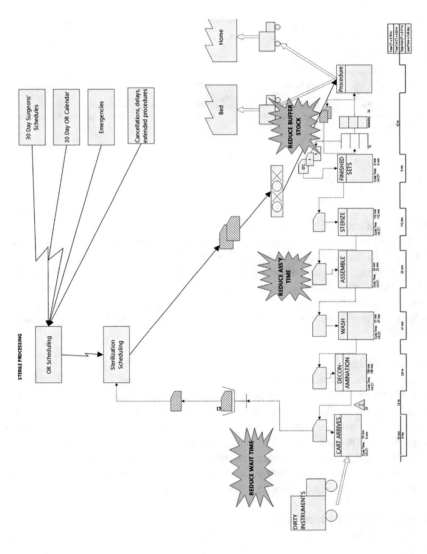

Fig. 5.10 Future state value stream map with Kaizen burst symbols

The Kaizen bursts show that improvements can be made by reducing wait time prior to moving instruments to the cleaning department, reducing assembly time, and reducing buffer stock. Kaizen is covered later.

Standardized Work Design

6

In previous lessons, you learned how to change a traditional batch-and-queue value stream into a Lean value stream. Now we will discuss the design of the actual work that will take place within the processes of the value stream. By going a level deeper we will be able to improve the flow of work *within* the different processes in the value stream. Specifically, you will learn how to design continuous flow work cells. The Lean principles described apply to any work, including that done in administrative areas, transactions (such as charging a credit card) services, and so on.

6.1 Selecting Subprojects

The first step in work design is to identify subprojects within the value stream. Subprojects, sometimes called project "loops," are determined by looking at the future state value stream map and choosing groups of related processes in the value stream for improvement analysis. Each subproject will probably require a different team with its own set of knowledge, skills, and abilities. However, it is desirable to have at least one member of the Lean team who participates on all of the subproject teams. Figure 6.1 shows a future state value stream map for identifying and processing stroke patients with subprojects identified with dashed boxes and Kaizen burst symbols.

Once subprojects are identified, the Lean team must decide which subproject to pursue first, second, third, and so on. As a rule, it is a good idea to begin at the customer end of the value stream and work backwards. This provides the customer with improved service that they can see and feel quickly. Another criterion is that the pacemaker process should be improved early, since it sets the pace for the rest of the value stream. The "Inside-Out Rule" should be observed: get your own house in order before extending your improvement efforts to include the value streams of outside customers and suppliers. Of course, your decision regarding the starting point should also take into account the likelihood that the subproject will have a big impact on the business and its customers.

© The Author(s), under exclusive license to Springer Nature Switzerland AG 2021
T. Pyzdek, *The Lean Healthcare Handbook*, Management for Professionals,
https://doi.org/10.1007/978-3-030-69901-7_6

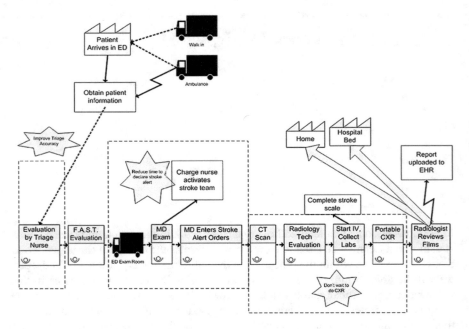

Fig. 6.1 Subproject loops

Do not think of the future state value stream map as untouchable. If, as you go through the exercise of selecting and prioritizing subprojects, you see an obvious improvement that is not on the map, revise the map. Remember, the goal is to improve as much and as quickly as possible.

Once the subprojects have been identified and prioritized, treat each of them as you would any project. I.e., for each project find a sponsor (the value stream owner is a good candidate) write a charter, select a team, develop a schedule, identify stakeholders, etc. Eventually these things will become second nature to you.

6.2   Elements of Work

Figure 6.2 shows the relationship between value streams, processes, operations, workplaces, and procedures in the creation of value. The relationship is hierarchical. To implement Lean all levels of the hierarchy are considered. In previous lessons, we discussed ways to change value streams by replacing batch-and-queue push scheduling systems with Lean value streams where work is scheduled to maximize flow. Several other lessons focus on ways to improve processes, the next level of the hierarchy. For example, by using process maps to see how work flows through processes or by identifying non-value-added work. In designing work cells we will go deeper than the process level and look at the design of operations, including the layout of workplaces and the standard procedures followed to perform the work in

Fig. 6.2 Value creation
hierarchy

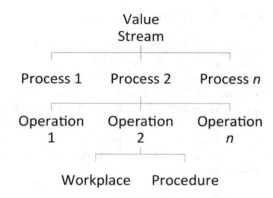

each operation. Such operations are known as standard operations, because the way work is performed follows strict standard procedures.

Processes are distinct sets of operations nested within a value stream. Process improvement requires knowledge of the root causes creating process problems. In the context of designing continuous flow work cells in Lean, we focus primarily on the things in a process that inhibit flow, such as

- Non-value added process steps, as defined in earlier lessons.
- The distance people, materials, or WIP travel between process steps (from the spaghetti chart).
- Changeover, setup, and adjustment time (discussed below).
- Identify the root causes that are creating quality issues that are responsible for scrap, rework, or problems downstream (discussed in later chapters on continuous improvement).

In Lean we design work cells that improve the processes as well as the specific operations within a work cell. We get into "nitty-gritty" details of the work itself, considering how materials are handled and moved, fixtures and instruments, work-place layout, movement of various workers, movement of "work objects" (e.g., patients), etc. The transfer of work elements (small units of work) between workers is carefully considered. "Work" is the sum of all of the work elements required to create one complete unit of product or service through the entire value stream.

Principles of Motion Economy[1]

The rigorous study of efficient work design predates Lean by several decades. As a Lean Healthcare Advisor, you should take advantage of this by learning the principles discovered long ago. Here are those principles most relevant to the design of work cells. You will see that we draw on these principles heavily when we discuss specific recommendations for work cells. Knowing the principles on which Lean is based will help you understand why the recommendations are made, and it will make it possible for you to go beyond what you learn in Lean Advisor training to discover improvements of your own. My goal is not just to teach you Lean, it is to teach you how to learn.

Use of the Human Body
- The two hands should begin as well as complete their motions at the same time.
- The two hands should not be idle at the same time except during rest periods.
- Motions of the arms should be made in opposite and symmetrical directions and should be made simultaneously.
- Hand and body motions should be confined to the lowest classification with which it is possible to perform the work satisfactorily.
- Momentum should be employed to assist the worker wherever possible, and it should be reduced to a minimum if it must be overcome by muscular effort.
- Smooth continuous motion of the hands is preferable to straight line motions involving sudden and sharp changes in direction.
- Ballistic movements are faster, easier, and more accurate than restricted (fixation) or controlled movements.
- Work should be arranged to permit an easy and natural rhythm wherever possible.
- Eye fixations should be as few and as close together as possible.

Arrangement of the Workplace
- There should be a definite and fixed place for all instruments, tools, and materials.
- Tools, materials, and controls should be located close to the point of use.
- Gravity feed bins and containers should be used to deliver material close to the point of use.
- Drop deliveries should be used wherever possible.[2]
- Materials and tools should be located to permit the best sequence of motions.
- Provisions should be made for adequate conditions for seeing. Good illumination is the first requirement for satisfactory visual perception.

---

[1]Ralph M. Barnes (1937) *Motion and Time Study Measurement of Work*, reprinted by John Wiley & Sons, New York, 1980. This is the classic, seminal work on the subject and these principles are still relevant today.

[2]Gravity feed bins, gravity chutes, and other mechanisms that "drop" the needed parts and tools to the proper place for use by the worker or for moving the part(s) to the next operation.

- The height of the workplace and the chair should preferably be arranged so that alternate sitting and standing at work are easily possible.
- A chair of the type and height to permit good posture should be provided for every worker.

Design of Tools and Equipment
- The hands should be relieved of all work that can be done more advantageously by a jig, a fixture, or a foot-operated device.
- Two or more tools should be combined wherever possible.
- Tools and materials should be pre-positioned whenever possible.
- Where each finger performs some specific movement, such as in typewriting, the load should be distributed in accordance with the inherent capacities of the fingers.
- Levers, hand wheels, and other controls should be located in such positions that the operator can manipulate them with the least change in body position and with the greatest speed and ease.

What Do We Need to Produce? How Many and When?

How fast do we need to produce in order to meet customer demand (takt time)? Goal: produce precisely this much just-in-time for use.

Takt Time
You learned about calculating and using takt time in the chapter Lean Value Stream Design. It is used again here when developing the continuous flow cell. You will recall that takt time, which is synonymous with cycle time in Lean, is calculated as using this equation which was introduced earlier:

$$\text{Takt time} = \frac{\text{Daily operating time}}{\text{Required quantity per day}} \tag{1.1}$$

Once this has been calculated the amount of work for each worker is determined so he can work at a constant cycle time. No extra margin "fudge factor" is allowed. In addition to takt time, the team also determines the speed, degree of skill, and other standards required. New workers are considered trainees until they are able to consistently produce quality work at the required rate.

As with value stream design, the work cell uses takt time as the standard cycle time. Since no fudge factor is included in the calculation, waste becomes obvious. There will also be individual differences in ability that will emerge. While all workers are required to match takt time, some people will be able to produce faster than others. Allowing them to do so in a work cell would be counterproductive, it would merely result in accumulated work-in-process inventory. The work cell must be designed to productively utilize the skills of the superior workers for the benefit of the team and the company. More about this later.

What Are the Requirements for Materials, Machines, and Manpower?

Can the Processes that We have to Meet this Demand? Identifying Work Elements

Decomposing a process into work elements helps you identify sources of waste and allocate work among people. This involves identifying and timing each work element. You will find that some of the work elements are repeated in every work cycle, while others are not. Examples of non-repetitive work are replenishing supplies or getting tools. Work cell design considers only work that is involved in every cycle. Non-repetitive work is either converted to repetitive work, eliminated, or done outside the cell.

To identify the work elements, begin by defining the scope of the work being evaluated. This will be a subset of the work done within the cell. Watch a qualified operator do the work several times. For a while, just observe the work being done to help you get a feel for what is involved. Once you have a sense of the whole, break it down into specific elements. Write down a description of each element and have the team participate until you arrive at a description that everyone understands and agrees upon. Be sure each element description has a clear start and end point. Describe the sequence in which the elements are performed. Identify which activities are done by people and which are done by equipment. Finally, record any non-repetitive work that needs to be done outside of the cell, or which can be eliminated.

What Are the Specific Tasks Required to Complete the Work?

Overall cycle time for the value stream and each process within the value stream is determined by customer demand and the time available for work. This also applies to the rate at which parts (e.g., filled prescriptions, completed lab tests, faxes sent, etc.) are produced *within* a cell. Since parts are completed as work elements are performed, work elements must be timed. When collecting data on work elements the time it takes a capable worker to complete each work element must be determined. Collect actual data from various people doing the work. Work element time will not be based on the very fastest or slowest time, rather you are looking for a representative time that can be performed repeatedly over a reasonable time period. The descriptive statistic most useful for this purpose will be a measure of central tendency, such as the mean (average) the median, or the mode.

Table 6.1 shows an example of a process study which recorded the time it took three different people to place prescription refill orders into a fax machine. Five times were observed for each person, the times recorded, and statistics calculated. There are three central tendency statistics recorded:

1. *Mean*. Sum divided by count. Means are heavily influenced by outliers, so they are less useful if there are one or a few values there are much different than the others.
2. *Median*. When values are put into rank order, the number in the middle is the median. If there are an even number of values, the median is the midpoint between the two middle values.

Table 6.1 Work element time data (seconds)

Process	Work element	Person	Time 1	Time 2	Time 3	Time 4	Time 5	Mean	Median	Mode
Refill prescription	Place fax in machine	A	5	3	5	5	4	4.4	5	5
		B	7	6	6	8	5	6.4	6	6
		C	5	4	4	4	3	4.0	4	4

3. *Mode*. The value that occurs most often. There can be more than one mode, i.e., if there are two different numbers that occur equally often. For example, if you have these numbers: 3, 3, 4, 4, 4, 5, 5, 5, 6, 7 then the modes are 4 and 5.

Based on these data the team will determine the standard time for this work element. (What would you choose to be the standard time for the process shown in Table 6.1?[3]) I suggest that work elements be timed by recording several cycles with a camera and evaluating the recording off-line. You can use a video timeline to identify precisely when an operation starts and stops, or you can get this information with the pause button and a stopwatch. Your team should all agree on the start and stop definitions. Getting to a consensus on this is often surprisingly challenging!

Take another look at Table 6.1 again. Note that Worker B takes longer than either Worker A or Worker C. Such person-to-person variability is to be expected; people are different after all. In the work cell designed for multiple workers, you want to arrange overlap in areas of responsibility so the faster workers can help whenever the slower workers fall behind. Lean recognizes that it is the team, not the individual worker, that produces value. It is not a contest or a competition. It makes no sense to have the faster workers in a cell producing at a rate that exceeds takt time while slower workers produce at a rate less than takt time. People must work together to help their company compete.

Example of Calculating Production Capacity

Once you have the cycle time data for all of the work elements, you can combine the data to determine the overall production capacity. Figure 6.3 shows this analysis for a surgical instrument cleaning process. The production capacity (column H) is based on the net operating time per three shift day, which does not include two scheduled 10-min breaks or a 30-min lunch break per shift (cell G7, 77,400 s) divided by the total time per piece. In this example, a "piece" is a set/cart of surgical instruments required for a procedure. The production capacity for the process is the smallest production capacity for all required operations. In this case, the value is 13 units, the production capacity for the mechanical clean operation. Since this exceeds the quantity needed per day of 12 (cell G5) this process has barely adequate capacity, assuming unplanned downtime, quality problems, etc. are held in check. A small buffer inventory is probably a good idea.

Bottlenecks

If the production capacity is less than the quantity needed per day we would have a *bottleneck* which we need to address so we can meet the required demand. In Lean a bottleneck is any process that has a cycle time that is greater than takt time.[4] It is

---

[3]I would choose 5 s. It is close to the overall mean, and it is the average of the three medians and also the average of the three modes.

[4]In the Theory of Constraints a bottleneck is defined differently.

	A	B	C	D	E	F	G	H
1								
2					Prepared By		Date	
3					Jane B. Campbell		31-Jul-17	
4			Process Name		Part Number		Quantity Needed per Day	
5							12 sets	
6			Surgical Instrument Cleaning		Surgical Instruments		Net Operating Time (sec)	
7							77,400	
8					Basic Time (sec)		Summary (sec)	
9		#	Operation Name	Manual Time	Auto Time	Completion Time per Piece	Total Time per Piece	Production Capacity
10		1	Initial Prep	1200	0	1200	1200	65
11		2	Pre-treatment	1500	0	1500	1500	52
12		3	Manual wash	2400	0	2400	2400	32
13		4	Ultrasound soak	300	1800	2100	2100	37
14		5	Rinse/soak	300	1200	1500	1500	52
15		6	Dry	120	3600	3720	3720	21
16		7	Mechanical clean	300	5600	5900	5900	13
17		8						
18		9						
19		10						
20		11						
21		12						
22		13						
23								
24		Total:		6120	12200		Max Output	13

Fig. 6.3 Production capacity for instrument cleaning process

possible to have multiple bottleneck operations. There are several ways of breaking bottlenecks:

- *Improve its cycle time*. Use Lean, Kaizen (discussed later) and other methods. You should review the Production Capacity Table for the process and focus your attention on the operation with the lowest production capacity. Look at the basic time and changeover time for ideas about improving the operation.
- *Improve quality*. It is vital that the units produced by the bottleneck conform to requirements. Take extra care that only acceptable quality materials are delivered to the bottleneck. Aggressively address any issues with the quality of production created by the bottleneck.
- *Supplement bottleneck production with purchased materials*. Use a supplier to fill the gap temporarily until the bottleneck is brought up to capacity.
- *Work the bottleneck longer hours*. This option will require using a batch-and-queue push system until a better option, such as one of the approaches above, can be implemented. The real-time output from the bottleneck can be supplemented with inventory produced earlier by the bottleneck. Try to keep this additional inventory to an absolute minimum.
- *Add capacity*. Purchase additional equipment to allow additional production. This is usually the least desirable option because it tends to lock in the added expense. If you need to do this, look into leasing equipment.

What Materials Do We Need to Have on Hand in Order to Produce the Items? (Standard Stock)

Standard stock refers to the materials that are needed to begin work within a process, such as work-in-process inventory (WIP.) The design of the work cell will influence the WIP requirements. Ideally, one piece will start at the beginning of the work cell and progress through each process step without the need to stop. However, there are circumstances that may require additional time to complete a step before beginning the next step. For example, if a culture is taken and needs to be incubated before it can be processed, then it makes sense to create several cultures for processing later. Or if there is a need to perform an inspection before an item is used in a place where it cannot be accessed afterwards (e.g., a stent is placed into a patient.) The bottleneck situation described above may require some amount of additional WIP.

What Equipment Do We Need in Order to Produce the Needed Items?

Small, Flexible/Mobile, "Fast-Enough" Machines

Equipment in work cells tends to be smaller and more flexible than the equipment used for mass production batch-and-queue operations. The machines used in Lean are also often slower than those used for batch-and-queue systems. There are several reasons for this:

1. Smaller machines can be placed closer together. This reduces the travel distance required by the workers. Since WIP inventory is small or non-existent, we do not need as much space between machines for storage of inventory.
2. Equipment used in Lean work cells can be slower, "fast-enough" is good enough. Unlike mass production equipment, the goal is not to produce a large batch for inventory, it is to produce at the pace of customer demand, takt. This means that a machine running at a rate faster than the required rate is wasteful.[5]
3. Smaller machines save space. Lean work areas often produce triple the value per square foot compared with their non-Lean counterparts.
4. Small machines can be moved more easily. A work cell can be quickly reconfigured by rearranging equipment to produce a variety of different parts.
5. Flexible machines must be easy to set up fast. If changeover and setup times are low, it is easier to complete a variety of items or procedures in small quantities.
6. Small, slower, and more flexible machines are less expensive, easier to operate, and easier to maintain.

---

[5]Cost accounting systems are often designed to measure output from individual pieces of equipment rather than from value streams. These systems need to be modified to accurately measure the Lean value stream; failure to do this can undermine the entire Lean program.

Equipment is also used in office environments. Computers, printers, fax machines, file systems, desks, tables, mail carts, etc. are needed to perform work in an office. The Lean equipment principles also apply here.

Autonomation (Jidoka)

Autonomation is Taiichi Ohno of Toyota's word to describe a production system that mimics the human autonomic nervous system, i.e., the system automatically adjusts to changes in external and internal conditions. For example, when we get too hot, our body automatically reacts to cool us down by making us sweat; we do not have to think about it. Similarly, production systems should react to customer demands, increasing production when demand goes up or decreasing production when demand goes down. They should react to Work-in-Process inventory buildup by producing less or producing on a different schedule. Lean mechanisms to accomplish this include Takt time, visual controls, pull systems, exploiting constraints, etc.

Actually, this concept was embodied in the very first product made by Toyota, a loom. From an early age Sakichi Toyoda worked on improving looms. In 1891, he obtained his first patent for the Toyoda wooden handloom. Among the innovations was the feature that the loom stopped if a thread broke. It can be argued that this invention led directly to the formation of the Toyota automobile company. A company was founded in 1926 as Toyoda Automatic Loom Works, Ltd. by Sakichi Toyoda. In 1933, the company established its automobile department, led by Kiichiro Toyoda, the eldest son of Sakichi Toyoda. This department was spun out as Toyota Motor Co., Ltd. in 1937 and is now the well-known Toyota Motor Corporation.

Autonomation within a work cell is used to eliminate the need for an operator to stand and watch a machine as it does its work. Work cell equipment is intelligent in the sense that it stops and signals when an operation is complete, or if there is a problem.[6] Although operators often load the machines, the machines usually unload automatically. More importantly, after the operators load and start the machines, they move on to other activities in the cell or elsewhere rather than watching or tending to the machines.

Modifying equipment to use Jidoka is usually quite simple and inexpensive. Microswitches, simple sensors, light beam, and other simple mechanisms are commonly used for the purpose. Poka-yoke is Japanese for mistake-proofing. These devices are used either to prevent the special causes that result in defects, or to inexpensively inspect each item that is produced to determine whether it is acceptable or defective. A poka-yoke device is any mechanism that either prevents a mistake from being made or makes the mistake obvious at a glance.

---

[6]This is an example of poka-yoke or mistake-proofing.

6.3   What Methods Should Be Used to Accomplish the Goal Using the Resources that We Have?

Standard Operations Routine Sheet

What standard work procedures should everyone follow? Designing continuous flow work cells involves developing standard operations. These are descriptions of work that combine people, equipment, and materials to create value as effectively as possible. The components of standard operations are:

1. Takt time.
2. The work procedure.
3. The parts and materials essential to start work within the process, including parts or materials at the machines.

If all three of these components are not present, standard operations cannot exist.

At companies like Toyota standard operations are determined by the foreman. Toyota foremen are masters of the work being done by their employees. Foremen are able to demonstrate the standards to their people. If an impartial observer agrees that the pace of work being done by the foreman following the standard is appropriate, then Toyota expects workers to adhere to the standards.

In many companies, however, things are done differently. It is my experience with non-Japanese clients that there are few supervisors who are able to do all of the work being done by their employees. The history of management in America and most European countries has led to a system where work is designed by experts in work design (industrial engineers) supervised by experts in management (foremen and supervisors) and performed by blue-collar specialists at a given trade (machinists, assemblers, welders, assembly line workers, etc.). This model worked adequately[7] in the past for batch-and-queue systems where specialization was the norm, but it is no longer possible to remain competitive using this approach.

This raises a question: if we do not have a well-rounded supervisor to design work, how can work design be done? The answer at many companies is to use teams. Teams designing and analyzing work are provided with basic training in the principles of work design, inventory control, and Lean; that is what this lesson and previous lessons are all about. The team must include at least one member who is highly skilled at the work done at each process in the subproject loop. Preferably this will be the same person, but if there is no such person available the team may have more than one skilled worker. Once the work of several people/machines is combined into a work cell, the company will need to cross train all of the workers in the cell so that they may help one another.

It may be that no one person on the team knows as much about work design as the industrial engineer, or as much about management as the business school graduate,

---

[7]This is a debatable premise today, but it isn't fair to judge past behaviors by current day standards.

or as much about any operation as the blue-collar journeyman, but experience has shown that tremendous improvements are possible using the team approach–if the company leadership truly embraces the Lean philosophy.

Standard operations are the sum total of all of the ways that people, materials, equipment, and information combine to create value. There are three components to standard operations[8]:

- Cycle time
- Work procedure (work sequence)
- Standard stock on hand (WIP)

Each of these items is required to standardize the operations.

Are There Any "Tips" that People Should Know About Doing the Work?

Knowledge of work is often a collection of insights. Experienced people have developed tricks that make it easy to do the task at hand, or help them avoid problems that might cause injuries or quality issues. When designing the work you should create a document that can be given to workers showing them what to look for. This will include such things as the work sequence, how to handle the items (e.g., lab specimens) how to set up the equipment needed for the job, and other relevant work details. The emphasis is on specific, concrete directions. Avoid abstractions. Include drawings, videos, pictures, animations, and other media to help show the proper way to do the work. Flowcharts are often helpful.

A model for work instructions is the instructions provided to customers for assembling consumer products. Figure 6.4 shows the instructions for assembling a baby's crib. It includes step-by-step directions, drawings, safety warnings, tips on how to put the crib together more easily. It also includes tips on maintenance, cleaning, and storage; guidance on how to test your work to assure that it is done correctly; instructions on changing the crib into a toddler bed; etc. There are also videos on YouTube. Think of work instructions as the workplace counterpart to assembly instructions for consumers and you will have a good idea of what is needed. The idea is to provide simple, easy-to-understand, and complete instructions.

Manual of Work Directions

The manual of work directions tells how to perform the standard operations properly. It is based on the production capacity table (e.g., Fig. 6.3) and the standard operations routine sheet. It describes the work to be done by each person in the work cell. In addition, the manual includes:

---

[8]*Kanban Just-in-Time at Toyota*, 1989, Lu, David J. translator, Productivity Inc., Portland, OR., p. 101.

CRIB ASSEMBLY INSTRUCTIONS
For cribs with hidden hardware.

DO NOT USE POWER TOOLS!

Step 1: Lay the Mattress Support Spring upside down on the floor (Scissor Lifts facing up). Unscrew the Nut and Hex Bolt at each of the four corners of the Spring. Rotate the short arm of the Scissor Lift away from the middle of the spring toward the outside of the spring, and screw the short arm back onto the Spring with the Nut and Hex Bolt you just removed. Repeat on each corner. *This configuration puts the Spring in the highest position, which is the height recommended for newborns. To select a lower position, unscrew the Nut on the long arm of the Scissor Lift and move it closer to the middle of the Spring. The closer to the middle, the lower the mattress height will be.*

Step 2: Attach one of the two Stabilizer Bars to the remaining holes in the Scissor Lift with two Hex Bolts and Hex Wrench. Make sure the metal inserts on the Stabilizer Bar are toward the floor and the Stabilizer Bar is on the inside of the spring assembly as pictured below. Repeat for the other Stabilizer Bar on the other side of the spring. Place one Wood Dowel in each of the holes on the ends of the Stabilizer Bars. Now flip the entire assembly over so that it rests on the stabilizer bars.

Step 3: Attach the Stationary Side to one of the End Panels with two Long Decorative Bolts using the enclosed Allen Wrench. Place the Bolts through the End Panel and secure the Side, but DO NOT tighten completely yet. Repeat this procedure with the other End Panel.

Step 4: Move the Spring and Stabilizer Assembly inside the End Panel and Side Assembly. Lift the Spring Assembly up and position the Dowels in the ends of the Stabilizer Bars into the dowel holes (the upper of the two) drilled in each End Panel. Use the four Short Decorative Bolts to secure the Spring Assembly in the bottom holes, but DO NOT tighten the Bolts completely yet. Leave at least half an inch on each Bolt in order to make the next steps easier.

Step 5: Place a Plastic Roller Wheel and Flathead Screw into the top insert on the inside of each End Panel. Tighten the Screw completely, then *back it off about a quarter turn so the Plastic Roller Wheel spins freely*. Place a Metal Guide Pin into the bottom insert of each End Panel using a Phillips Head Screwdriver to tighten securely.

Steps 1 & 2   Spring and Stabilizer Bar Assembly

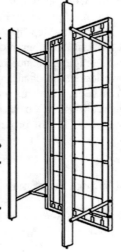

Steps 3, 4 & 5   End Panel and Stationary Side Assembly

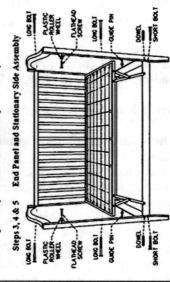

Fig. 6.4 Crib assembly instructions

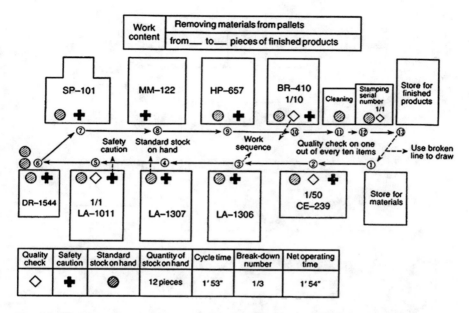

Fig. 6.5 Manufacturing standard operations bulletin example (*Kanban Just-in-Time at Toyota* (1989), Productivity Press, Portland, OR. P. 114.)

- Safety and quality items for each step in the work sequence
- Illustrations of machine placement for work performed by each individual worker
- Cycle time for each operation
- Work sequence
- Standard stock on hand
- Instructions for checking quality

Machine placement is shown on a separate sheet of 11 × 17 paper (A3 size paper.) The sheet will have columns showing work sequence, standard stock on hand, cycle time, net operating time, and safety and quality checks. The completed sheet is called a *Standard Operations Bulletin*. Figure 6.5 shows a Standard Operations Bulletin for a manufacturing process. A healthcare standard operations bulletin is shown in Fig. 6.6 Standard Operations Bulletin Example (Surgical Instruments Cleaning).

Standard Operations Bulletins are displayed at the workplace and show the workers what is expected of them. In addition, supervisors can use the bulletins as visual control tools to audit compliance with work instructions. Managers and Process Improvement Teams can study the bulletins for ideas on improving the work.

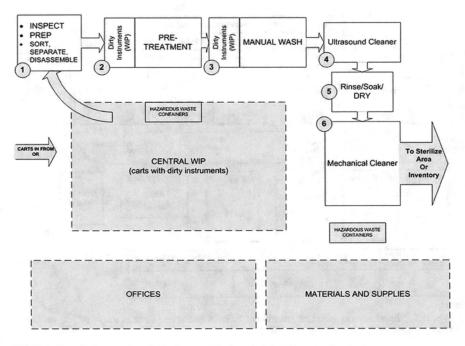

Fig. 6.6 Standard operations bulletin example (surgical instruments cleaning)

Which Non-Value-Added Activities Can Be Eliminated Immediately?

Of course, the standard work description, including the work element times, is just a starting point. Constant improvement is expected in the way the work is done and the time it takes to do it. For the long term, consider creating an opportunity map for the work within the cell and pursuing the opportunities over time. It is a good idea to do this even before the original work cell design is complete. You can use the work element time data you collected for this purpose. Create a stacked bar chart showing all of the work element in the work cell (Fig. 6.7). One of the bars is for the work elements used currently, the other will show only the work elements that are actually included in the work cell design. In particular, you need to focus on eliminating non-value added work. You may recall that work is considered value added only if *all* of the following are true:

1. It is done right the first time. Rework does not count as value-added work.
2. The customer is willing to pay for it.
3. It changes the thing being worked on. Moves, inspection, or storage are not value-added.

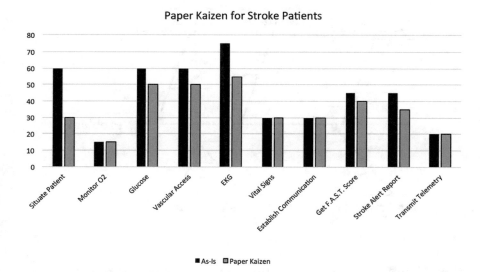

Fig. 6.7 Paper Kaizen

Figure 6.7 shows a bar chart of the initial improvements that can be made to a stroke patient treat and transport by ambulance process. To create the paper Kaizen teams focus on identifying non-value work elements such as waiting and moving. The team's paper Kaizen indicates that a 20% reduction in total cycle time in the stroke patient treatment process (excluding transportation) should be possible.

6.4   How Should the Workplace Be Arranged?

Lean work takes place in work cells. Work cell design is performed in two phases.

- *Phase 1*: Document the current state. This topic has been covered in several earlier chapters. At this point in your Lean project, you have already created a Lean value stream at the process level. Cell design begins from there.
- *Phase 2*: Convert to a process-based layout. How should these elements be combined to achieve the maximum flow of value? Cause-and-Effect Diagrams are a useful tool here. Cause-and-effect diagrams are used to identify the causes of a problem you are trying to solve. Here the problem is one of achieving continuous flow. When creating a cause-and-effect diagram use the "5 Ms" as a starting point: **M**en (and women) **M**ethods, **M**achines, **M**aterials, and **M**easurements (see Fig. 6.8). Each "twig" on the diagram will be something that causes or might cause the problem.

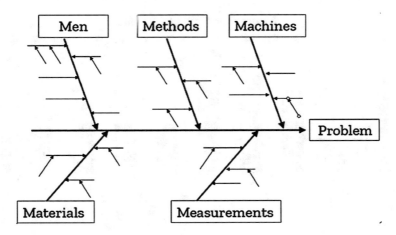

Fig. 6.8 Cause-and-effect diagram template

How Should We Layout the Equipment so Movement of People and Materials Is Efficient?

Continuous flow work cells are nearly always shaped like either "U" or "C" to minimize walking. The equipment and workstations are arranged close together in the sequence of the work steps. This arrangement reduces the walking distance to a minimum and results in the worker being near the start point of the next work cycle when he completes the work cycle. It is different than many traditional work arrangements where a worker sits or stands in one position and does a very simple repetitive task all day, such as loading and unloading a machine or typing on a computer. The traditional non-Lean work arrangement leads to psychological issues such as boredom or mental fatigue that lead to errors and poor morale, as well as physical problems from repetitive stress injuries. In Lean work, people perform a variety of different tasks and work is much less boring.

Ambulances are examples of healthcare work cells. They are compact, efficient work spaces that can be used for a variety of different situations. Even so, Lean can often be used to improve the efficiency of these work spaces by evaluating things like material storage and non-value added work (Figs. 6.9 and 6.10).

Where Will WIP Be Stored?

Standard stock refers to the materials that are needed to begin work within a process, such as work-in-process inventory (WIP.) The design of the work cell will influence the WIP requirements; conversely, WIP requirements will influence the design of the work cell. Ideally, one piece or work unit will start at the beginning of the work cell and progress through each process step without the need to stop. This is not always possible. For example, if a basket of instruments is placed in an enzyme soak for

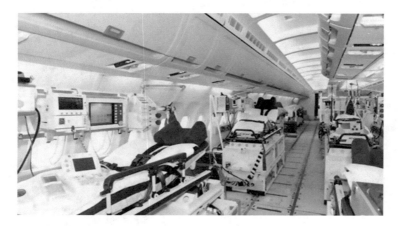

Fig. 6.9 Air ambulance work cell layout

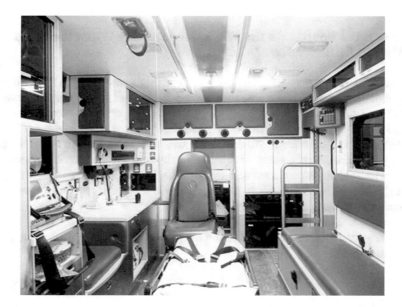

Fig. 6.10 An ambulance as a work cell

some period of time. Or if there is a need to perform an inspection before the item is placed somewhere that it cannot be accessed afterwards, such as inside of a patient. Bottlenecks, by definition, cannot produce enough to meet takt time requirements. The bottleneck problem is sometimes solved by additional WIP to supplement the bottleneck's output (Fig. 6.11).

Fig. 6.11 Material storage in an ambulance

How Can We Rearrange the Workplace Quickly When We Need to Make a Different Item?

As discussed earlier, the equipment used for Lean production tends to be smaller and more mobile. It is usually possible to rearrange the equipment in a work cell quickly so different things can be produced using the same equipment. Work cell design should make this as simple to do as possible. Also consider where equipment, fixtures, WIP and other items will be placed when not needed for the item currently being produced. Storage areas should be nearby and clearly marked so workers know where to store unneeded resources, and where to find them when they are needed again. It should be easy to physically move the equipment and, if necessary, reconnect to power, plumbing, etc.

Healthcare examples where changeover is crucial include operating rooms, emergency department and physician practice examination rooms, ambulances, and many others.

6.5 How Many People Are Needed?

Consider the process described in Fig. 6.3. The requirement for this process is shown in the figure to be 12 sets of surgical instruments. The team's idea for the process was to set it up as shown in Fig. 6.12, which you will recall having seen used previously for a different purpose in Fig. 6.6. The partial-U shape will minimize the distance that people need to move. It is not a completed U or C because the cleaned instruments exit via a connected sterilized area. However, when the operator completes the last step they are at the Central WIP area where they can pick up the next cart for cleaning.

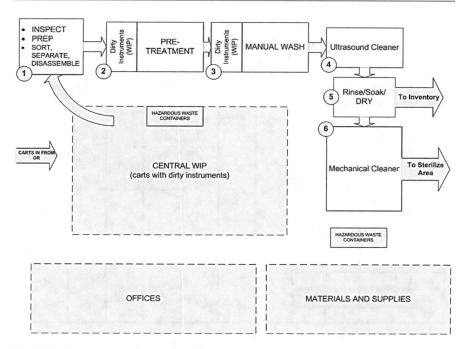

Fig. 6.12 Instrument cleaning work cell layout

Figure 6.13 shows the standard operations routine sheet for the process. This sheet graphically shows a time line for each operation, the manual time, the automated machine time, and the travel time. The total time to complete a full cycle for this process is 12,200 s (see either Fig. 6.13 or Fig. 6.3).

An additional advantage to the continuous cell layout is that workers do not waste time standing around waiting for a machine to finish a task. Instead, they load one machine, start it, and move to the next operation in the cell while the machine completes its automatic cycle. Although some machines continue to operate automatically at this time, the operator can return to the beginning of the process and start another cycle. By the time the operator reaches each operation on the next cycle, the machines will have completed their cycle and, due to autonomation (Jidoka) they will have automatically stopped and, in some cases, unloaded. In the example surgical instrument cleaning process shown in Fig. 6.13, the ultrasound soak, rinse/soak, dry, and mechanical clean processes continue to operate well after the 6120 s mark when manual operations are concluded.

What Skills Do the People Need?

The Lean cell layout requires that workers be multi-skilled and able to handle as many of the tasks as possible in the work cell. This differs from an operations-based

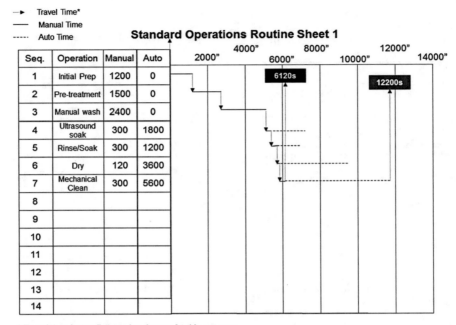

Seq.	Operation	Manual	Auto
1	Initial Prep	1200	0
2	Pre-treatment	1500	0
3	Manual wash	2400	0
4	Ultrasound soak	300	1800
5	Rinse/Soak	300	1200
6	Dry	120	3600
7	Mechanical Clean	300	5600
8			
9			
10			
11			
12			
13			
14			

* Travel time is small enough to ignore for this process

Fig. 6.13 Instrument cleaning work flow

layout where, in a medical test lab for example, all tissue dissection is done by one individual, all tissue freezing by another, etc. In contrast, a Lean lab where everyone was cross-trained would have all workers know how to perform all of the tasks competently.

Cross-training in many healthcare facilities is complicated by the need for advanced education and training and credentialing for many positions. Table 6.2 provides a case in point that is not atypical. Nevertheless, whenever possible cross-training should be seriously considered. Having flexible workers is very important in Lean.[9]

How Can We Keep Track of Cross-Training?

Of course, this cross-training standard of perfection is seldom achieved. In the vast majority of cases some people are qualified to perform some tasks, but not others. Because of this, it is a good idea to keep track of which person has which skill in a Lean work cell. Figure 6.14 shows an example of how you might keep track of who is trained to do which task.

---

[9]http://bit.ly/2tz0p4l.

Table 6.2 Roles and responsibilities in the lab

Position	Education & training	Responsibilities
Laboratory director	Doctoral degree (e.g., MD or PhD); sometimes a medical laboratory scientist Board certification recommended	Directs and manages all lab operations and ensures quality patient care; Interprets test results, with consulting pathologist
Technical supervisor	Doctoral degree (e.g., MD or PhD); may be Master's or bachelor's degree with experience Board certification recommended May be the same person as the lab director	Provides oversight of technical and scientific functions of the lab
General supervisor	May be the same person as the lab director or technical supervisor Depending on lab and experience, MLS/MT or MLT may qualify	Provides oversight of day-to-day functions of the lab
Medical Laboratory Scientist (MLS) or Medical Technologist (MT)	Bachelor degree in clinical/medical laboratory science or life sciences and completion of accredited MLS/MT program Licensure/certification may be required by employers	Performs routine tests; develops new test methods under supervision; performs quality control tests; becomes group or team leader; supervises, teaches, delegates
Medical Laboratory Technician (MLT)	Associate degree and completion of accredited MLT or certificate program Licensure/certification may be required by employers	Performs routine tests and quality control tests under supervision on MLS/MT
Specialized fields		
Pathology assistant	Master's degree and board certification	Gross examination and dissection of tissue samples sent to anatomic pathology lab; assist with autopsies
Cytogeneticist	Doctoral degree (e.g., MD or PhD) and board certification	Performs cytogenetic analyses to diagnose chromosomal abnormalities in human genetic diseases
Cytogenetic technologist	Bachelor degree (B.A. or B.S.) in the sciences or clinical/medical laboratory science CG certification recommended	Prepares biological specimens for cell culture and microscopic analyses as part of cytogenetic studies; assists the cytogeneticist
Cytotechnologist (CT)	Bachelor degree and completion of accredited CT program	Examines human cells under the microscope for signs of pathology (e.g., Pap smears for signs of cancer); with appropriate experience, may supervise a cytology laboratory

(continued)

Table 6.2   (continued)

Position	Education & training	Responsibilities
Histotechnologist (HTL) or Histologist	Bachelor degree and completion of accredited HTL program	Prepares tissue samples for microscopic examination by the pathologist and performs complex procedures; can supervise histologic technicians and, with appropriate experience, may supervise histology laboratory
Histologic technician (HT)	High school degree and completion of accredited histology program	Prepares sections of body tissues for microscopic examination by pathologist, processes tissue biopsies, assists histotechnologists
Phlebotomist (PBT)	High school degree and training or work experience	Collects blood samples from patients for lab tests

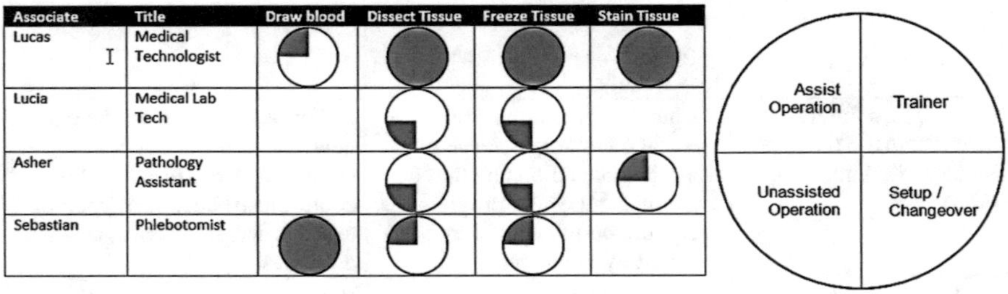

Fig. 6.14   Cross-training chart

How Can We Arrange the Workplace and Assign Workers so Those Working in it Can Easily Help One Another?

Yet another efficiency enhancement is that when more than one person is working in the cell the workers can help each other if one of them falls behind. Quality also improves as workers are able to check on each other's work and often catch quality problems right away. Work cell layout should deliberately take this into account, making it easy for a more experienced worker to help a fellow worker. Worker assignment should also consider this. Try to assign workers so new or slower people have more experienced and faster workers on either side or immediately after them in the flow.

Keeping the workplace clean and organized is an essential part of Lean. The standardized approach to work is completely dependent upon maintaining discipline in the workplace. Procedures are useless if they are not maintained and followed. Change is not only inevitable, it is desirable and pursued continuously. When the favorable change has been discovered it is made part of the standard.

The workplace itself is the physical manifestation of the standard. It includes the materials, equipment, and tools needed to do the work according to the standard. It does not include anything that is *not* needed. Just as the work cell is laid out to produce maximum efficiency, the details are also arranged to achieve this goal. The necessary tools are placed where they can be easily and immediately accessed when needed. Strict housekeeping is enforced to assure that clutter is non-existent; clutter is not needed to do the work, so it is to be eliminated. In Lean the system used to create and maintain an efficient, clutter-free, and clean workplace is known as "5S." 5S is the starting point for Lean deployment. 5S stands for Sort, Set in order, Shine, Standardize, and Sustain. These terms are defined as follows:

- *Sort*. Clearly distinguish what is necessary to do the job from what is not. Eliminate the unnecessary.
- *Set in order*. Put needed items in their correct place to allow for easy accessibility and retrieval.
- *Shine*. Keep the workplace clean and clear of clutter. This promotes safety as well as efficiency.
- *Standardized cleanup*. Develop an approach to maintaining a clean and orderly work environment that works.
- *Sustain*. Make a habit of maintaining your workplace.

T. Pyzdek, *The Lean Healthcare Handbook*, Management for Professionals, https://doi.org/10.1007/978-3-030-69901-7_7

7.1   Sort

Earlier in the training, we focused attention on process steps and operations activities that were non-value-added. The same search for waste occurs with 5S during the Sort phase. Sort means that you vigorously search for items in the work place that are not needed to perform the value-added work being done. This is much more difficult than it sounds. People tend to want to hold on to things "just in case" they are needed at a future time. This mentality is an artifact that results from the pre-lean era when unforeseen problems–for example, equipment failures, quality defects, bottlenecks, etc.—created such needs. This hoarding behavior results in the accumulation of things that are not needed in a well-designed Lean work cell. They take up space that is needed for production and they get in the way of smooth movement within the work cell.

Red-Tagging

To deal with the "we may need this later" mentality, and the general uncertainty and psychological distress regarding what is and is not needed, it is best to proceed by placing an item in a holding area before discarding it completely. In Lean, this is done by using physical pieces of paper called red-tags. When a red-tag is placed on an item the team is asking three questions:

1. Is this item needed in this work cell?
2. If the answer to #1 is yes, is it needed in this quantity?
3. Does this item need to be located here?

Items that are red-tagged are considered one-by-one and one of the following actions is taken:

- They are left where they are.
- They are moved to another location for storage.
- They are held in a local red-tag holding area for a specified period of time to see if they are needed or not.
- They are disposed of, i.e., thrown away, sold, used elsewhere in the company, or moved to a central red-tag holding area.

If large equipment is red-tagged it should be handled as described above if possible. If the equipment cannot be moved it can remain where it is for a while, but it should be removed when it is determined that it is not needed where it is.

> **Aren't You Ashamed?**
> One evening, near the end of a long and arduous day, a team led by Dr. Bob Mecklenburg, Chief of Medicine, and Charleen Tachibana, Chief of Nursing, was huddled with a sensei who had been pushing them for hours. The team was studying a schematic of a section of Virginia Mason when the sensei pointed to an area on the graphic and asked what it was. Dr. Mecklenburg told him it was a waiting room. "Who waits there?" the sensei asked. "Patients," Mecklenburg said. "What are they waiting for?" "The doctor." The sensei asked more questions, learning that there were dozens and dozens of waiting rooms spread throughout the medical center—waiting rooms in every division of every department and most crowded much of the time. The sensei reacted as though an invisible line had been crossed; as though he was deeply offended by this news. "You have one hundred waiting areas where patients wait an average of 45 min for a doctor?" He paused and let the question hang in the air, and then asked, "Aren't you ashamed?" It stunned the team, and yet they all knew the answer was yes, of course—they were ashamed.

The results of the red-tag effort should be documented to show the value of the effort. It is not uncommon for companies to actually postpone or scrap plans to add facility space after seeing the amount of floor space freed as a result of the red-tag program. This is the infamous "hidden factory" made visible. I witnessed an instance where a Sensei walked up to a wall where a facility layout blueprint was tacked up and proceed to mark areas of waste with a red sharpie pen. Waiting area? *Slash*! Rework area? *Slash*! Excess inventory storeroom? *Slash*! When the Sensei finished fully 40% of the facility was shown to be unneeded. The company did not need a new facility, it needed Lean! If you think this does not apply in healthcare, think again (see sidebar "Aren't you ashamed?") (Kenney & others, 2001).

7.2   Set in Order

Once the Sort phase has been completed, it is time to set the remaining needed items in order. Items are arranged and labeled so they are easy to find and use when needed. When this is done a great deal of waste is eliminated in production and office activity. For example, it will no longer be necessary to waste time searching for the needed item, nor will it be necessary to return an item because it was not the item you actually needed. You will make fewer errors due to using the wrong tool or material or form.

Setting in order revolves around standardization, and, conversely, standardization revolves around setting things in order. The key principle is visual control. For example, Fig. 7.1 makes it clear to the surgical team which instrument goes where by providing drawings and verbal descriptions. In factories, Lean teams often keep things simple by drawing outlines of the tools on simple pegboards, as shown in

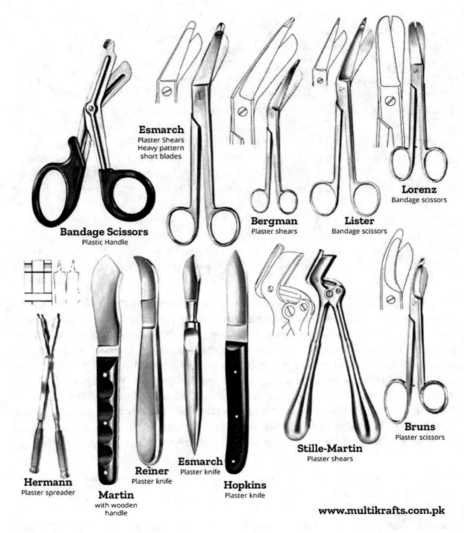

Fig. 7.1 5S surgical instruments organizer

Fig. 7.2. It is then easier to see which items are currently in use, as well as where a given item needs to go when it is returned. If possible, attach the tool to a retractable cord so it automatically returns to the correct location when released. Color-coding the tools helps reduce errors (Fig. 7.3).

To further simplify, teams should organize tools so they are presented in the order of use and are easily accessible to operators. Ideally, operators will be able to get the needed tool without even looking at the tray or pegboard. This may require

Fig. 7.2 Pots and pans
outlined on pegboard

providing storage areas with additional space between tools to make it easy to reach them.[1]

As a general set in order rule, frequently used items are located nearer to the work cell than items used less frequently. Items that are seldom used are usually stored in a remote location to reduce clutter.

Locations (5S Map)

The locations where WIP, jigs, tools, and other equipment are stored can be determined by evaluating the "5S Map." The work flow layout, such as that

---

[1]In the case of the surgical instruments tray, a person normally hands the needed instrument to the surgeon.

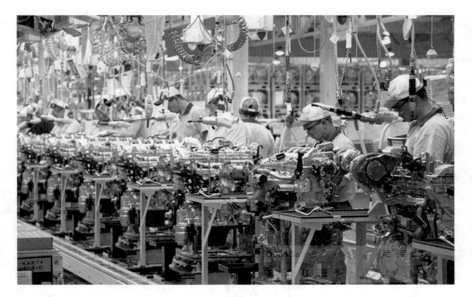

Fig. 7.3 Engine assembly line in Poland with color-coded overhead tools on retractable cords

shown in Fig. 6.12, can serve as the starting point for the 5S map if it is drawn to scale. Creating a 5S map is done as follows:

1. Draw the 5S Map on a floor plan, preferably drawn to scale. Indicate the location of WIP, fixtures, tools, etc. on the scale drawing.
2. Draw a spaghetti diagram of the work flow on the 5S map. Identify wasted motion.
3. Create alternative 5S maps that reduce or eliminate wasted motion.
4. Simulate the work flows represented by the various 5S maps and choose the best alternative. This can be done in the actual work area, or by creating a simulated work area in an empty space such as a warehouse area (Fig. 7.4).
5. Create the new work cell layout, including locating the WIP, tools, fixtures and jigs, etc.

Once the improved layout has been determined, create "signboards" to identify the locations for the various items needed in the work cell. This includes *location indicators* that show where the various items go, such as marking floor areas with tape or paint (Fig. 7.5). It also includes *item indicators* which show the specific items that belong in each location. Finally, you will need *amount indicators* to specify how many of each item are needed. Signboards are used to identify machine locations, locations for standard procedure displays, storage of equipment when it is not being used, location of WIP and finished goods inventory, racks and spaces within racks for various items, and named work areas.

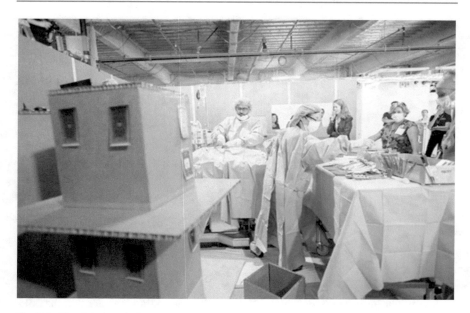

Fig. 7.4 Simulated workplace

Fig. 7.5 Location indicator

Floor locations are often shown in places other than the work cell itself. For example, paint (or colored tape) is used to show aisles and aisle direction, door swing space, storage locations, zones that are off-limits for storage, hazardous areas, etc. Additional information can be conveyed by the use of color-coded paint. For example, red might show off-limit areas, green might show operations areas, and

Fig. 7.6 Lean aisle marked
with colored tape

yellow might indicate divider lines.[2] If you use color-coding, be sure that the color
uses are standardized. See the example in Fig. 7.6.

7.3   Shine

Shine can be thought of as the Lean version of housekeeping. It involves making
sure that dirt, grease, and grime are eliminated from the work place. The goal is to
make the workplace a safe and pleasant place to work. Shine also assures that items
and equipment will be ready to use when needed. Shine is an ongoing activity, not a
once-in-a-while "spring cleaning" type of event.

---

[2]Color-coding has other uses as well. For example, it can be used to show which tools are used
together, which equipment make up a "set" for producing a particular item, etc. Be creative and use
your imagination to identify how to use simple, visual means of conveying information at a glance.

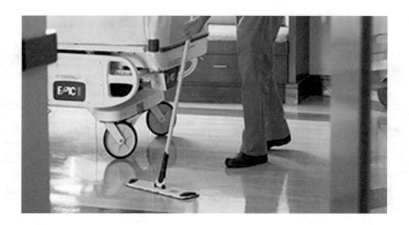

Cleaning and inspection go hand-in-hand. When you clean an area you automatically inspect the working surfaces, floor, equipment, parts, etc. that you are cleaning. This is a side-benefit of cleaning because it highlights issues and opportunities that would otherwise be overlooked. To get the full benefit from this you will need to incorporate a method for easily reporting any problems discovered.

Shine Steps

1. *Identify the shine targets.* What warehouse items (medical instruments, sterile linens, medical supplies, etc.) equipment (lumens, instruments, carts, worktables, desks and chairs, etc.) and spaces (floors, work areas, beams, windows, shelves, lights, plumbing, etc.) will be cleaned?
2. *Assign responsibilities.* Use the 5S map to create specific areas that will be assigned to individuals. Set up and post a schedule showing when each area is to be cleaned. Be sure that shine activities take place throughout each day.
3. *Determine the shine methods.* Start and end each shift with a shine inspection. Determine what will be cleaned and how it will be cleaned, including the cleaning supplies and equipment needed. Implement the "5-minute shine" drill. You will be surprised at how much can be done with an intense 5-minute effort. Develop standard cleaning procedures that assure that time is spent on actual cleaning rather than on preparation for the task.
4. *Tools.* Apply the Set In Order approach to your cleaning tools, thereby making them easy to find and easy to use.
5. *Shine!* Now it is time to get to work on the targets. Have the responsible people follow the shine procedures and, using the proper tools, clean the work area to the required standards.
6. *Deal with issues identified during cleaning.* Finally, respond to any problems found during the shine process. When possible, fix things immediately. The standard cleaning procedure should include what steps to take to deal with

		Div./Dept./Section		Prod. Div.									
	5S Job Cycle Chart	Entered by:		Date:			JOB CYCLE						
No.	5 S Job	Sort	Set in order	Shine	Standardize	Sustain	A	B	C	D	E	F
1	Red-tag strategy (occasional, companywide)	O									O	
2	Red-tag strategy (repeated)	O					O					
3	Place indicators (check or make)		O						O			
4	Item indicators (check or make)		O						O			
5	Amount indicators (check or make)		O						O			
6	Sweep around line			O				O				
7	Sweep within line			O				O				
8	Sweep around worktable			O				O				
9	Sweep on and under worktable			O				O				
10	Sweep work areas and walkways			O					O			
	Job Cycle Code											
	A Continuously											
	B Daily (mornings)											
	C Daily (evenings)											
	D Weekly											
	E Monthly											
	F Occasionally											

Fig. 7.7 5S job cycle chart

problems that cannot be fixed at once. To whom should they be reported? What forms, etc. are needed? It is a good idea to attach a tag to any equipment where maintenance has been requested to remind workers and supervisors that maintenance is pending.

7.4 Standardized Cleanup

Standardized cleanup is used to maintain the 5S activities described so far. The definition is somewhat circular: when the 5S activities of Sort, Set in Order, and Shine are properly maintained, then you have standardized 5S. When 5S has been standardized you avoid backsliding.

Determine Responsibilities

The tools needed for standardized cleanup include the tools already introduced: 5S maps and 5S schedules. In addition, you will need a new tool: the 5S Cycle Chart (see Fig. 7.7) To create such a chart, you sort the duties into Sort, Set in Order, and Shine categories and use a letter code to identify the cycle period. The resulting 5S Job Cycle Chart can be used as a checklist by the personnel responsible for the various 5S activities.

Integrate Sort, Set in Order, and Shine with the Work Routine

Make these three 5S activities a part of the normal work done in the work cell. This integration will reinforce the idea that 5S is not something added on to the work being done, it is an integral part of it. One mechanism for implementing this is "Visual 5S." As with the visual workplace in general, the purpose of visual 5S is to be able to tell at a glance that 5S activities are being done on an ongoing basis. For example, if Set in Order requires that tools are kept on a pegboard, then the tool outlines on the pegboard will indicate which tools are currently in use. This means that any blank space observed on the pegboard at the start or end of the shift is an indication of a problem.

Another mechanism is 5-minute 5S. This is similar to the 5-minute shine described earlier, only the scope is the entire 5S program. Do not get hung-up on the "5-minute" part of this activity, it is just an easy to remember the descriptive label. Just think of it as something you do quickly. You may want to use a visual display to make it easier to track your 5-Minute 5S activities, such as that shown in Fig. 7.8.

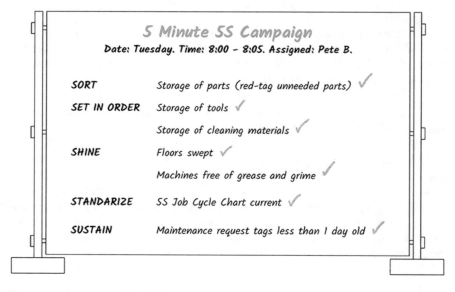

Fig. 7.8 5 Minute 5S signboard

7.5   Sustain

Sustain is the name of the whole 5S game. You gain nothing by deploying the first 4S's, only to let things go back to business as usual in the long run. In fact, it is actually worse to do this than to do nothing because you create an attitude among workers and supervisors that management is not really serious about Lean.

Things tend to get worse unless we pay close attention to them. There is an analogous concept used in thermodynamics: entropy. One definition of entropy is applied to human systems, "The inevitable and steady deterioration of a system or society."[3] In physics entropy is inevitable *in closed systems*. These are systems where there is no additional input of energy. The same applies to Lean 5S systems: if no additional effort is put into sustaining the improved state, then deterioration is inevitable and steady. You simply have no choice. If you want to sustain the benefits of 5S you must put forth the required effort to do so. Here are some guidelines to help you do so.

- Provide periodic refresher training on 5S.
- Schedule the required time to perform 5S on a daily basis.
- Create a standardized approach to 5S that clearly spells out how 5S will be implemented.
- Have your Lean process owner acknowledge and accept ownership of 5S.
- Create programs to recognize 5S efforts and reward compliance with standards.
- Keep 5S fun! Think of creative ways to keep 5S from becoming drudgery. (5-Minute 5S contests anyone?)

7.6   Safety: The Real First S

A workplace where 5S is practiced is not only clean and well-organized, it is also safe. Clutter and unnecessary materials and equipment contribute to accidents. People can locate the tools and materials they need without searching among unneeded objects and moving them out of the way. There are no oil spills where people can slip and fall. Adequate and clearly marked aisles make transportation safer. Marked storage areas that contain only what is needed are less likely to have excess inventory that can fall and injure people.

7.7   How Can We Continue to Reduce Waste? (Kaizen, Lean)

Continuous improvement is, well, continuous! Chances are that your new work cell will be a dramatic improvement over the previous workflow arrangement. You will compare the before and after numbers and be astonished at the improvements in

---

[3]http://dictionary.reference.com/browse/entropy.

cycle time, quality, inventory, accident reductions, and the overall appearance of the workplace. The temptation will be to shout Hooray! ... and stop. Do not give in to this temptation. There is always room for improvement. Continue to work to reduce cycle times even further by using the Lean methods you already know and others you will learn later in this course. Employ Kaizen in its two flavors: looking for ways to improve each and every day, and Kaizen Events focused on particular areas of opportunity. Apply the quality tools learned in this course to improve conformance to customer requirements.

Fast Work Changeover

8

Changing from producing one kind of work to another is an area worthy of special attention. This topic, like many in Lean, is a big one. Entire books have been written on the subject. We will present a brief overview of the main ideas here.[1]

8.1 · History

Fast changeover has its roots in a manufacturing method known as Single Minute Exchange of Die, or by its acronym SMED. It is one of the many lean production methods for reducing waste in a manufacturing process. In the mass production manufacturing world such rapid changeovers was, before Lean, unthinkable. It often took several hours, even days, to change equipment to make a different part. An extreme example is when Henry Ford switched from making only Model T automobiles to making other models (and colors). Ford factories shut down, 60,000 workers were laid off and no cars were produced from May 26 until October 20, 1927, while Ford changed over to the new Model A. These days models change from one car to the next on the assembly line.

Personally, when we move out of the manufacturing realm I would like to change SMED to something new, like Single Minute Work Transition, but I do not think the world is ready for a new acronym so I will stick with SMED in this book. The *principles* of SMED apply perfectly in healthcare. For example, getting an examination room ready for a new patient or getting an operating room ready for a different type of surgery. The important thing is to be able to quickly change from doing one thing to doing something else. That is where SMED comes in. SMED provides a rapid and efficient way of converting any process from creating the current product

---

[1]The material on SMED is from a particularly good article on Wikipedia at http://en.wikipedia.org/wiki/Single-Minute_Exchange_of_Die.

© The Author(s), under exclusive license to Springer Nature Switzerland AG 2021
T. Pyzdek, *The Lean Healthcare Handbook*, Management for Professionals,
https://doi.org/10.1007/978-3-030-69901-7_8

Table 8.1 Changeover time versus operation time

Changeover time (h)	Lot size	Process time per item (min)	Operation time (min)	Ratio (%)
8	100	1	5.8	480
8	1000	1	1.48	48
8	10,000	1	1.048	5

or service to creating a different product or service. This rapid changeover is key to improving work flow (Mura).

The SMED concept is credited to Shigeo Shingo, one of the main contributors to the creation of the Toyota Production System, along with Taiichi Ohno. The phrase "single minute" does not mean that all work changeovers should take only one minute, but that they should take less than 10 min (in other words, "single-digit minute").[2] In either case, the objective is the same: change fast!

As mentioned, SMED originated with Toyota. Toyota's problem was that land costs in Japan are very high and therefore it was very expensive to store its vehicles. The result was that its costs were higher than producers in other countries because it had to produce vehicles in uneconomically small lots. That is, the lots were uneconomical until SMED came along!

8.2   SMED for Healthcare

SMED is the key to healthcare flexibility and efficiency. Changing over quickly has numerous benefits, including increasing the time available for productive work, or operation time (Table 8.1).[3]

With the increasing pace of change in healthcare, it becomes critical to be able to change quickly from one service to another. Surgery teams, for example, have to change from one patient within the operating theater to another one. SMED is a Lean changeover tool that avoids the dead time and improves changeover operations increasing productivity. SMED techniques provide a rapid and efficient way of converting an activity from one type to another. There are many benefits of fast changeovers, for example,

- Less capital is needed which drives capital turnover rates and improves profitability.
- Reduction in the footprint of processes with reduced inventory freeing floor space.
- Productivity increases or reduced production time.

---

[2]Study of TOYOTA Production System, Shigeo Shingo, 1981, p 70.

[3]The term "operation time" is from manufacturing, but it transfers well to healthcare too, do not you think?

- Increased equipment and other capital work rates from reduced changeover times even if the number of changeovers increases.
- Elimination of changeover errors and elimination of trial runs reduces error rates.
- Improved quality from fully standardized operating conditions in advance.
- Increased safety from simpler changeovers.
- Simplified housekeeping from fewer tools and better organization.
- Lower expense of setups.
- Increased employee satisfaction since changing is easier.
- Lower worker skill requirements since changes are now designed into the process rather than a matter of skilled judgment.
- Elimination of unusable stock from obsolescence and forecast errors..
- Goods are not lost through deterioration or expiration.
- The ability to mix production gives flexibility and further inventory reductions as well as opening the door to revolutionized production methods (large orders $\neq$ large production lot sizes).
- New attitudes on controllability of work process amongst staff.

Implementation

Shigeo Shingo listed eight techniques that should be considered in implementing SMED.[4] I have reworded Shingo's techniques for healthcare and added a ninth of my own for good measure.

Separate Internal from External Setup Operations

Internal tasks are those changeover activities that require work to be stopped on the equipment. For example, if you are changing the surgery in an operating room, an

---

[4]A study of the Toyota Production System, Shigeo Shingo, Productivity Press, 1989, p 47.

internal task might be gathering instruments from the previous surgery or washing the floors. External tasks can be done while the current equipment is still in use. An external task example would be sterile packaging the instruments for the next surgery.

Convert Internal to External Setup

Since internal tasks require halting the use of the equipment, they add to wait time, and therefore they are Muda. Change as many internal tasks as possible into external tasks. For example, if you had a suitably equipped "shadow operating room" adjacent to actual operating rooms, you would be able to stage a great deal of the setup for upcoming surgeries while current surgeries were in progress.

Once these two steps have been completed you can perform the tasks below (see Fig. 8.1 for a graphical illustration).

(a) Streamline the remaining internal activities, by simplifying them (D). Focus on fasteners—Shigeo Shingo rightly observed that it is only the last turn of a bolt that tightens it—the rest is just movement.
(b) Streamline the External activities, so that they are of a similar scale to the Internal ones (D).

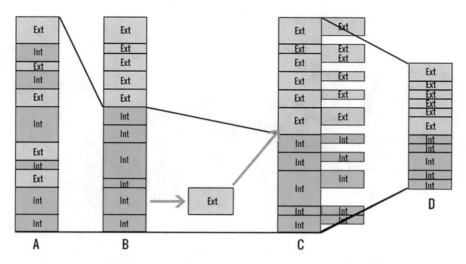

Fig. 8.1 SMED method illustrated

Standardize Equipment

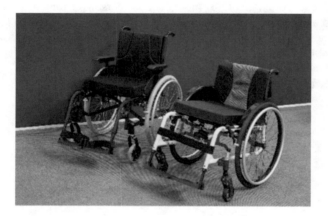

Whenever possible use the same equipment or similar equipment for a given purpose. Standardized equipment may vary in size and shape, but they will have identical or similar ways to load, restrain, manipulate, move, process, and unload their payloads.

Hospitals, clinics, physician offices, etc. all have equipment for moving patients from point A to point B, getting patients on and off of examination tables, repositioning patients, etc. Try to make the equipment the same from department to department and room to room so people do not need to learn different ways of doing similar things.

Quick Fasten and Release Mechanism

Find quick and easy ways to fix patients, containers, materials, and other things in the desired place and position regardless of shape and size. Preferably, restraint clamp or release mechanisms should involve a quick, obvious single motion, such as closing a clamp or pulling a strap tight.

While car seats do a great job of reducing childhood injuries from automobile accidents, from the viewpoint of the adults who must use them they are examples of poorly designed constraints. To install a vehicle correctly requires studying manuals and a lot of effort, often involving more than one person. Getting a child in or out of one is often an exercise in frustration, at least it is the first dozen or so times you do it. There are similar examples in healthcare, for example, raising or lowering side rails on hospital beds.

Adjustments

Adjustments involve changing something that has been previously set, for example, changing the volume setting for an IV drip. Reduce the number of things that require setting or adjusting. Get patients and equipment set correctly before a procedure begins to minimize adjustments during the procedure. Stabilize to prevent settings from changing after they are set.

Parallel Activities

It is often possible to do two or more things at once. This is called parallel processing. Parallel processing reduces total cycle time, which can speed changeovers considerably.

Non-parallel and Non-sequential Activities

For activities that cannot be done in parallel, but that do not need to be done in a particular sequence, do them in the shortest-to-longest order to reduce average cycle time. For example, if you come into the pharmacy and there are three prescriptions to fill that will take 10, 20, and 30 min to fill, and none are more urgent than others, fill the 10-min prescription first, 20-min prescription second, and the 30-min prescription last. The average time to do all three in this sequence is $(10 + 30 + 60)/3 = 33$ 1/3 min. If you did them in reverse order it would take an average of $(30 + 50 + 60)/3 = 46$ 2/3 min.

Fast Patient Transfer

Find safe and efficient ways to transport and move patients. (Transport changes the location of the patient. Move changes the position of the patient.) Transportation is one of the classic types of waste. Moving is another. Think of ways to minimize these wastes. Both might well be necessary, but the faster they are done without error, the better.

Pre-prepared Workers

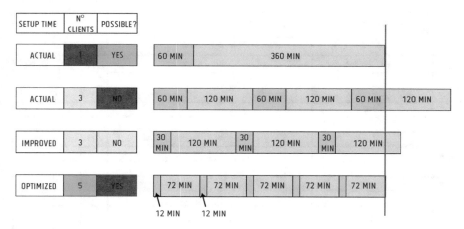

Fig. 8.2 Four successive runs using SMED

Have people who are on the same work team ready to begin a new procedure immediately, while workers who have just completed a procedure prepare for the next procedure.

In healthcare, a great deal of time is spent getting people ready for an event, such as a patient arriving at the emergency department or for a surgery. Things like scrubbing, dressing, getting to the right place, etc. take time. To the extent possible, all actors in a given situation should be on location and ready to go before the activity actually begins.

Once the above steps have been successfully implemented,

1. Document the new procedure, and actions that are yet to be completed.
2. Do it all again: For each iteration of the above process, a 45% improvement in setup times should be expected, so it may take several iterations to cross the 10-min SMED line.

Figure 8.2 shows four successive runs with learning from each run and improvements applied before the next.

- Run 1 illustrates the original situation.
- Run 2 shows what would happen if more changeovers were included.
- Run 3 shows the impact of the improvements in changeover times that come from doing more of them and building learning into their execution.
- Run 4 shows how these improvements can get you back to the same production time but now with more flexibility in production capacity.
- Run N (not illustrated) would have changeovers that take 1.5 min (97% reduction) and whole shift time reduced from 420 to 368 min a productivity improvement of 12%.

LINE			STANDARD
MACHINE	REQUIRED SETUP		SETUP TIME
OPERATORS	TOOLS		

N°	TASK / OPERATION	ACTUAL TIME		IMPROVEMENT	TARGET TIME		NECESSARY
		INTERNAL	EXTERNAL		INTERNAL	EXTERNAL	ACTIVITIES
1							
2							
3							
4							
5							
6							
7							
8							
9							
10							
11							
12							
13							
14							
15							

Fig. 8.3 SMED data recording form

Key Elements to Observe

When implementing fast changeover look for:

1. Shortages, mistakes, inadequate verification of equipment causing delays and can be avoided by check tables, especially visual ones, and setup on an intermediary process such as a shadow operating room.
2. Inadequate or incomplete repairs to equipment causing rework and delays.
3. Optimization for least work as opposed to least delay.
4. Using slow precise adjustment equipment for the large coarse part of the adjustment.
5. Lack of visual lines or benchmarks for part placement on the equipment.
6. Forcing a changeover between different raw materials when a continuous feed, or near equivalent, is possible.
7. Lack of functional standardization, that is the standardization of only the things necessary for setup, e.g., all faucets have the same hot and cold directions.
8. Much operator movement during setup.
9. More attachment points than actually required for the forces to be constrained.
10. Attachment points that take more than one turn to fasten.
11. Any adjustments after initial setup.
12. Any use of experts during setup.
13. Any adjustments of assisting tools such as guides or switches.

Record all necessary data using a form such as that shown in Fig. 8.3.

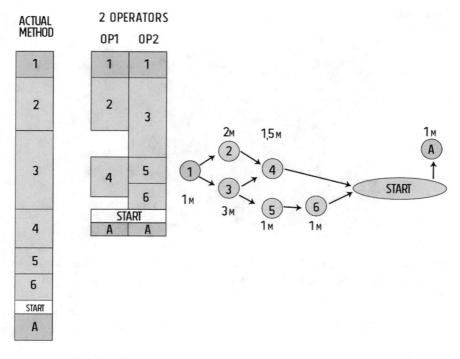

Fig. 8.4 SMED with multiple operators

Parallel Operations Using Multiple Operators

By taking the "actual" operations and making them into a network that contains the dependencies it is possible to optimize task attribution and further optimize setup time. Issues of effective communication between the operators must be managed to ensure safety is assured where potentially noisy or visually obstructive conditions occur. This idea is illustrated in Fig. 8.4.

Automating

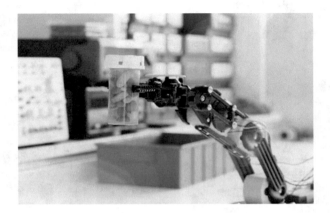

Automate as a last resort. If the above steps are not sufficient, consider leasing or purchasing additional equipment and facilities or using automated equipment.

Part II
Continuous Improvement and Kaizen

Introduction to Continuous Improvement

9

9.1 Kaizen

The Kaizen approach focuses attention on making ongoing improvements that involve everyone from the top executives to the workers on the floor. Its domain is that of small local improvements from ongoing efforts. Over time these small improvements produce changes every bit as dramatic as the "big project" approach. Kaizen does not concern itself with radically changing or designing fundamentally new systems. Rather, it works to optimize existing systems.[1]

Responsibility for Kaizen

All processes in any given organization have two components: process improvement and process control. Control involves taking action on deviations to maintain a given process state. In the absence of signals indicating that the process has gone astray, control is achieved by adhering to standard operating procedures (SOPs).[2] In contrast, improvement requires experimentally modifying the process to produce better results. When a successful improvement is identified, the SOPs are changed to reflect the new way of doing things. Since work is always done according to standards, the standards must be viewed as dynamic documents.

The perception of job responsibilities (improvement or control) is based on job function. In Fig. 9.1 the lower portion of the chart involves controlling the process at its current level by following the SOPs and solving problems as they occur. Kaizen fits into the upper portion of this picture. It can be seen that although all levels of

---

[1]If you want to design a new process or product from scratch I recommend that you use Design for Six Sigma, or the Lean 3P process. These topics are not discussed in this book.

[2]If something has gone astray, problem solving is required to identify the root cause. See X-Charts.

© The Author(s), under exclusive license to Springer Nature Switzerland AG 2021
T. Pyzdek, *The Lean Healthcare Handbook*, Management for Professionals,
https://doi.org/10.1007/978-3-030-69901-7_9

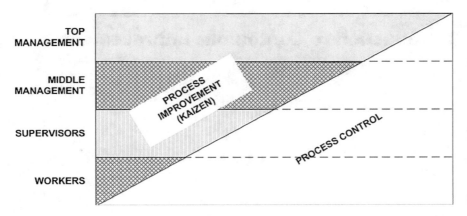

Fig. 9.1 Kaizen responsibilities

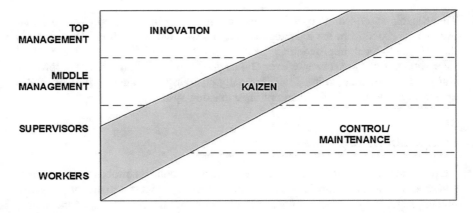

Fig. 9.2 Kaizen versus innovation

employees share responsibility for Kaizen, the responsibility for improvement increases as one goes to higher levels of management.

Kaizen does not cover radical innovations or breakthrough improvement, that is where Design for Six Sigma comes in. As shown in Fig. 9.2, Kaizen occupies the middle ground between process control and radical innovation.

Process Owner Responsibilities

The process owner, the person in management whose authority covers all processes in the value stream, must take responsibility for continuously improving with Kaizen as well as maintaining control of the process. The Process Owner's responsibilities for Kaizen are a mixture of middle-management and supervisory responsibilities. Of

Table 9.1 Topics that may be taught in Kaizen training

Types of waste
Value added/Non-value-added work
Process maps: L-maps, value stream maps, opportunity maps, spaghetti charts
Group dynamics, team member roles
GEMBA (learning to see the process)
SMED (techniques for fast changeover from one type of work to another)
Brainstorming

course, their first responsibility is to use Kaizen and not simply settle for current levels of performance. However, standards are an important part of the Kaizen process and the process owner must assure that they receive the attention they deserve and that the staff understands and uses them. Employee training is another key aspect of Kaizen. Training should impart the skill set and the awareness of Kaizen, that is what this book is all about.

A big part of Kaizen is identifying and solving problems. Employees need training to acquire the skills and tools needed for this, it is not something that comes naturally. Table 9.1 lists some of the topics that might be taught to employees. The Process Owner must understand the importance of statistical thinking, especially of special cause and common cause variation (see Special and Common Cause Variation below.) The process owner should see to it that employees are allowed to make contributions individually and as members of their work group.

Quality requires that discipline be practiced. It is surprising how often quality problems occur simply because someone ignored a procedure that they were well aware of.

Finally, the Process Owner needs to offer his or her own ideas for improvement.

PDCA

The Kaizen process is actually an implementation of plan-do-check-act, or PDCA. *Plan*ning occurs when someone has an idea for doing the job better. These ideas are actively solicited in Kaizen. A change is made to determine if the idea actually works, which is the *do* step. Then the results are *check*ed to see what happened when the change was made. If the results indicate that the process operates better after the change, the procedures are revised to make the change permanent. This is the *act* stage. See Fig. 9.3 for an illustration of the PDCA framework.

Benefits of Kaizen

Kaizen is all about improving people as well as processes. Participants benefit from involvement in Kaizen by improving the skills needed to work on teams and to

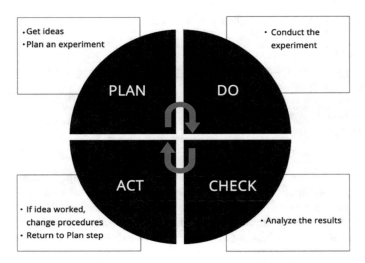

Fig. 9.3 PDCA improvement cycle

improve business processes. Participants also learn a great deal about their organization, its customers, and its business through their involvement in Kaizen.

Leaders are also improved when they create and lead Kaizen in their organization. The Kaizen improvement process helps leaders do a better job of leading, especially leading change in their organizations. Leaders also learn about the core processes (e.g., design a product, create product, acquire customers, etc.) and enabling functions (accounting, IT, quality control, etc.) which comprise their organization. Most business leaders are trained to think of their organization in command-and-control and functional terms. Kaizen helps them understand a process-oriented view of their business. These learning experiences are the result of efforts to improve the business processes by enhancing their ability to efficiently create customer value.

Kaizen Events[3]

Kaizen events are short, focused projects conducted to improve value streams. During value stream mapping and work cell design you will have identified a number of problems and opportunities that kept you from completely eliminating waste. These were marked with Kaizen burst symbols on value stream maps (see Fig. 5.10). Now is the time for the new process owner to apply Kaizen to these issues. Usually the new owner will want to begin at the pacemaker process or as near to the customer as possible. Lean Advisors or Lean Six Sigma belts usually co-lead the first few Kaizen events to help the new process owner and his team learn the

---

[3]Kaizen event organization is discussed in greater detail in Chap. 18.

Kaizen event process. Eventually this activity is handed over completely to the process owner.

Kaizen events are much more tightly focused than most Lean Six Sigma projects. Unlike Lean Six Sigma projects, Kaizen projects are seldom cross-functional. They also have a much shorter timeframe.

Typically, there will be a preparation period approximately 3 weeks long. During this time the team leader will create a project charter and conduct a project assessment. The leader will also find a sponsor, recruit the team, and communicate with all stakeholders.

Next the team will conduct the actual Kaizen event, using either the Lean Six Sigma Define-Measure-Analyze-Improve-Control (DMAIC) or PDCA framework. This phase usually takes 3–5 days. As many improvements as possible are actually implemented during this phase.

Last, the team will follow up on changes that were identified as being necessary, but that could not be made during the event. They will also confirm that the changes they made worked as planned and assure that standards were updated.

Training for Kaizen Teams

The guiding rule for training Kaizen team members is to give the team the training they need, but no more. Of course, if you read this entire book you will have learned a great deal more. If you decide that the team needs to know something that you learned, then teach it to them. Often you can give the team the background they need in a few minutes, so long as you yourself actually apply the technique. Table 9.1 lists topics commonly taught to Kaizen team members.

Transfer Ownership

Once a Kaizen team has improved a process and modified the SOP, the team leader needs to work with the process owner to identify new key process outcomes and critical to quality metrics. The team leader will create dashboards to monitor these metrics on an established schedule. But it is still not enough to just maintain the status quo. Even though the process the team designed might be much better than the process it replaced, continuous improvement is *still* necessary. While this is not the team's direct responsibility, the team leader should encourage the process owner to hold regular huddles with the process operators and supervisors to continue to streamline the work. The A3 approach is useful for huddles and other continuous improvement activities (see Chap. 19, A3 thinking).

Process Mapping

10

Process maps are used to make processes visible. You have already seen some process maps earlier in this book, for example, spaghetti charts and 5S diagrams. In this chapter we will show you additional process maps that can be used to create different views of what happens within a process. The information can be used to help you better understand how the process creates and delivers customer value.

10.1 Activity Maps

Activity maps produce a detailed picture of the process as it currently exists. This serves as a documentation of the current state and a basis for establishing a shared vision of the as-is process at a relatively detailed level. Activity maps are a starting point for two other process maps you will learn about later: opportunity maps and deployment or swimlane maps.

What Is a Process?

A process acts on inputs to produce outputs of greater value. Thus, processes consist of inputs, actions, and outputs. Processes can be thought of as "transfer functions" that turn *causes* (resources, labor, procedures, etc.) into *effects* (products or services.)

Inputs are the factors of production: land, materials, labor, equipment, and management.

Actions are the way in which the inputs are combined and manipulated in order to add value. Actions include procedures, handling, storage, transportation, and processing. Note that not all actions are value added. One goal of Lean is to improve processes by reducing the non-value activities in them.

Outputs are the products or services created by acting on the inputs. Outputs are delivered to the customer or other user. Outputs also include unplanned and undesirable results, such as scrap, rework, pollution, etc.

© The Author(s), under exclusive license to Springer Nature Switzerland AG 2021
T. Pyzdek, *The Lean Healthcare Handbook*, Management for Professionals,
https://doi.org/10.1007/978-3-030-69901-7_10

Why Activity Maps Are Important

Activity maps help all contributors, including team members and process workers, see how their work helps build the final result. They show the process in sufficient detail to get a good idea of what root causes are driving the final results. And they help teams and workers identify process costs, bottlenecks, waste, and other opportunities for improvement.

Many computer simulation software products use activity maps as the starting point for simulations. If your process is complex, or if the inputs and activity times are highly variable, simulation will help you see things you might not see otherwise. They also help you perform "what if" analysis, which lets you try changes in the virtual simulated world before trying them in the workplace. This has numerous advantages, such as letting you try many different changes very quickly and saving on scrap and rework when changes do not work as planned.

When processes have many steps or many decision points, it can be difficult to understand how they work. Process maps show the complexity as a picture. Most people find it much easier to understand a picture than a written or verbal description. Activity maps show decision branching. They also show both negative and positive outcomes simultaneously.

Activity Map Symbols

Figure 10.1 shows the process mapping symbols you will use most often. Popular computer programs include these symbols, which are called flow charting symbols. You will find these symbols in Microsoft Office products such as Word and PowerPoint by entering the term "flowchart" in the search box.

Figure 10.2 is an example of an activity map made with standard flowchart symbols.

How to Create an Activity Map

1. Create the team
   Get the right people involved. Be sure to include people with hands-on knowledge of the way things are actually done.
2. Go and look (Go to the Gemba)
   You cannot learn what you need to know unless you leave the conference room and go watch the work being done. Going to the Gemba will provide insights that often get you half way to your goal instantly.
3. Record the work
   Write down what people do on post-it™ notes, one activity per note. Include unintended and undesirable consequences. My mentor Dr. W. Edwards Deming used to point out that accidents are outcomes of processes too. Show categories of work (e.g., different kinds of services, different shifts, different people doing the

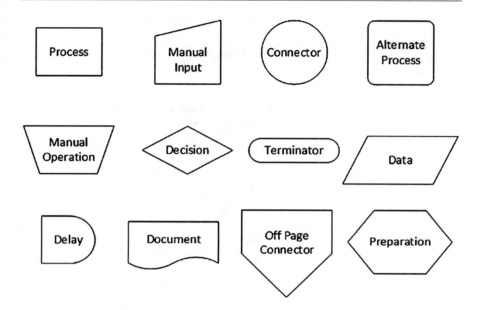

Fig. 10.1 Standard flowchart symbols

work, etc.) using colored post-it™ notes. This will make it easier for you to create more detailed process maps later on. Display the record of what you have found in the workplace for all to see. Invite people who are not on the team to contribute.

4. When all of the activities have been listed put them in the order in which the work is actually done
5. Determine the level of detail for your activity map
   This is another instance where we invoke the Goldilocks principle. There should be just the right amount of detail, not too much and not too little. The correct amount of detail depends on how you will use the activity map. You want the map to point you to the right course of action.
6. Draw the map and distribute it for the input of others
   Use the map to get shared vision from team members and other stakeholders. If processes are highly complex, you might want to form sub-teams to create maps of the different parts of the process. Create a high level map of the main process and use off-page connector symbols to indicate where to find maps of sub-processes. Post what you have publicly to encourage others to contribute. I prefer to have physical process maps posted, but computerized distribution also works, especially if the process spans multiple locations.

Fig. 10.2 Activity map
example

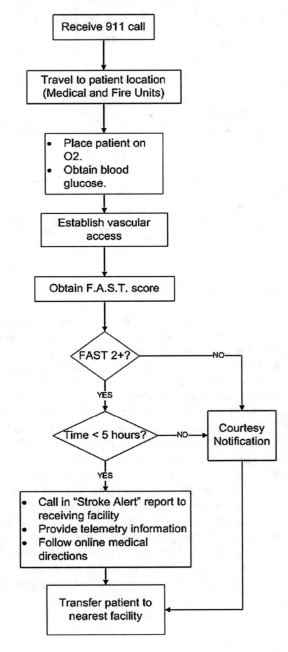

EMS ADULT STROKE PROTOCOL

How to Use Activity Maps

Be sure that you have consensus that the activity map is accurate. As-is activity maps provide a graphical picture of the process as it is now. But that does not mean that everyone sees the same thing when they look at the picture. Be sure that the entire team, the sponsor, and the process owner agree that this picture is accurate.

Use the activity map to validate procedures. Does the map match what the procedures say? If not, either change the procedure or the map.

Some big Lean projects take months to complete. But there is no point waiting if you can make improvements right away. Look at the activity map for easy and obvious changes. Eliminate unnecessary complexity immediately if it can be done quickly and easily. Other changes will be made when the time is right.

The activity map can make it easier to see where you can place your process controls when you change the standards as a result of your work. As with all improvements, there is no need to wait to make immediate changes that can be done quickly and easily.

You can also use the activity map to make deployment and opportunity maps, which are discussed later.

10.2 Opportunity Maps

The activity maps that you drew show the process as it is. Opportunity maps will show the process as it should be. Opportunity maps are a graphical stepping stone between the current state and the future state. Opportunity maps enhance activity maps by highlighting which activities and choices add value and which do not. Value, as always, is defined from the customer's perspective. Although it's true that activities might add value for other stakeholders, that is not the focus of opportunity maps.

Why Opportunity Maps Are Important

The creation of opportunity maps creates a forum where the team can discuss the nature of customer value. It helps team members understand the reason that the process exists in the first place. Opportunity maps show value graphically. Conversely, they also show a picture of process waste. This picture helps the team understand the causes of process outcomes, both good and bad. The fact that this display of value-added and non-value-added work is graphical is important because visualizing waste has more impact on people than numbers or words.

What Makes Opportunity Maps Unique

Opportunity maps are the only mapping tool to show whether an activity adds value or not. When combined with deployment map swim lanes, the opportunity map shows the team and project sponsor who is primarily responsible for eliminating waste.

How to Create Opportunity Maps

Opportunity maps begin with activity maps (see above.) The value-added activities shown on the activity or deployment map are then determined. An activity is classified as value added if three conditions are met.

First. The activity is not rework, repair, or any other activity that is a "do over." Quality can be defined as doing the right thing right the first time. Only quality activities are value added.
Second. Only activities that the customer is willing to pay for are value added. Because of waste we end up charging customers for many things that they would rather not have if they had a choice.
Third. The activity changes the flow object that is moving through the process. Activities such as internal movement, inspection, or storage do not count as value added.

Once non-value-added activities have been identified, modify the as-is activity map by marking non-value-added activities in a way that makes them easy to see, for example, by making them a different color or shading them. Next, create a map showing both value-added and non-value-added activities together to make it easier to see the extent of the opportunity. Finally, create a new process map that shows only value-added activities. This is your ideal future state map. Although you may not ever reach this level of perfection, it helps to know what it looks like.

Opportunity Map Example

We have all made copies, but have you ever thought about what is actually involved and whether or not there is an opportunity to improve? Let us do this for the process of making copies in an office environment.

Figure 10.3 shows the as-is process for making copies. (Admit it, you have had similar experiences!) It will serve as our starting point for creating an opportunity map. Take a moment to study this figure before going on. Feel the frustration and pain!

Next, for each box on the activity map ask yourself the three value-added questions posed above. Draw another version of the activity map showing this information. Assuming that you agree with my choices Fig. 10.4 shows how this

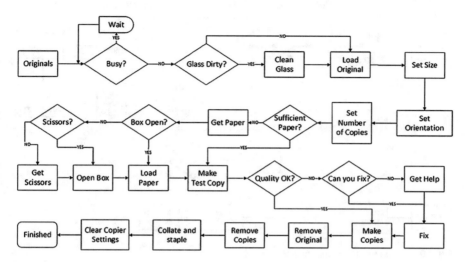

Fig. 10.3 Make a copy as-is process

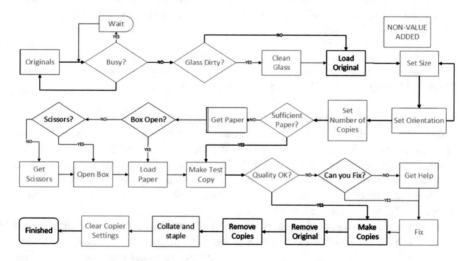

Fig. 10.4 Opportunity map example (Gray activities are NVA)

map would look. This is called an opportunity map because it highlights the non-value-added activities and helps you see the opportunities to remove NVA work. Of course, discussions as to which activities are VA and which are NVA can get quite spirited, but whatever your team agrees to in the end will always help point the way forward.[1]

---

[1]Do not let the discussions drag on too long. This is one place where voting is allowed.

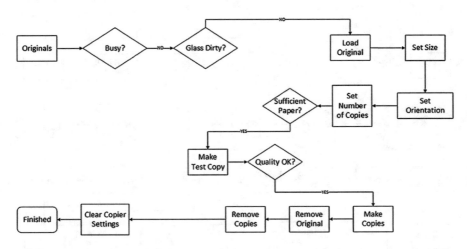

Fig. 10.5 Future state process map example

To really drive the point home, you can make a new map showing only the value-added process steps, as in Fig. 10.5. Getting from the as-is state to the future state is what Kaizen is all about!

10.3   Deployment Maps (Swimlane Maps)

Deployment maps are useful tools that show decisions, activities, responsibilities, and timelines. Unlike functions in an organization, processes in an organization are often unmanaged. Sometimes it is even difficult to determine who is responsible for doing something or for making a particular decision. Deployment maps show a detailed picture of workflow, including information on responsibility for decisions and actions. Once responsibility is determined, deployment maps provide a clear picture of the work done in a process, when, and by whom.

Deployment maps provide a more complete picture of a process than the process maps that have been presented so far. The handoffs between departments is shown. Until the deployment map is created, the contributors to the process often do not know who is responsible for other activities. This is because very often no one is responsible for managing the process. Deployment maps show responsibilities, when this is known. When it is not known, it requires that the team determine this. Deployment maps show when an activity is performed or when a decision is made.

Differences Between Deployment Maps and Activity Maps

Activity maps show what is flowing, how the flow object is being handled or changed, and where decisions and choices occur. Deployment maps often begin

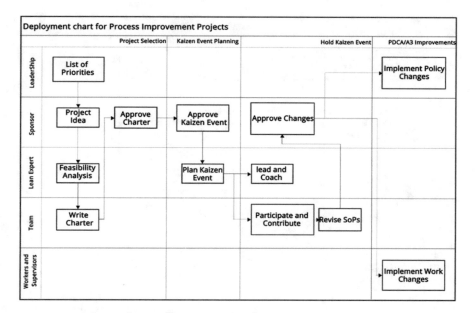

Fig. 10.6   Deployment (swimlane) map example

with activity maps. But activity maps do not show when activities occur or who is responsible. Deployment process maps also show what and how, and include the who (the person or function handling or doing the work). Deployment maps show multiple handoffs and accountability. Figure 10.6 is an example of a deployment map for process improvement events. Note that it shows five groups of responsible parties: leadership, sponsor, Lean Advisor, the team and workers and supervisors. It also shows that the activities involved occur in four different phases: project selection, Kaizen event planning, the event itself, and post-event activities (PDCA and A3). The entire picture of what is to take place, who is responsible for the different activities, and when the activities occur makes it easier to assure that improvement projects are successful.

Variations of Deployment Maps

Not all deployment maps look the same. Figure 10.7 is a deployment map where the responsible departments are shown in separate boxes and there is no timeline. As a Lean Advisor team leader you will have to decide when it is best to force the team into a standardized format and when it is okay to let them experiment with other looks. Figure 10.7 is a "Vertical" deployment map that has an orphan activity. No one seems to know who is responsible for processing orders. Perhaps that is why the company might ship an order even though Accounting fails to approve the

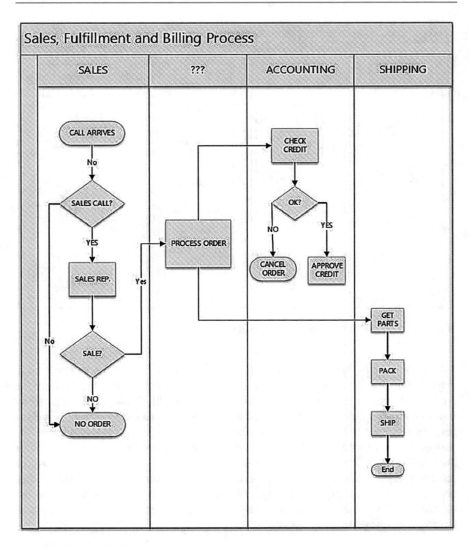

Fig. 10.7 Vertical deployment map of process with a problem

customer's credit, or fails to invoice some customers! Such discoveries are not uncommon when you look for ways to improve.

Other variations on deployment maps are maps that exclude the swimlanes showing responsibilities and others that exclude the timeline. Usually these are simply bad deployment maps, but on occasion they may serve some useful purpose.

What Makes Deployment Maps Unique?

Deployment maps are the only process mapping tool that shows process activities, decisions, responsibilities, and timelines in a single display. Even though this is a great deal of information, deployment maps are very easy to understand. This makes them a great tool for communicating with groups and for getting shared vision.

How to Create a Deployment Map

Deployment map creation is a step by step process, which is described here.

1. *Activity Map*. Start with the activity map. The deployment map is an enhanced activity map, so it makes sense to begin by creating an activity map (see above).
2. *People*. Bring together people who understand the process you are mapping. The deployment map should be created by a team of people with detailed knowledge of the process being mapped. This is probably already your team, but you may want to bring in outside experts, process operators, or others.
3. *Detail*. Determine the Goldilocks optimum level of detail. The level of detail required is determined by the question the deployment map is solving for. In the case of maps of processes improved by Kaizen, you are solving for the successful deployment of your improvement plan and control plan to operations.
4. *Timeline*. When are activities performed? The top of your deployment map will include a timeline showing when a given activity is performed. The timeline might be calendar time, such as months, weeks, or days. Or it may be phases, such as those in PDCA. Your team must then determine when each activity will be completed. Note that some deployment maps show the timeline as horizontal zones rather than vertical zones as you saw in Fig. 10.7.
5. *Swimlanes*. Who will perform the activities? Modern organizations are divided into functionally specialized areas, represented on the deployment map by horizontal bars called swim lanes. The term "Swim lanes" is merely a useful metaphor. You can show shared responsibility by drawing an activity or decision box across the two or more departments responsible.[2] Your team must determine who is responsible for completing each activity.
6. *Draw the map*. You can draw the deployment map by hand or by using specialized process mapping software. You can also use the drawing capabilities of general purpose software such as word processors, spreadsheets, graphics programs or presentation packages. Microsoft Office or Open Office includes

---

[2]This is how I like to show joint responsibility, however this approach does not comply with some flowcharting standards, such as BPMN and if you use some flowcharting software it may not allow it. If this is the case you can create a separate swimlane for the joint responsibility team. Sometimes you need to get creative to get the process map you want.

several programs capable of drawing deployment maps. Online software programs are also available.

Note that some deployment maps show swim lanes as vertical zones rather than as horizontal zones, as shown above. (See Variations of Deployment Maps.)

How to Use Deployment Maps

The additional information on deployment maps makes it possible to find problems that are not so obvious with other process maps. Look for unnecessary handoffs. Every handoff is an opportunity for miscommunications and problems. Complexity may also appear in the form of too many activities or decisions. Are responsibilities unclear or overlapping? Is the timeline efficient and reasonable?

Statistical Thinking

11

In this chapter, we will discuss statistical principles. Statistics are data summaries based on numbers. You will learn principles for designing statistical studies and for summarizing the numbers you obtain. To be specific, we will discuss enumerative statistical studies, analytic statistical studies, statistical process control principles, and operational definitions.

11.1 Enumerative Studies (Classical Statistics)

If you studied statistics in college, chances are you learned about enumerative studies. An enumerative study is one where the action will be taken on a well-defined and static universe. In statistics, the universe is called the population. The universe is the entire group of interest. Examples are people, materials, units of product, or other things that possess certain properties of interest. A universe might consist of customers who spend more than $1000 with your company in a given calendar year. The statistical methods used to analyze enumerative studies are primarily numerical. Enumerative studies are assessed using deductive reasoning, like the reasoning used in mathematical proofs or formal logic. Just like a proof, you will reach a definite conclusion when you assess an enumerative study. Although this approach has a certain elegant beauty to it, few situations in the real world of Lean projects meet these requirements.

Enumerative Study Example

Here is an example of how an enumerative statistical study would be used. *A sample of 100 bottles of sterile disinfectant for soft contact lenses is taken from a filling machine. The sample average fill level is 353 mL. 95% Of the sample measurements are within ±6 mL of the mean. The specifications are 355 mL ±3 mL.* Based on these results, should you:

© The Author(s), under exclusive license to Springer Nature Switzerland AG 2021
T. Pyzdek, *The Lean Healthcare Handbook*, Management for Professionals,
https://doi.org/10.1007/978-3-030-69901-7_11

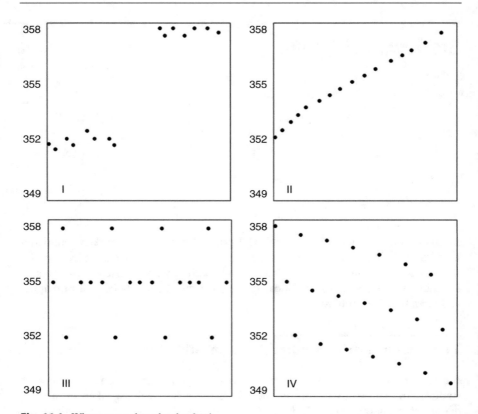

Fig. 11.1   Why you need to plot the data!

A. Do nothing?
B. Adjust the filling machine average upwards by +2 mL?
C. Do something else?

   Go ahead and make a choice as to how you would proceed, even if you are not sure. When you are ready, read on.
   Figure 11.1 quadrant I shows a pattern that would produce these statistical results. Based on this pattern did you make the right choice?
   But wait! Quadrant II shows another pattern that would also produce these statistics. Did your decision change?
   Hold on! The pattern in quadrant III matches the statistics too. Now what would you do?
   Quadrant IV is yet another matching pattern.
   In fact, there are virtually limitless patterns that could produce any given set of statistics, and the correct response depends on the pattern. This is a serious flaw in enumerative statistical methods. It also highlights the three rules of data analysis: 1. *Plot the data!* 2. *Plot the data!* And 3. *Plot the data!*

11.2   Analytic Studies

The problem with the statistics taught in college is that they assume that samples are drawn from a static population. This is virtually *never* true in the real world. In the real world, we are sampling from processes that are dynamic and constantly changing. In this world, graphical methods are far more valuable than numerical statistical methods.

Another kind of study is the analytic study. Analytic studies are conducted to help you understand how to improve *future* performance, exactly what we are looking for with continuous improvement. The focus of analytic studies is understanding a process so you can effectively improve it. With analytic studies, the "universe" we are interested in has not been created yet. Analytic studies use numbers, of course. But the numbers are nearly always shown graphically. If the time-order is available, the numbers are plotted in this order to extract information from the time series patterns. Analytic studies employ *inductive* reasoning rather than deductive reasoning. Rather than provide hard and fast decision rules, analytic studies produce useful guidelines. You probably have already guessed that in the real world these methods are more useful than enumerative studies.

Let us compare the two types of studies. The aim of enumerative studies is parameter estimation. For example, what is the population average? The aim of analytic studies is prediction. What will the process do in the future? The focus of enumerative studies is the universe or population. This is what we will act upon based on the study results. The focus of analytic studies is the process. We will act on the process based on the study results. We access the object of focus using counts or statistics when using enumerative studies. With analytic studies, we access the process by creating predictive models relating causes to effects. With enumerative studies, the major source of uncertainty is sampling variation in the parameter estimates. With analytic studies the major source of uncertainty is that we are extrapolating our conclusions into the future, always a risky business. The uncertainty in an enumerative study can be measured, but the future is inherently unknowable. The enumerative study environment is a static universe or population, while analytic studies are conducted on dynamic and constantly changing processes. In Lean, you will find applications for both enumerative and analytic studies, but analytic studies will be much more common Table 11.1.

Table 11.1 Comparison of analytic and enumerative studies

Item	Enumerative study	Analytic study
Aim	Parameter estimation	Prediction
Focus	Universe	Process
Method of access	Counts, statistics	Models of processes
Major source of uncertainty	Sampling variation	Extrapolation into the future
Uncertainty quantifiable?	Yes	No
Environment for the study	Static	Dynamic

Statistical Control

Next we will look at the principles that underlie what is called statistical process control or SPC. SPC is the name given to a set of techniques used to operationally define a controlled process. A controlled process is as close as we can get to a static universe in the real world. While variety may be the spice of life, variation is the bane of quality. In Lean, less variation is better. While we will never get to a process with zero variation, we may be able to get a controlled process. We say a process is in control if there is no statistical evidence that any identifiable cause is having a big impact on the measured variation of the process. A process that is *not* in control is said to be being influenced by "special causes" or "assignable causes" of variation.

We determine when a process is in control or out of control[1] by using statistical methods. SPC is one of the most important topics you can learn for continuous improvement because the proper action needed to improve depends on whether or not you have statistical control.

Distributions

All processes vary and all variation is caused. There are two sources of process variation: special causes and common causes. Special causes are not an inherent part of the process, they come and go. Common causes are built into the process and they influence every observation obtained from the process. You cannot know what to do to improve until you know what kind of variability you are seeing. SPC will tell you which type of variation you are seeing. If special causes are eliminated or accounted for, the variability from the process will be predictable. A predictable pattern of variation is referred to as a distribution. In continuous improvement, we fit mathematical models to stable distributions, which allows us to predict the long-term performance of the process (Fig. 11.2).

Having a mathematical model that predicts what the process will do going forward is like having a crystal ball that tells us the future. Can you imagine how powerful it is for you, your project sponsor, and your leadership team to be able to *predict* future process performance? With this knowledge, you can successfully manage hiring decisions, costs, delivery schedules, inventory level, transportation and storage needs, and profits.

Process Control Versus Quality Control

Many people believe that they can control quality by looking at results. If the output does not meet requirements, then the action is taken. This is output control. A better

---

[1]The unwritten word "statistical" is important to keep in mind. I.e., in *statistical* control and out of *statistical* control are understood.

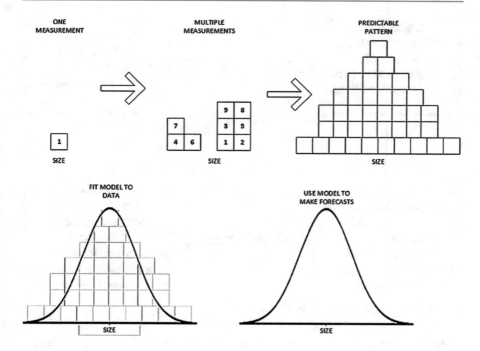

Fig. 11.2   Models for forecasting

way to achieve quality is by controlling the *causes* that create the results. This is process control. A process control system is a feedback system that links process outcomes with process inputs. But process improvement takes things one step further. It acts not only on special causes that temporarily impact the process, but also on common cause variation. That is, on variability that is built into the process. This is the primary focus for Lean improvement projects. And it is the biggest source of variability. 85% To 95% of the variability in most processes is common cause variability (Fig. 11.3).

Special and Common Cause Variation

When process control is based on statistical guidelines it is known as *statistical process control* or SPC. Control is defined as follows:

   a phenomenon will be said to be "controlled" when, through the use of past experience, we can predict, at least within limits, how the phenomenon may be expected to vary in the future.

   This means that statistical control is achieved when variability is predictable, not when it is zero. This is achieved when you have eliminated special causes, which create unpredictable variation. Since common cause variation is present in each and every observation, it is predictable, within limits. It is not easy to tell when the

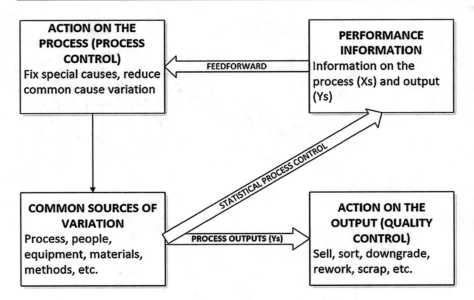

Fig. 11.3 Process control versus quality control

variation is created by special or common causes, you need statistical guidelines to help you separate the two types of causes. That is where SPC comes in.

In his seminal book on SPC, Dr. Walter A. Shewhart showed the two charts on the left side of Fig. 11.4 and asked if the observed variation should be acted upon or left to chance. In other words, should you look for a problem or not? The two charts both show the fraction of defective product created by a process month-by-month. In healthcare, it might be the percentage of in-patients who fell or the percentage of insurance claims rejected because of an error.

One of the charts presents variability that should be investigated, the other presents variability that should be, as Shewhart says, "left to chance." Can you tell at a glance which is which? I certainly cannot. That is why we need help in the form of statistical guidelines which are called "control limits," as shown on the right side of Fig. 11.4. Variation between the two control limits designated by the dashed lines will be deemed as the variation from the common cause system. Any variability beyond these fixed limits will be assumed to have come from special causes of variation. We will call any system exhibiting only common cause variation "statistically controlled." It must be noted that the control limits are not simply pulled out of the air, they are calculated from actual process data using valid statistical methods. Without statistical guidance there could be endless debate over whether special or common causes were to blame for variability.

Let us use control limits to answer Shewhart's question about the two process charts (Fig. 11.5). Since the top chart has one or more points outside of the control limits, we should look for a special cause of variation. However, the similar-looking pattern on the lower process chart does not have any points outside the control limits,

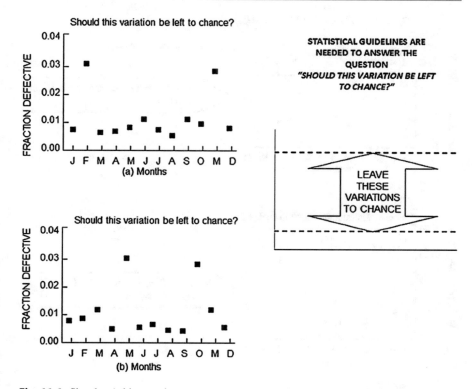

Fig. 11.4 Shewhart's big question

so the variability from this process should be, in Shewhart's terms, "left to chance." implies that the type of action needed to reduce the variability in each case is of a different nature. In the special cause case, we should look for something different that caused the process to change. In the common cause case, we should look at the process design.

Using Process Knowledge to Make Improvements

Let us take a closer look at the implications of having the ability to separate special and common cause variation. We always want to improve, the only question is how best to do it. There are two choices: we can look for the reason that a given result occurred and, based on our findings, take action. Or we can look for ways to redesign the process to reduce the variability. Consider that there are two types of variability: common cause and special cause.

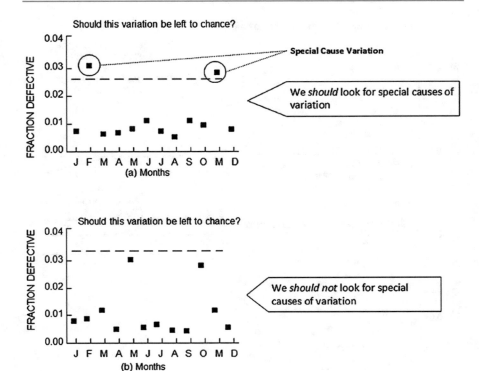

Fig. 11.5 Shewhart's big question answered

Making Matters Worse When Variation Is from Common Causes

Let us say that your process is only showing common cause variation, as shown in the bell curve on the left side of Fig. 11.6. You make a measurement and obtain the result shown by the black dot. The result is below the target. The target we are talking about is not based on the control limit, it is the target based on the management or engineering requirement. Let us also assume that you erroneously decide to look for the "problem" and you adjust the process to move closer to the target. Before you made the change the process was already centered on the target and the variation was just the common cause variation shown by the bell curve on the left. However, the adjustment you made caused the process means to move upward, above target, which is shown by the bell curve on the right side of the figure. The overall result is a process that has much greater variability, which was caused by your adjustment. This is shown in Fig. 11.6 by the dashed line curve. If you continue you will be constantly making adjustments upward and downward, which will cause a huge increase in the total variation of the process.

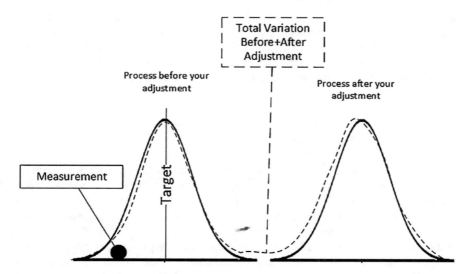

Fig. 11.6 Wrong common cause improvement strategy

Superstitious Learning

Even though your actions made matters worse, you may actually believe that your action made an improvement, which is called superstitious learning. For example, often supervisors react to measurements that are relatively far off-target by "talking to the workers." In statistics, there is a phenomenon called "regression to the mean." It means simply that results that are far from the mean will usually be followed by results that are closer to the mean. It is a natural result of the fact that measurements closer to the mean are more common. When a result is noticeably off-target, chances are the next result will be closer to the target even if nothing is done. But if you intervene it is very likely that you will believe that your intervention *caused* the improved result, leading to "learning." Superstitious learning is responsible for a great deal of counter-productive management behavior, such as employee ranking systems.

Making Matters Worse When Variation Is from Special Causes

What happens when special causes of variation are addressed by treating them like common causes? In other words, the system is redesigned based on data from out-of-control processes. Since special causes are not part of the system in the first place, the redesign has very little effect. The special cause variation is still there, and time and money were wasted.

Reacting Properly to Special and Common Cause Variation

What happens when the manager reacts to common cause variation appropriately by designing a new system? Overall process variability is reduced, perhaps six sigma performance is achieved. Finally, what happens when a special cause is treated as a special cause? In short, the reason for the transient problem is found and corrected. The process is returned to the state it was designed to be in and total variability is decreased. In addition, you will learn something meaningful about the process. If the process was properly designed in the first place, it will now produce results that achieve the goal of meeting the management or engineering requirements.

11.3   Operational Definitions

In continuous improvement work, you will frequently discover that the opportunity your project is addressing cannot be reliably measured because it has not been operationally defined. An operational definition is a definition that includes a detailed specification of measurement. The side bar contains an example of an actual operational definition used by a carpet manufacturer to define "Dark Blue Carpet."[2] Note that this example describes the qualifications of the person making the evaluation, the standard of comparison, and the conditions under which the judgment is made. These are the essential elements of operational definitions.

Dark Blue Carpet
A carpet will be deemed to be dark blue if:
    Judged by an inspector medically certified as having passed the U.S. Air Force test for color-blindness.
    It matches the PANTONE color card 7462 C when both carpet and card are illuminated by GE "cool white" fluorescent tubes.
    Card and carpet are viewed with the naked eye at a distance between 16-in. and 24-in.

Examples of Operational Definitions

Intelligence
Operational definitions are needed for non-physical properties as well. Intelligence is an elusive and debatable concept, but it has been and is measured. Note that the validity of the operational definition is not resolved by the definition, but it cannot even be discussed until it is first defined. Here is an operational definition that might be used:

---

[2]Early in my career I inspected the lithography process at a can plant. Our best customer returned a shipment because, they said, the cans were off-color. Both my boss and I re-inspected the cans and agreed that the color met the standard. Later on eye tests showed that both of us were colorblind!

Administer the Stanford-Binet IQ Test to a Person and Score the Result. The Person's Intelligence Is the Score on the Test

Acceptable Waiting Time

One common practice in Lean is to get operational definitions directly from customers. For example, waiting time acceptability can be defined by asking customers for their judgments. Of course, different customers may have different judgments: a busy professional may have a different standard than a casual consumer. Your team will need to carefully determine which operational definition applies to their project.

A Support Call's Waiting Time Will Be Deemed Acceptable if a Customer Agrees Or Strongly Agrees with the Survey Item "The Waiting Time Was Acceptable"

While the definition will always be the same, the results of using this definition may vary with customer segment, time of day or season of the year, etc. Be sure your sponsor and other stakeholders agree with your choice.

Control Charts

In this chapter we have talked a lot about common cause variation and special cause variation. These types of variation are operationally defined by graphical tools called control charts. A particularly useful type of control chart, known as an X chart, is discussed in Chap. 13.

Descriptive Statistics

12

It is vital that you measure the current state before you begin your project. This is the only way you will be able to document the impact of your project, and it will tell you a lot about what is wrong and how to move forward. Be forewarned that there will always be some debate over the impact of your project because it is likely that other activities are also taking place that might have improved things. Still, if you do not have data, it will not be possible to make your case. The way you make sense of the data is by using statistics. Statistics are data summaries. That is, they are a small set of numbers used to represent a larger set of numbers. Descriptive statistics are data summaries that describe the process distribution in numbers.

12.1 Properties of Distributions

Distributions have certain properties that can be described using statistics. In this lesson, you will learn about statistics for three of these properties: location, spread, and shape. You will also learn what outliers are.[1]

Let us take a graphical look at these ideas (Fig. 12.1). The location refers to the center of the distribution. The spread of the distribution is the amount by which smaller values differ from larger ones. In other words, how wide is the distribution? The shape of a distribution is its pattern, peakedness, symmetry, etc. A given phenomenon may have any one of a number of distribution shapes, such as skew to the right or skew to the left. Finally, there are outliers. These are observations that are not from the system's distribution, but from a different cause system entirely.

Here is a link to online programs to calculate the statistics discussed in this chapter http://bit.ly/2uVuua5.

---

[1] Because outliers are data points that do not come from the distribution so they cannot be called a property of the distribution per se. But that is just a technicality.

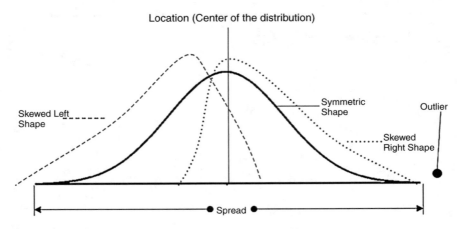

Fig. 12.1 Distribution properties illustrated

Table 12.1 Physician	Physician	Panel size
panel sizes	Dr. Linder	1200
	Dr. Bessette	1100
	Dr. Lorenz	1300
	Dr. Varga	1300
	Dr. Robertson	1500

Statistics to Measure the Central Tendency

The most commonly used statistic for measuring the central tendency of a distribution is the average or *mean*. This statistic is calculated by adding up all of the measurements and dividing by the number of measurements. The symbol used to show that you should add up a set of numbers is the upper case Greek letter sigma, Σ. The equation for the mean is shown in Eq. (12.1). The numerator is simply the sum of all of the measurements Σx. The denominator is the number of measurements, n.

$$\text{Mean} = \frac{\sum x}{n} \tag{12.1}$$

For example, if you measure the panel size (number of patients) for family care physicians in a group practice you might get the numbers shown in Table 12.1 physician panel sizes.

The mean panel size for this practice is $(1200 + 1100 + 1300 + 1300 + 1500)/5 = 6400/5 = $ **1280 patients per physician**. The mean can be thought of as the point that balances the distribution. Think of a data set as a teeter-totter. Just as a teeter-totter is sensitive to both the weight on each side of the center point and the distance the weight is from the center point, the mean is sensitive to *outliers*. I.e., a single

Table 12.2 Physician panel size in rank order by panel size

Physician	Panel size
Dr. Bessette	1100
Dr. Linder	1200
Dr. Lorenz	1300
Dr. Varga	1300
Dr. Robertson	1500

point far away from the mean will have as much influence as many smaller points close to the mean. This is something to keep in mind when you interpret any mean.

The *median* is another measure of the center of a distribution. It is found by ranking the data in order and finding the value in the middle. If there are an even number of values, the median is the midpoint between the two middle values. If we sort Table 12.1 according to panel size we get Table 12.2. Since there are 5 physicians, the median is in row 3, 1300 patients. Unlike the mean, the median is not influenced by outliers so comparing the median of a data set to the mean is often useful.

The final location statistic we will talk about is the *mode*. The mode is the measurement that occurs most often. If no measurement shows up more than once, then there is no mode. If multiple measurements occur the same number of times, then there is more than one mode. For the physician panel sizes, the mode is 1300, which occurs twice. This is easiest to see in the sorted data shown in Table 12.2.

Sometimes the location statistics for a distribution are all the same, such as for the normal distribution bell-shaped curve. However, this is not always the case. At times the mean, the median, and the mode will all be different. This indicates an asymmetric distribution shape. This does not necessarily indicate that there is any problem, but it might be useful to plot a histogram to study the shape of the distribution for clues as to ways to make improvements. Histograms are discussed in another chapter of this book (see below).

Most computer spreadsheets have built in functions for calculating the location statistics described above. If you are using Microsoft Excel, turning on the included Data Analysis add-in gives you access to all of these statistics.

Statistics to Measure the Spread of a Distribution

There are statistics that measure the amount of dispersion or "spread" in a data set. The easiest spread statistic to calculate is the sample *range*. The range is just the difference between the extreme values in a sample. To calculate the range, find the largest sample value and the smallest sample value, then subtract. The range is usually shown using the upper case R. It is commonly used in continuous improvement when working with control charts, which are discussed in the chapter X-Charts.

$$R = \text{Largest value} - \text{Smallest value} \qquad (12.2)$$

The range is not very efficient statistically when sample sizes become large and it is usually not used for subgroups sizes larger than 9. However, it has the advantage of being very easy to calculate even without a calculator or computer, and it has face validity as a measure of spread. Most spreadsheets have built in functions for finding the minimum and maximum values, making it even easier to calculate the range. For the data in Table 12.1 $R = 400$.

Another common statistic for measuring spread is the *standard deviation*, or *s*. *s* is a bit more complicated to calculate. Here are instructions on how to find *s*:

1. Finding the mean as described above.
2. Subtract the mean from each observation.
3. Square the result.
4. Sum the values found in step 3.
5. Divide the sum by the sample size minus 1.
6. Take the square root. This is *s*.

This procedure is shown by Eq. (12.3), where *x* stands for each measurement and *n* is the sample size.[2]

$$s = \sqrt{\frac{\sum (x - \text{mean})^2}{n - 1}} \qquad (12.3)$$

Using the above procedure for the data in Table 12.1 we get[3]:

x	x-mean	(x-mean) squared
1100	−180	32,400
1200	−80	6400
1300	20	400
1300	20	400

(continued)

---

[2]I am simplifying a vast quantity of math here, but there is plenty of information on the math in any statistics book or in my *Six Sigma Handbook*.

[3]Of course, it is easier to use the built in spreadsheet function =STDEV(1100, 1200, 1300, 1300, 1500).

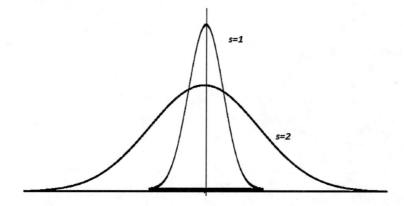

Fig. 12.2 Visualizing *s*

1500	220	48,400
	SUM	88,000
	SUM/(*n*-1)	22,000
	s	**148.32**

12.2   What Does *s* Mean?

For normal distributions (bell curves) about 95% of the data are within about 2 standard deviations of the mean, and nearly all data are within 3 standard deviations of the mean. One of the distributions shown in Fig. 12.2 has a standard deviation of 2. About 95% of the data from this distribution will be between −2 standard deviations below the mean (mean-4) and +2 standard deviations above the mean (mean +4). About 99.7% will be between −3 standard deviations below the mean (mean −6) and +3 standard deviations above the mean (mean +6). The distribution labeled *s* = 1 has only half the spread. The percentages between any two standard deviation values will, however, be the same. In short, the dispersion statistic will be larger for distributions that are more spread out.

X-Charts

13

Figure 11.5 Shewhart's Big Question Answered shows that you need statistical guidelines to help identify when special causes are present. Control charts are used to show you these guidelines. In this chapter, you will learn about a particular control chart called an x-chart that will indicate whether the process is in control or not in control. I will not go into the math of x-charts. Instead I will give you links to computer spreadsheets that do the math for you.[1]

13.1 Sampling for Process Control

Of the many important differences between enumerative and analytic studies, few are more fundamental than the way we select our sample units. The basic sampling method used for enumerative statistics is the random sample. The sampling method used for control charts is based on the rational subgroup. Rational subgroups are composed of items or observations which as far as we know were produced under essentially the same conditions. Our statistical process control (SPC) samples will be small and they will be taken frequently. We do this because we are looking for patterns in the process over time. When we receive action signals from the control chart our actions will address the root causes of process variation and will impact future process performance. Contrast this with the classical approach taught in college statistics classes. Instead of rational subgroups, the classical approach uses random samples, instead of small samples, large samples are used. Studies are infrequent due to the expense of taking large samples. Rather than looking at patterns of variation to identify special causes of variation, parameters are estimated from the samples. And rather than looking at the future, the population from which samples are drawn are the focus of conclusions. Table 13.1 summarizes these differences.

---

[1]If you're interested in learning more about the math behind x-charts, go to this website http://bit.ly/2uHzwHQ

Table 13.1 Statistical process control versus classical statistical studies

Sampling for SPC (analytic methods)	Classic approach (enumerative methods)
Rational subgroups	Random samples
Small samples	Large samples
Frequent samples	Infrequent studies
Dynamic process	Static universe/population
Focus on the future	Focus on the population
Infer the state of the process	Inference on population parameters

13.2   Control Charts for Process Metrics

There are many different types of data: measurements, counts, percentages, etc.. However, a single type of control chart will give you good insights into all of these types of data. That control chart is called the individuals' chart, or the x-chart.

For x-charts our rational subgroup consists of measurements obtained from consecutive units of production, or as close as feasible. By the unit of production I mean the product or service or transaction being created. For example, a blood draw, a patient visit, a bill prepared and sent. Control charts for individuals compare variation over the long-term with limits that are calculated from observations of the process taken at close to the same time. If the process is in control, then nearly all of the measurements should fall within the control limits.

For x-charts we measure process variability by looking at the absolute value of the difference between measurements taken on consecutive units of production. An absolute value ignores whether an observation is less than or greater than the previous observation, in other words, if the difference is negative we ignore the minus sign. For example, assume that we observed that it took 110 min to process a patient through the ED process and the next patient took 103 min. The measured difference between these two times is $110 - 103 = 7$ min. This is the range discussed earlier in this book. If the third patient took 117 min, then the second range would be $103 - 117 = -14$, which would become simply 14 because we ignore the minus sign. Note that the range measurements "move" from one pair of values to the next (e.g., the 103-min observation is included in two range calculations). Because of this, the range is called the moving range.

The moving range is used to determine the control limits for the patient ED times (the Xs on the x-chart.) The control limits are operational definitions of special causes. I.e., if a measurement falls outside of a control limit, we will conclude that a special cause of variation is acting on the process. Here is a link to an online tool that will create x-charts for you http://bit.ly/2w4oNvf.

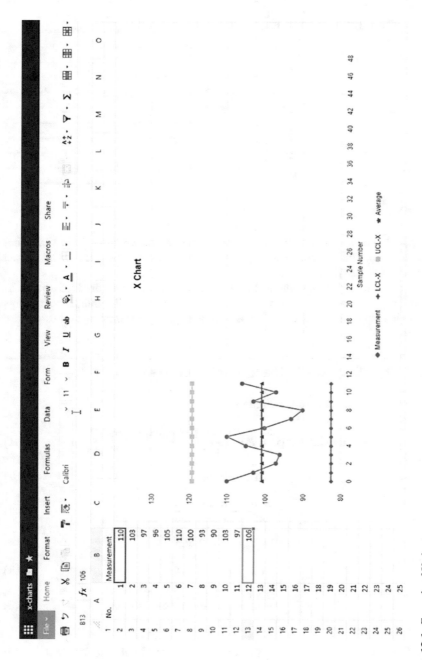

Fig. 13.1 Example of X chart

Table 13.2 Sample data for X-chart	Patient ED time	Moving range
	110	
	103	7
	97	6
	96	1
	105	9
	110	5
	100	10
	93	7
	90	3
	103	13
	97	6
	106	6

X-Chart Example

Figure 13.1 shows an x-chart plot of the ED processing time data in Table 13.2 using the online tool. The plot shows that the process is in control, i.e., there are no special causes of variation present.

Enter your own data in column B of the online tool and it will produce an x-chart control chart. Points outside of the control limits will be highlighted. Such points indicate that special causes of variation were acting on your process at those times.

13.3   Equations for X-Charts (Optional Material)

Here are the equations used for X-charts.

$$\text{Average moving range} = \overline{R} = \frac{\text{Sum of moving ranges}}{\text{Number of moving ranges}} \tag{13.1}$$

$$\text{UCL}_R = 3.267 \times \overline{R} \tag{13.2}$$

$$\overline{x} = \frac{\text{Sum of measurements}}{\text{Number of measurements}} \tag{13.3}$$

$$\text{LCL}_x = \overline{x} - 2.66\overline{R} \tag{13.4}$$

$$UCL_x = \overline{x} + 2.66\overline{R} \tag{13.5}$$

$$\widehat{\sigma} = \frac{\overline{R}}{1.128} \text{ where } \widehat{\sigma} \text{ is an estimate od sigma.} \tag{13.6}$$

- LCL = Lower Control Limit = the lowest value you should see for the statistic if the process is in control.

- UCL = Upper Control Limit = the largest value you should see for the statistic if the process is in control.
- A statistic with a line or bar above it is an average and is pronounced [statistic] bar. E.g., $\bar{x}$ is the average of the x values and is pronounced x bar. $\bar{R}$ is the average moving range and is pronounced R bar.
- If a control limit is below a bounded value, it is not shown on the chart. For example, if the lower control limit is below zero and it is not possible to get a measurement less than zero, do not show the LCL on the chart. (The online tool will show *all* values.)

Pareto Analysis

14

Vilfredo Federico Damaso Pareto was a nineteenth century renaissance man. He was an Italian engineer, sociologist, economist, political scientist, and philosopher. He made several important contributions to economics and he also contributed to the fields of sociology and mathematics.[1] But, more important for our purposes, he is also known for the 80/20 rule, named after him as the Pareto principle. For continuous improvement purposes, the 80/20 rule states that 80% of the problems are due to 20% of the causes. For example, a few suppliers were responsible for most supplier-related quality problems. When you are trying to improve a process, the Pareto Principle is an excellent way to sharpen your focus to the critical few sources that are causing most of the problems.

Pareto analysis is simply the process of looking at opportunities, which are often disguised as problems, to find the few big opportunities that should be pursued first. Pareto analysis is a tool that is used over and over again in Lean to progressively break a big project into easier to manage subprojects. Early in your project, you will use Pareto analysis to answer questions like what project should I pursue? After choosing a project Pareto analysis can help you answer the question "which problem in this project should I address first?"

14.1 How to Perform Pareto Analysis

Performing Pareto analysis is quite simple. Here are the steps you should follow.

First decide on how you will "slice and dice" the data into categories. For example, if your project involved quality problems with bacteremia infections of central venous catheters (CVCs) you might categorize quality problems according to

---

[1] I could not find anything that tells us what Mr. Pareto did in his spare time!

the type of patients with CVCs, the place the IV was inserted, whether a physician or a nurse placed the IV, the day of the week the IV was placed, et cetera. If your project involved order processing cycle time you might look at late orders by order type, day of the week, order taker, or customer.

Second select a time interval for your Pareto analysis. You do not want an interval that is too short to be meaningful or so long that the old data are irrelevant or the time to get useful data is too long. Think about what a "typical" time period might be. This may require breaking your problem into pieces, such as weekdays versus weekends, day shift versus night shift, or just the Christmas season.

Third find the total for each category and the sum total for all categories combined. A common rule of thumb is to lump many categories with small totals into a catchall category called "other." I recommend that you show separate categories until approximately 20% or less of the total are unaccounted for, then put all of the remaining data into the "other" category. This will keep the resulting Pareto chart from being distorted by having a long "tail" of trivial problems.

Fourth compute the percent contribution each category makes to the total.

Fifth rank order the categories from largest to smallest.

Finally, compute the cumulative percentage up to and including each category. The total for all categories combined should be 100%.

Principles of Good Charts

Before I launch into the step-by-step instructions for constructing a Pareto Chart, let me provide some principles to guide you. Charts provide a picture of the data. They tell a story about the real world thing that is represented by the numbers. Like all stories and pictures, the story that the chart tells can be accurate and illuminating, or distorted and misleading. It is vitally important that your Pareto Chart tell the correct story. The story may be why you are doing this particular project or why you are starting the project by focusing on this particular problem or why the study of this problem should begin by addressing this particular cause. But if not told properly, the story may do more harm than good.

Table 14.1 Newspaper sales

Who?	Sales
Us	485,720
Them	446,954

14.2   The Graphical Story of Me

This is a photo of me. The scale of the photo has not been altered and it is pretty accurate, except that in real life I am in color!	Here is what happens when I change the scale. I look heavier, do not I?	But I can be made to look slimmer by merely changing the scale again.

Of course, I could also change the photo in other ways, for example, I could chop off the bottom of the photo. However, the *reality* behind the photo is still the same, and it is an accurate graphic depiction of the reality that we are striving for.

These sorts of distortions are common in real life. Take a look at Table 14.1, which shows the sales of two different newspapers.[2]

If you enter this data into an Excel spreadsheet, select it, and tell Excel to create a bar chart without changing the default settings, Fig. 14.1 shows what you get.

Since the first bar is physically 250% taller than the second bar, your eyes tell you that "Us" outsold "Them" by more than two-to-one. However, the *numbers* tell you that the sales difference is only about 10%. In the world of humans, visuals trump numbers, so Fig. 14.1 will leave the audience with a false impression. No matter how much you *say* that the difference is small, your audience will have trouble accepting it in their hearts because of what they *see*. To make the picture match the numbers you need to manually change the scale of the chart to what is shown in Fig. 14.2. Now you can see the 10% difference more clearly. The bottom of the chart's vertical axis now starts at zero. It is still not perfect because I allowed the computer to make the top of the chart's vertical axis a nice round 500,000 instead of 485,720, but it tells the story much more accurately than the chart that was created using Excel's default

---

[2]These are actual data that were published. For other egregious distortions visit http://www. statisticshowto.com/misleading-graphs/.

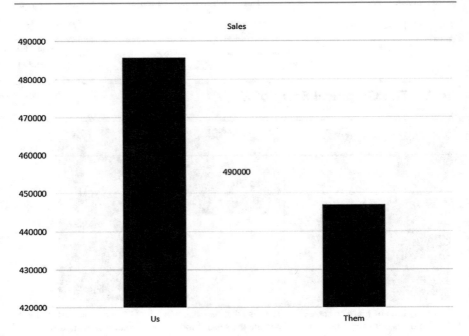

Fig. 14.1 Newspaper sales

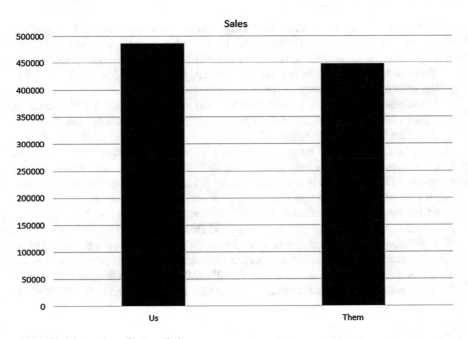

Fig. 14.2 Newspaper sales rescaled

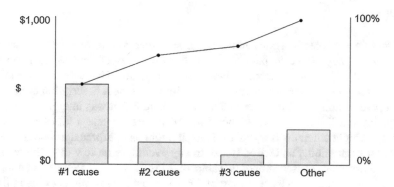

Fig. 14.3 Pareto chart structure

settings. This is what we want to do when we tell our Lean process improvement
story using Pareto Charts.

How to Create a Pareto Chart

A Pareto chart is two charts in one: one of the charts is a bar chart, the other a line
chart. The bar chart will show the contributions of each separate problem category to
the total problem, the line chart will show the cumulative total up to and including a
given problem category.

The left axis of the chart is in the original units, such as dollars, customer
complaints, quality problems, errors, et cetera. The right axis is in percentage
units. The bottom on both axes will be zero. The top of the vertical axis will be
the total size of the problem in original units on the left axis and 100% on the right
axis. The 100% tick mark will be directly across from the total if the chart is properly
scaled. The bottom axis will show the categories of the problem in descending rank
order, from largest to smallest. The bars will get smaller as you go from left to right.
The last bar may be an "other" category bar where you aggregate several small
categories to avoid having a Pareto chart where a lot of insignificant problem
categories cause the chart to stretch too far to the right. The Other category may
be larger than some of the other categories, which is okay. The line chart makes it
easier to see how much of the *total* problem can be accounted for by several
categories.

A rule of thumb is that approximately 20% of the causes or categories should
account for approximately 80% of the total problem. In real life, this may not be the
case, which is helpful in deciding if you have a useful Pareto Chart. If your Pareto
analysis does not show a relatively small number of big categories dominating the
chart, take another look at the problem to see if you can come up with different
categories that will help you focus the problem. A Pareto chart where all of the bars
are about the same size is not very helpful in setting priorities (Fig. 14.3).

Example

A team of employees in a community hospital wished to improve the satisfaction of in-patients. They spoke to patients about to be discharged and asked them what problems, if any, they had experienced during their stay. The team listened to what patients said and interpreted their comments into consistent descriptions. For example, if patient said "I did not care much for the pudding" it was interpreted as a food complaint and listed as Food. If they said "The nurses made a lot of noise in the hallway at night when I was trying to sleep" it might be interpreted as both Noise and Staff Not Professional and listed twice. In any event, after a few days the team had the list of problem causes shown in Table 14.2 Problems Reported by Patients. The list was sorted in a spreadsheet program. Data in most organizations exists in lists of text descriptions like this one.

Microsoft Excel has a menu called Data. If you choose this menu in a recent version of Excel you will see a submenu labeled Outline. Within this menu is an option called Subtotal. If you select the list of problems and click the subtotal choice, Excel will let you calculate subtotals for the different problems. Then you can use the subtotals to create the Pareto chart, as shown in Fig. 14.4 Pareto Chart of Reported Problems. To watch a video showing how this chart was created type this link into your browser http://bit.ly/2g0LEBc.

Discussion

I advised the team to group the two staff categories into a single "Staff" category and to lump the Policy issues and Restroom cleanliness issues into an Other category. This tightened up the Pareto chart and made it easier to see the priorities. After these changes, it was clear that three problems dominated the customer feedback. Note that in Fig. 14.5 I changed the colors to simple black and white. Research shows that colors influence the way people interpret charts. However, there is a point where it takes more time than it is worth to dress up the graphics, so I will not object if you let Excel choose the colors for you.

Table 14.2 Problems
reported by patients

Problem
Food
Food
Food
Food
Food
Food
Food
Food
Food
Food
Food
Food
Food
Noise
Noise
Noise
Noise
Noise
Noise
Noise
Noise
Noise
Noise
Noise
Policy issues
Policy issues
Policy issues
Restroom cleanliness
Restroom cleanliness
Restroom cleanliness
Staff not courteous
Staff not courteous
Staff not courteous
Staff not courteous
Staff not professional
Staff not professional
Staff not professional
Staff not professional

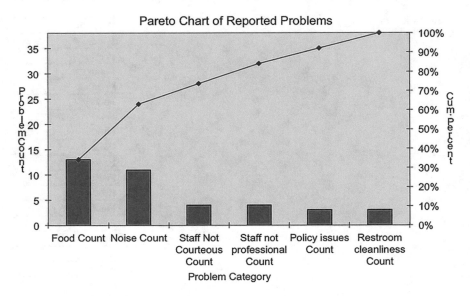

Fig. 14.4   Pareto chart of reported problems

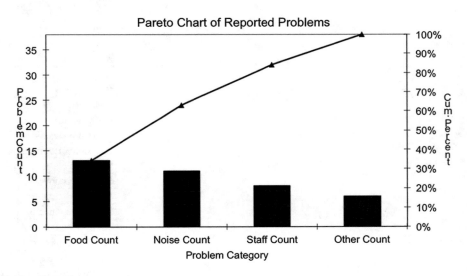

Fig. 14.5   Final pareto chart

Graphical Data Analysis

15

Remember when I said in Chap. 11 that the three rules of data analysis were "(1) Plot the data! (2) Plot the data! And (3) Plot the data!"? The previous chapter on Pareto analysis showed you an example of plotting the data and discussed the importance of properly scaling a chart. This chapter will discuss several other powerful graphical tools that will help you understand what your data is begging to tell you.

15.1 Correlation Analysis Using Scatter Plots

The dictionary defines a variable as something that may or does vary or change; a variable feature or factor. Correlation is defined as the degree to which two or more attributes or measurements on the same group of elements show a tendency to vary together. Correlation analysis is the evaluation of the joint variation of a set of variables. By studying the correlation among variables in a process you can get insights that can be very helpful in improving the process.

One tool that is very useful in displaying the joint variation of two variables is the scatter plot. A scatter plot is a simple dot plot of one variable versus another. If we have process knowledge that one variable is causing the other variable to change, then one variable is called the independent variable and it is usually shown on the horizontal (bottom) axis. The other variable is called the dependent variable and it is shown on the vertical (side) axis. If scatter plots are used to examine the joint changes of variables not known to be related by cause and effect, the terms dependent and independent variable are not used.

Even if you use advanced statistical methods of analysis (which are usually not necessary for Lean continuous improvement) scatter plots are must-have supplement to these statistical tools, as well as a useful stand-alone tool. In the early part of a Lean project scatter plots are often applied to "historical data," i.e., data that already exists.

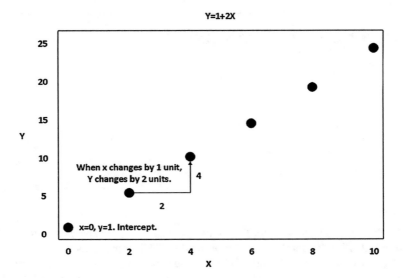

Fig. 15.1 Linear relationship

Linear Models

A linear model is simply an expression of a type of association between two variables, x and y. A linear relationship simply means that a change of a given size in x produces a fixed change in y. Linear models have the form: $y = a + bx$, where a and b are constants. The equation simply says that when x changes by one unit, y will change by b units. This relationship can be shown graphically as a set of points that fall on a straight line. The term a is called the intercept and b is called the slope. The intercept is the value of y when $x = 0$. Figure 15.1 depicts an example of a perfect linear fit, I.e., if x is known we can determine y exactly.[1] The equation for the relationship in the figure is $y = 1 + 2x$, so $a = 1$ and $b = 2$ for this example. The intercept is what the equation gives when $x = 0$. In this case when $x = 0$ $y = 1$ so the intercept, $a = 1$.

If we know from our knowledge of the process that x causes y then we can say that a change of 1 unit in x will *cause* y to increase by b units. If we do not know if x causes y then we say that a change of 1 unit in x is *correlated with* a 2 unit change in y. This is not mere semantics, it is an important distinction to understand. Misunderstanding can result, for example, in mistakenly believing that x causes y, when in fact y causes x. Or we might miss the fact that a third variable, z, is causing *both* x and y to change. These misunderstandings can result in making ineffective or unnecessary process changes, or in failing to make a change when we should. Sometimes the action we take or fail to take can even be harmful.

---

[1]Of course, perfect fits are virtually unknown when real data are used.

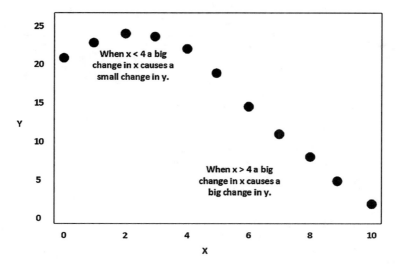

Fig. 15.2 Curvilinear relationship

Curvilinear Relationship

Many types of associations are non-linear. For example, over a given range of *x* values, *y* might increase, and for other *x* values, *y* might decrease. This curvilinear relationship is shown in the scatter plot in Fig. 15.2. Here we see that *y* increases when *x* increases and *x* is less than about 2 and decreases as *x* increases when *x* is greater than 2. Curvilinear relationships are valuable in the design of robust processes. A process is robust when a big change in a cause variable results in a relatively small change or no change in the effect variable. Notice that at the top of the curve a large change in *x* produces a small change in *y*. In fact, when *x* = 0 or 4, *y* is about the same. If you are interested in reducing the variability of *y*, this relationship is worth knowing about. It is also important because you know that if *x* is allowed to go beyond 4, *y* will change a lot. A wide variety of processes have such relationships.

How to Create Scatter Plots

Constructing a scatter plot is quite straightforward.

First, gather several paired sets of observations, preferably 20 or more. A paired set is one where the dependent variable can be directly linked to the independent variable. For example, measurements were taken on the same patient.

Second, find the largest and smallest independent variable and the largest and smallest dependent variable.

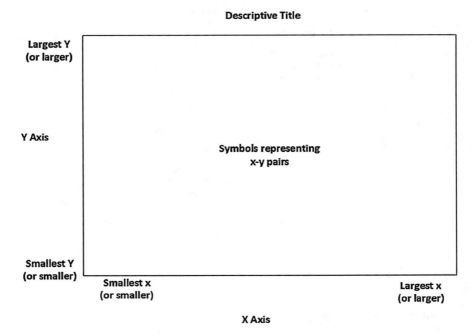

Fig. 15.3 Structure of scatter plots

Finally, construct the vertical and horizontal axes so that the smallest and largest values can be plotted. Figure 15.3 shows the basic structure of a scatter diagram.

If you have Microsoft Excel you can create a scatter plot with a few clicks.[2] Excel can also fit a straight line to your data to help you see the relationships. Figure 15.4 shows a basic scatter plot created in Excel for the linear relationship described in the Linear Models section above.

Tips for Using Scatter Plots

Here are some tips to help you use scatter plots effectively.

- Be sure that the independent variable, x, is varied over a sufficiently large range. When the range of x is too small it is called range restriction. You might miss a relationship that is really there. Figure 15.5 shows an example where the correlation between x and y does not show up when x is varied over a range of less than 2 units. Many times management or engineering specifications call for restricting a metric to a tight range. This is fine practice for maintaining process control.

---

[2]Here is a video showing you how to do this http://bit.ly/2vb6PXO.

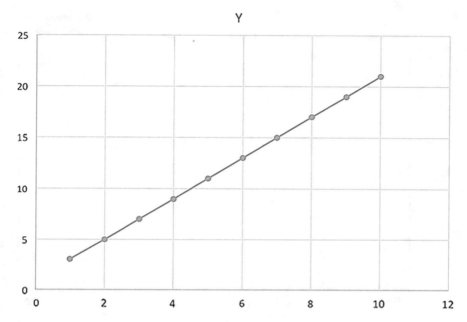

Fig. 15.4 Excel's scatter plot

However, if you experiment you might find a hidden correlation or curvilinear relationship that you can use to make the process robust and easier to manage.

- Predicting a y value beyond the x range actually tested is called extrapolation. Avoid doing this if at all possible. If you must extrapolate, try to get at least one *x-y* pair at the extrapolated value.
- Keep an eye out for the effect of variables you did not evaluate. Often, an uncontrolled variable will wipe out the effect of your *x* variable. It is also possible that an uncontrolled variable will be causing the effect and you will mistake the *x* variable you are controlling as the true cause.
- Beware of "happenstance" data! Happenstance data are data that were collected in the past for a purpose different than constructing a scatter diagram. Since little or no control was exercised over important variables, you may find nearly anything. Happenstance data should be used only to get ideas for further investigation, never for reaching final conclusions.
- If there is more than one possible source for the dependent variable, try using different plotting symbols for each source. For example, if you have measurements for different shifts, plot each shift using a different symbol.
- Although it is possible to do advanced analysis without plotting the scatter diagram, this is bad practice. It misses the enormous learning opportunity provided by the graphical analysis of the data.

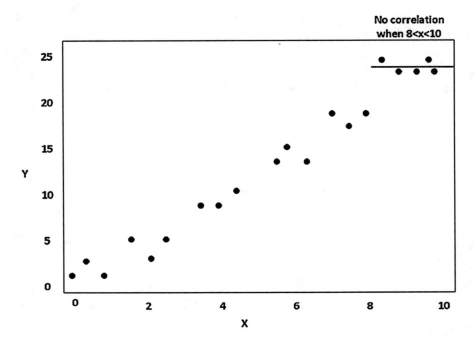

Fig. 15.5   Range restriction effect

Scatter Plot Interpretation Guide

With scatter plots you see what happens to one variable when another variable changes. There are several possibilities. When y increases as x increases we say the correlation is positive. When y decreases as x increases, we say the correlation is negative. If y increases over some range of x values and decreases over some other range of x values, then the relationship is non-linear. If a smooth curve can be drawn through the data points, the non-linear relationship is called curvilinear. Do not forget that correlation does not equal causation. We create scatter plots from historical data to develop hypotheses, not to prove them.

Figure 15.6 is a guide to help you quickly assess scatter plot patterns.

1. Pattern #1 shows that the two variables being studied are tightly linked (or strongly correlated) and positively correlated. Positively correlated means that when x increases, y does so too, and the size of the increase in y for a given sized change in x is very consistent. The consistency indicates that x is dominant and few other factors are impacting y. If there is process knowledge to show that x causes y, then controlling x will probably be sufficient to control y.
2. Pattern #2 shows a pattern similar to pattern 1 except that there is less consistency in the amount of increase in y for a given increase in x. This means that something other than x is having an influence on y. If x is known to cause y, then controlling

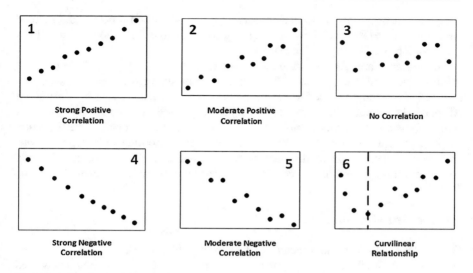

Fig. 15.6 Scatter plot interpretation guide

x will be helpful in controlling y, but other causes of the variation in y need to be identified and controlled as well.

3. This pattern shows that x and y are probably unrelated. Controlling x will not do much to control y. A control chart for y should be considered to keep its variability within limits. Process studies and experiments should be conducted to determine what is causing y to vary. Kaizen Events (Chap. 18) and A3 projects (Chap. 19) should be considered.
4. Pattern #4 is similar to pattern #1 except that increases in x are associated with decreases in y. This is called negative correlation.
5. This pattern is similar to pattern #2 except that increases in x are associated with decreases in y.
6. This pattern in curvilinear. When x is equal to or smaller than the value indicated by the dashed line, an increase in x is associated with a decrease in y. When x values are beyond the dashed line an increase in x is associated with an increase in y. The value of such a relationship in process control was discussed earlier in this chapter.

15.2 Histograms

Histograms are tools that can be used to create pictures from data that help you see the distribution of your process metrics. By studying the distribution you will obtain insights that can be used to troubleshoot and improve processes. Frequency distributions are empirical presentations of observations. Ungrouped frequency distributions show each observation and how often it occurred. Grouped frequency distributions show a range of observations and how many times observations in the range occurred.

Histograms are grouped frequency distributions. A histogram is a pictorial representation of a set of data. It is created by grouping the measurements into "cells." Histograms are used to determine the shape of a data set. Also, a histogram displays the numbers in a way that makes it easy to see the dispersion and central tendency without needing complicated calculations and to compare the distribution to requirements. Histograms can be valuable troubleshooting aids. Comparisons between histograms from different shifts, personnel, pieces of equipment, etc. often reveal important differences that can be used to improve processes.

Histogram Structure

Let us take a look at the structure of histograms (Fig. 15.7). The left axis of the histogram shows the frequency or count of observations in a cell. It should be scaled starting at zero and go to a frequency that is at least as large as the largest cell frequency, but not too much larger. This will assure that the picture presented is not distorted. The bottom of the histogram will show the cell boundaries. The lower leftmost cell boundary must be equal to or smaller than the smallest value in the data

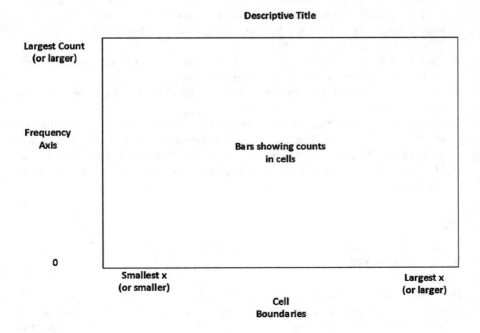

Fig. 15.7 Histogram structure

Table 15.1 100 ED times in minutes

112	99	112	100	98	88	77	145	86	62
108	113	96	99	124	109	125	102	63	103
128	100	107	75	83	76	122	108	130	115
103	119	85	119	124	99	130	108	122	93
116	93	85	126	98	88	116	91	109	109
105	118	82	100	64	82	112	48	101	107
97	126	86	106	109	120	104	127	75	90
79	85	79	103	156	128	120	69	108	110
84	118	109	86	114	80	116	101	96	120
68	125	115	105	130	112	99	96	137	136

set. The upper rightmost cell boundary must be equal to or larger than the largest value in the data set. Cells are usually of equal size, but this is not always true. This is commonly the case when outliers exist and the lower or upper cells have boundaries such as "x or less" or "x or greater." The top of the histogram should briefly describe the data shown, including the process, the metric plotted, and the date range covered by the data.

15.3 Example of a Histogram

The numbers shown in Table 15.1 are how long it took to process patients through the emergency department, in minutes. Although the numbers contain all of the information, humans have a difficult time understanding tables of numbers. A histogram will make it easier to see the information.

The histogram shown in Fig. 15.8 was created using Microsoft Excel's built in analysis toolpak, which has histograms.[3] The bottom axis is the ED time. Each bar represents the ED time from the previous time up to the time shown. For example, the number 59 represents all times from the smallest time (which was 48 min) up to 59 min. The 70 represents all times between 59 and 70, and so on. The height of the bar represents the count of ED times in the range. For example, there was 1 patient with an ED time of 59 min or less, 5 with ED times of 59–70 min, and so on. It is easy to see from the histogram that the distribution of ED times is approximately normal (bell shaped) and it is centered at about 113 min. So the typical patient spent about 113 min (nearly 2 h) in ED. Since the sample size was 100, the counts are also percentages. In the sample, 4% of patients spent more than 145 min in ED (2 h 25 min). All patients were processed in 156 min or less (2 h 36 min).

---

[3]To see the data analysis tools you need to turn on the data analysis toolpak in Excel.

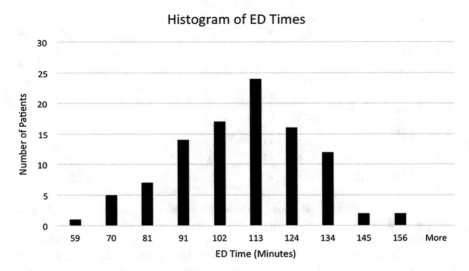

Fig. 15.8 Example of a histogram

Creating Histograms by Hand

Histograms are easy to construct by hand as well.

1. Find the count, the smallest value (minimum), and the largest value (maximum) in the data set.
2. Take the integer of the square root of the count. This is approximately the number of cells your histogram will have.
3. The size of each cell will be (Maximum-Minimum)/Number of cells. You may wish to round this up. At times there will be a logical reason to deviate from this norm, e.g., using common time periods like hours, days, weeks, etc..
4. The first cell in the histogram will start at the minimum value and will end at the minimum value plus the cell size.
5. Subsequent cells boundaries will start at the upper boundary of the previous cell plus the cell size. Continue until the upper cell boundary is equal or greater than the maximum.
6. Go through each number in your data set and make a mark in the cell for that value.
7. Plot the counts on a bar chart.

Example of Creating Histogram by Hand
We will use the data in Table 15.1 to illustrate the above procedure.

1. Count = 100, smallest value = 48, largest value = 156.

2. Square root of $100 = 10$.
3. Size of cell $= (156 - 48)/10 = 10.8$. We will round this to 11.
4. First cell: start at 48, end at $48 + 11 = 59$.
5. Other cell boundaries: 59–70, 70–81, 81–92, 92–103, 103–114, 114–125, 125–136, 136–147, 147–159.[4]

You can complete steps 6 and 7 on your own for practice.

Pointers for Using Histograms

- Histograms can be used to compare a process to requirements if you draw the specification lines on the histogram. Be sure to scale the histogram accordingly.
- If you know the time-order of the measurements always construct a control chart to supplement your histogram. They are needed because histograms will often conceal out of control conditions due to the fact that they do not show the time sequence of the data.
- Evaluate the pattern of the histogram to determine if you can detect changes of any kind. For example, if there are two humps on the histogram it may indicate two different sources of variation such as different shifts or suppliers.
- Compare histograms from different periods of time. Changes in histogram patterns from one time period to the next can be very useful in finding ways to improve the process.
- Stratify the data by plotting separate histograms for different sources of data. For example, with the ED times histogram, we might want to plot separate histograms for different shifts or different triage categories. This can sometimes reveal things that even control charts do not detect.

---

[4]These are slightly different than the histogram in Fig. 15.8 because the computer did not round off as we did in step 3.

Problem Solving Tools

16

In Lean, problem solving addresses root causes of problems, not symptoms. This is in stark contrast to what most organizations do. We discussed this in the earlier section on Process Control versus Quality Control. While we do not ignore Quality Control, which focuses on the *results* of problems, we emphasize Process Control which focuses on the *causes* of problems. Previous discussions covered ways to identify that problems are present in a process, i.e., **special cause variation**. This chapter will present methods of identifying what is causing the special cause variation. The same methods can also help you when only common cause variation is present and you want identify these common causes.

16.1   Cause and Effect Diagrams

Cause and effect diagrams are tools that organize group knowledge about causes of a problem and display the information graphically. They were invented by Dr. Kaoru Ishikawa and are therefore often called Ishikawa diagrams. Dr. Ishikawa developed these tools spontaneously when he was working with engineers who needed a tool to display information on a variety of possible causes to a given problem. A properly built cause and effect diagram resembles a fish skeleton and they are sometimes often called fishbone diagrams.

How to Create Cause and Effect Diagrams

The creation process I will describe here utilizes some of the tools you have already learned. For a short cut approach that you can teach to people who have not learned to use the other tools, start with step #5.

1. *Map the process.* To begin, develop an activity map of the area to be improved. Activity maps are discussed in Chap. 10.

© The Author(s), under exclusive license to Springer Nature Switzerland AG 2021   177
T. Pyzdek, *The Lean Healthcare Handbook*, Management for Professionals,
https://doi.org/10.1007/978-3-030-69901-7_16

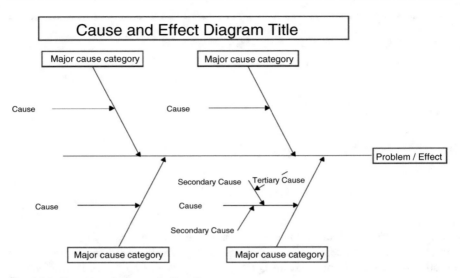

Fig. 16.1 Structure of cause and effect diagram

2. *Define the problem.* Here you answer what you are solving for with this cause and effect diagram by defining the problem in detail. Although traditionally the problem is only very briefly described in a text box on the cause and effect diagram, I recommend that you get as much detail as possible about the problem and its effects (see Enhanced Cause and Effect Diagram.)

3. *Brainstorm.* Use the brainstorming approach to identify all possible causes of the problem you are solving. Brainstorming is discussed in greater detail in the subsequent chapter on Kaizen Events.

4. *Affinitive.* Use affinity analysis to identify rational categories of causes. Break large categories into subcategories. Affinity analysis is discussed in greater detail in the chapter on Kaizen Events below.

5. *Draw the basic diagram.* Draw a box on the far right hand side of a large sheet of paper and draw a horizontal arrow that points to the box. Inside of the box, write a brief description of the problem you are trying to solve. Use the information from step #2 to arrive at the description.

6. *Add cause categories as branches.* Write the names of the major categories on branches above and below the horizontal line (see Fig. 16.1). You should come up with your own categories, subcategories, and root causes based on your affinity analysis or some other categorization method.

After the initial cause and effect diagram is drawn have the team brainstorm about additional major causes, secondary causes, and root causes. Try asking "Why?" five times to get to the root cause. E.g., (1) why did the power go out? Because the circuit breaker tripped. (2) Why did the circuit breaker trip? Because the circuit was overloaded. (3) Why was the circuit overloaded? Because a four slot toaster and an electric grill were operating on the circuit at the same time, etc. Typically the further you can drill down, the easier the cause is to resolve. Draw in the detailed cause data for each category, using the subcategories of your affinity analysis. I think of these detailed causes (shown as secondary causes on Fig. 16.1) as limbs and twigs on the branches. If you have a team with detailed knowledge of the problem, you should have a final diagram with quite a few twigs. If your cause and effect diagram does not have very many twigs, you probably need to expand your team to include someone with a deeper understanding of the process, such as a front-line worker.

Computer graphics programs such as Visio and Lucid chart include templates for creating cause and effect diagrams.

Example of Cause and Effect Diagram

Figure 16.2 shows an example of a cause and effect diagram for a clinical problem. These diagrams are also useful for administrative and other non-clinical problems. In fact, whenever a team is interested in identifying what is causing any problem cause and effect diagrams should be considered.

Narrowing the Focus

Cause and effect diagrams will show a large number of possible causes. Ideally your team would investigate and address every possible cause. However, in a world with limited resources, including limited time, it is often not possible to do this. In most cases teams address this by voting on which of the potential causes are most likely to be big contributors and then focusing their attention on these. I find this approach to be very dissatisfying on several levels. For one, it is not data based. People have a number of inherent biases that affect their judgment and make it unlikely that they will pick the most important causes. For example, people tend to pick things that they remember, and the reason they remember it may have nothing to do with how important it is. People also tend to remember things that occurred recently, but less recent causes may be more important.

Rather than relying on people's opinions about what is important, I like to enhance cause and effect diagrams with as much additional data and information as possible. The traditional cause and effect diagram presents information as text on a graphical layout. There are no numbers. Also, the cause side of the diagram is much more detailed than the effect side, which consists of a box with a simple description of the effect being studied. When I do consulting work my approach to cause and effect analysis, or root cause analysis, is to supplement both sides of the diagrams as much as possible. I have teams meet in a conference room with a very large table, such as a board room. Team members are instructed to gather as much information as they can before the meeting on each and every cause listed, and on the effect too. This information will include such things as

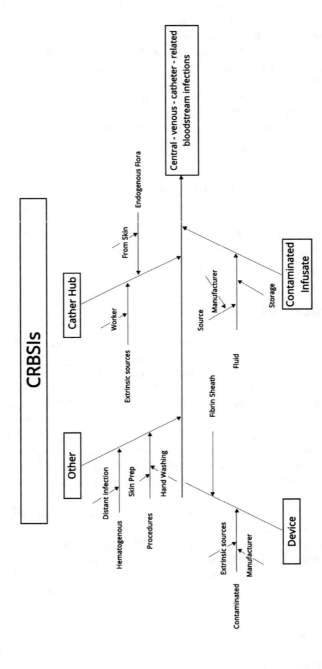

Fig. 16.2 Potential causes of CVC bacteremia infections (The diagram shown here is based on this NIH article http:/bit.ly/2iznSx4)

- Engineering studies.
- Specifications.
- Supplier reports and information.
- Quality control data.
- Test data.
- Data in Microsoft Excel pivot tables.
- Memos about the problem.
- Photos of the problems.
- Videos of the work areas (usually on computers or mobile devices).
- Control charts on metrics relating to the effect and/or the causes.
- Scatter plots of cause metrics to other cause metrics and to the effect metrics.
- Historic information from the organization's computer databases on the problem and the effects. Spreadsheets and pivot tables of the data are especially valuable.
- Lab notes on the problem.
- Anything else the team members deem relevant to the problem.

Once the meeting starts I create an area on one end of the table for the cause information and another area on the other end for effect information. We post the cause and effect diagram drawing in as large a format as possible on the wall, such as a flip chart. Then we discuss each cause on the diagram, constantly referring to the information laid out on the table. For example, someone might say, "I think there are more bacteremia infections when the IV is placed on the night shift." The team would then look at the information for evidence that confirms or contradicts this statement/hypothesis. If there are data on which shift placed the IVs, then someone can quickly create a bar chart showing the percent of day shift placed IVs that become infected versus night shift placed IVs. A Lean Six Sigma Black Belt or statistician might be asked to more rigorously evaluate the data at a later time, or it may be obvious that there is not an important difference. The resulting discussion and analysis are recorded for that particular cause and hypothesis.

Or someone may say "The problem is worse on the weekends." If there is a control chart of the problem, then the weekends can be marked on the chart. There are several possibilities:

1. There is little or no observed difference.
2. There is an obvious difference.
3. It is hard to tell if there is a difference.
4. Sometimes there is a difference, and sometimes there is not.
5. Additional questions result from discussing the marked-up control chart.

As the team goes through the causes one by one, they can determine what to do next. Is the problem metric in statistical control? If it is out of control, do any of the cause metrics go out of control at the same time? Can we rule this cause in or out based on what we have in front of us? Do we need information that is not here? For example, do we need to conduct experiments to see how a given cause relates to the effect? If a cause can't be definitively ruled in or out, does the information in front of us now help us determine how likely is it to be an important contributor to the problem? What additional information would allow us to make that judgment? For problems ruled in, what steps should be taken to mitigate their impact?

Enhanced Cause and Effect Diagram

Since we are all about putting information into the graphical form for better communication, it makes sense to add the above information to the cause and effect diagram in some way. Figure 16.3 shows how you might do this using the same basic format as used for traditional cause and effect diagrams. In addition to an arrow on the left showing what might be causing the problem, an additional arrow extends to the right showing what is caused *by* the problem. Some of the effects can be correlated to causes, while others are useful when considering the costs and benefits of proposed problem solutions. The enhanced cause and effect diagram gives a more complete picture of the situation. The diagram shown is "generic" in the sense that the causes and effects are not specific to any problem, they are shown to stimulate thought and discussion. In practice, you will replace the non-specific categories with the causes and effects for your particular situation. Using Fig. 16.2 as an example, one can consider a CVC bacteremia infection as an internal failure. The Cost Impact effect major branch has a sub-branch for failure costs, and there is a sub-sub-branch for internal failure costs. You could replace the word "Internal" with "uncompensated hospital time" because Medicare does not pay for hospital-acquired conditions.[1] Of course, the problem of CVC bacteremia infections also contributes to many other effects that can be shown on the diagram in the appropriate places. Feel free to modify the diagram to suit your needs.

---

[1] http://bit.ly/2wEh704.

Fig. 16.3 Generic enhanced
cause and effect diagram

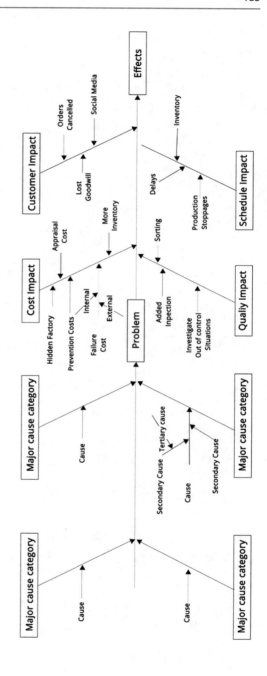

Project Management

17

Lean projects must help the organization achieve its goals. To accomplish this you must take actions that guarantee that your improvement activities are directly linked to the goals specified by your leaders. You will learn how to do this in this chapter.

17.1 True North Projects

Lean begins with the vision of the owner or the Board of Directors for the organization. This vision will be the ultimate focus of Lean projects, providing it is properly communicated. Table 17.1 illustrates the mechanism by which this is accomplished.

The organization's CEO has the difficult challenge of balancing short- and long-term goals and balancing goals for different stakeholders. Examples of goals for patients and their loved ones might include increasing the number of patients who recommend you to their friends and family or decreasing the number and percentage of the patient who say they would *not* recommend you. For employees the CEO might look at making employees feel like they are part of a high-performing organization, increasing employee satisfaction as measured by surveys, becoming the employer of choice in their area, or becoming a recognized leader in developing employees. For shareholders of publicly held entities, the CEO might have specific numerical targets, such as earnings per share or price-earnings ratios, or he may target a qualitative goal such as consistent growth and performance. For their community, the CEO might want to improve the organization's contribution to the overall health of its residents and visitors or its ability to help in case of disaster or emergency. Regardless of what the top-level and mid-level goals are, as a Lean team leader you need to assure that your projects have a direct "line of sight" to them. I.e., you should be able to trace your project's purpose to the vision for the organization. If that is the case, then your projects are helping the organization move towards the True North envisioned by its Leadership and they can justifiably be called True North projects.

© The Author(s), under exclusive license to Springer Nature Switzerland AG 2021
T. Pyzdek, *The Lean Healthcare Handbook*, Management for Professionals,
https://doi.org/10.1007/978-3-030-69901-7_17

Table 17.1 True north roles and responsibilities

Role	Responsibility
Member of the Board of Directors	Develop and articulate the organization's vision for each major stakeholder group.
C-Level Executive (CEO, COO, CFO, etc.)	Translate the vision into concrete goals and metrics. Provide leadership to management and feedback to the Board.
Management	Develop goals for your area that support the goals of your leadership team. Develop plans for achieving the goals. Communicate plans and goals to value stream owners.
Value Stream Owners	Identify project candidates that support management's goals. Find sponsors for projects. Support project sponsors.
Improvement Teams	Execute projects that support sponsor's goals. Improve root causes that drive process and value stream improvements.

Transfer Function

Goals do not just achieve themselves, they are the result of hard work. Achieving a top-level goal is too big a task for normal humans to accomplish by themselves and all at once. All you can do is help. To help you must determine what you need in to do in your own area of influence. This begins by thinking of your project goal as an end result that is driven by a number of causes, kind of a modified cause and effect diagram where the project goal rather than the problem being addressed is the effect. In Lean we say that we are "solving for" the end result. In high school math you are taught that in an equation y is a solution that depends on some other variables, which your math instructor referred to using one or more terms identified with the letter x. In Lean the equation that shows the relationship between the xs and the y in a process is called a "transfer function." For Lean purposes, the transfer function is usually only conceptual, not mathematical. The process inputs are the xs and the process output is the y. The transfer function is a helpful way of thinking about goals. Think about the ys as the goals that your leaders want to achieve for customers, shareholders, and employees. There will also be xs for customers, xs for shareholders, and xs for employees. Identify which xs need to be improved to reach each y. Also think about how you will measure each x and y. The transfer function idea is shown in Eq. (17.1)[1] and illustrated in Fig. 17.1.

$$Y = f\left(\vec{X}\right) \tag{17.1}$$

The essential take away here is that goals (Ys) are not pursued directly. Rather, we identify what causes we need to address to make these goals a reality.

---

[1] In the transfer function equation the X with an arrow above it represents all causes of the y. There can be several xs.

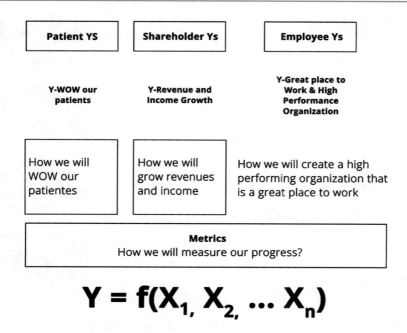

Fig. 17.1 Transfer function illustrated

Linking Lean Projects to Leadership Goals

It is helpful if you think of defining a suitable project as a "drill down" process. Start with the objectives for each stakeholder. These are your leaders' *ys*. Then determine how each *y* might be measured. These are called critical to quality metrics, or CTQs, because they will determine how well the higher level *ys* are accomplished. Now go down another level to plans and projects that can make the CTQ metric move in the desired direction. At some level, you will be able to identify a Lean improvement project candidate that you could undertake to help your organization achieve one or more of its *ys*. By using this process you will know precisely how your activity links to the vision of your senior leadership.

Figure 17.2 shows an example of how this might work. Starting from the top we see that the leadership team in a hospital would like to increase revenues. One way to do this is to perform more surgical procedures. More procedures could be performed if the ORs could be turned over more quickly between procedures. OR turnover might be improved by cleaning the OR instruments more quickly to have them ready for the next procedure. This is impacted by Jane Doe's Lean project. Jane and her team will need to keep the top-level goal in mind as they develop the charter, select metrics, etc. This will be useful in preventing the project from going off-track or from "scope creep" which occurs when projects become bigger and bigger.

Fig. 17.2 Cascade leaders'
goals to your project

The Effect → Cause → Effect → Root Cause Cascade

It all starts with external stakeholders: patients and their families, payers, investors, the community, etc. The transfer function shown in Eq. (17.1) actually repeats at several different levels of the organization. At the executive level, the CEO will choose a result, a Y, to meet a stakeholder demand and will identify several drivers, or xs, that they believe will have an impact on the y. Each x will become a y in a new transfer function that the next lower level of management will use. This process will continue until it reaches a level where a Lean project can be chartered to drill all the way down to root causes, the CTQs. These projects will address the root causes, and the results will flow back upwards to the top-level goal. The procedure is illustrated in Fig. 17.3.

The linkage back to the true north shown in Fig. 17.3 is as follows: the projects selected at L_4 will impact Y_4, which will impact X_{31}, which will impact X_{21}, which will impact X_1. X_1 will impact one or more of the items that are important to a customer, identified by getting the voice of the customer. This one-to-one correspondence will be very hard to prove with certainty, but the Leadership should verify that all projects are linked by logic and expertise to their goals. If the projects are successful in achieving their goals, then there should be positive movement at L_1. If there is not, Leadership and Management need to confirm their logic to keep the organization moving in the right direction. In other words, transfer functions are testable hypotheses. The scientific method is integral to Lean improvement.

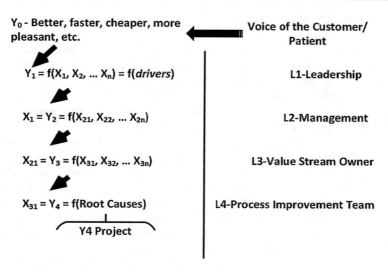

Fig. 17.3 Effect → Cause → Effect Cascade

Note that the transfer function at L_1 says $Y_1 = f$(drivers). Actually this terminology can be applied at any level above the root causes. Until we determine the root causes of some effect that we are interested in we do not have anything *actionable*.[2] I.e., we do not really know specifically what to change. As we go from higher levels to lower levels the drivers become more detailed and more numerous. The project will explore a large number of drivers using things like the categories on a cause and effect diagram. The team will decide when it is reasonable to take action. At that point, the driver becomes a root cause.

Perhaps an example will be helpful here. Let us say that leadership wants to increase profits (duh!) Since profits = revenues – costs, revenues, and costs are drivers. Leadership owes it to management to not merely dump such meaningless top-level drivers on them, so they take it down a step or two themselves: costs $= f$ (uncompensated costs) $=$ f(hospital-acquired conditions, uncompensated readmissions). Leadership decides to tell management to try to reduce the number of HACs so $Y_2 = f$(different HACs). This cascade continues all the way down to Lean improvement projects. At perhaps the L_3 level bacteremia infections are identified and projects are chartered to find the root causes of this problem. One of the teams drills down to the causes shown in Fig. 16.2 Potential Causes of CVC Bacteremia Infections. At this point, the team has a number of root cause candidates to address.

---

[2]By the way, actionable is how I *define* "root cause." In continuous improvement we are not seeking root causes in the philosophical sense of an uncaused first cause. We drill down until it is no longer reasonable to drill down any further, then we act. Use good judgment to determine where reasonable is.

17.2   Project Assessment

If you follow the steps above you will now have several excellent Lean project candidates. Before you launch into a project, however, you should carefully assess the project to be sure it has a good chance of success. I developed a process for making this determination by working with numerous clients. Project success, or lack thereof, was determined by a consensus of business leaders, sponsors, and Six Sigma Master Black Belts involved with the projects. Many of the unsuccessful projects failed because they were not linked to top-level business goals, which is why it is so important that you rigorously ensure that your candidate is a true north project. However, many true north projects also failed for various reasons. Here are some of the things to look for when deciding if a project is good-to-go. These factors were derived in a somewhat backwards fashion, by studying hundreds of both successful and *unsuccessful* projects. The factors should not be considered the only factors that are important to success. Instead, think of them as things that differentiated successful projects from unsuccessful projects.

Sponsorship. The most important success factor is sponsorship. Rate each project's sponsorship on a scale of Unacceptable to Ideal. For Lean projects, sponsors should have responsibility for the value stream being improved. Unacceptable indicates that there is no named project sponsor. Marginal indicates that the sponsor is known and they have accepted the project charter (see below) but have not yet agreed to meet with the team leader. Good would mean that there is a sponsor at the proper level and they know what their duties are, but they still have not blocked out time for the project. Better is a sponsor who has agreed to spend time on the project, but have not yet put the time into their calendar. E.g., "I'll meet with you as needed." An Ideal rating signals that the project sponsor is a value stream owner who knows what is expected of them and has set aside sufficient time to help the project team succeed. "We will meet to discuss this project every other Friday from 10 am to 10:30 am." An unacceptable rating in sponsorship, or any other assessment area, is a deal breaker. It indicates that the project should be rejected until the problem can be fixed. When looking at the factors, do not automatically reject projects that fail to meet the criteria. And do not automatically accept anything that is less than Ideal. Always work to improve the probability of project success by trying to make the project's sponsorship, benefits, etc. even better.

Stakeholder Benefit. Stakeholder benefits must be identified. The stakeholder can be patients or other customers, investors, employees, payers, or an interested third party such as a regulator. Determine which stakeholder group is the *primary* beneficiary of the project. Then describe precisely how the project will benefit this stakeholder. You can also list secondary stakeholders who would benefit from the project, but do not get carried away with this exercise. You will reach the point of diminishing returns pretty quickly.

Availability of Resources. If the project requires access to special resources, such as a computer database or special equipment, be sure that the resources will be available when needed. Your sponsor can help secure these resources.

Time Commitment. How much of your time will be spent on this project? Guestimate the percentage of your time you will devote to the project in a week, then guestimate how many weeks it will take to complete the project. Review the stakeholder benefits when making this decision. Think about whether the project justifies this time commitment before saying yes. Do not be afraid to say NO!

Team Membership. Lean improvement projects are not conducted by Lean Advisors alone. It is critical that you have a team of dedicated and qualified people who will be allowed to spend the necessary time on the project. You will want the best people to be on your team. Such people are in high demand so you will need to work hard to get them. But do not settle for less. Your project's success depends on the team.

Project Charter. There is a section later in this chapter about the Project Charter. The charter is the document that describes and authorizes the project. Do not start a project until this important document is complete and accepted by the team and the sponsor.

Value of PDCA/Lean Approach. A Lean improvement project is one that meets all of the criteria described in this lesson, including the need for the Lean Advisor's skill set. A critical differentiator between Lean improvement projects and other projects is that Lean improvement projects need analytical and statistical tools to identify what needs to be done to achieve the desired results. In other words, the path to success is unknown because the root causes driving success are unknown at the outset. If the path to the desired state is known in advance, it is not a Lean improvement project, it is a "Just Do It!" project.

17.3   Project Charter

Lean improvement projects are usually chartered by value stream owners or managers with responsibility for all of the processes targeted by the project. A charter form that you can use is shown in Fig. 17.4. Download the Charter form here or by entering the link in the footnote into your browser.[3] After downloading, open the document and click the review menu and select "All markup" from the download list to see the instructions for completing each field in the form. The instructions are also shown here should you be unable to open the charter document.

Charter Form Completion Instructions

1. Complete the header (see Table 17.2). Describe the information necessary to identify what this project is, who the key players are, expected savings, and the date range for the project.

---

[3]http://bit.ly/2jmHR2t.

Project Charter			
Project Name		Projected Annual Savings	
ID Number		Type of Savings:	
Black/Green Belt Name		Telephone Number	
Sponsor Name		Team Leader	
Start Date		Target Completion Date	

Project Details

Opportunity Statement (Current State):

Project Objectives (Future State):

Business Case:

Approach: ☐ DMAIC | ☐ DMADV | ☐ LEAN | ☐ JUST-DO | ☐ _____

Metrics

Opportunity Definition:

Defect or Error Definition:

Metric	Before Project	After Project

Scope

The segment of the manufacturing or service process this project is focused on. This defines to Management which steps of their process this project will be working with and what is outside the scope of this project. Refer to this often during the project to be sure the project's scope hasn't "creeped" into new areas.

Process Scope:

Project Scope:

Potential Adverse Impacts

Potential Barriers

Milestones	**Expected or Actual Date**
Project start	
Milestone 1 Completion	
Milestone 2 Completion	
Milestone 3 Completion	
Milestone 4 Completion	
Milestone 5 Completion	
Final Tollgate Review	
Best Practice Sharing	
Core Team Member	DACI Role

Fig. 17.4 Charter form

Table 17.2 Charter header

Project charter	
Project name	Projected annual savings
ID number	Type of savings:
Black/Green belt name	Telephone number
Sponsor name	Team leader
Start date	Target completion date

2. Opportunity Statement (current state). Very briefly describe the opportunity. What is the important problem or new opportunity that your project will address?

3. Project Objectives (future state). How will things be better after you have completed the project?

4. Business Case. Not every opportunity is important to the organization. What makes this a true north project? This is where you describe the "burning platform" for your project. Why is it urgent to successfully complete this project? What Ys and Xs on your business dashboard does this address?

5. Approach. Does this project need your skillset as a Lean Advisor? A Lean/PDCA project is one where you do not know what is causing the problem. Since a project addresses root causes, not knowing the causes means that you do not know what you need to do to fix the problem. If you already know what needs to be done, just do it!

6. Metrics. What will you measure to determine project success?

7. Metric Opportunity Definition. Describe what provides the opportunity to produce (or NOT produce) a defect or to make a mistake. For example, a customer transaction that may or may not have a mistake, a patient treatment that may or may not have a complication, an item produced that may or may not be defective.

8. Metric Defect or Error Definition. How do you describe it when things go wrong? For example, a customer transaction done incorrectly, a patient treatment that results in a complication, a defective item produced.

9. Scope. The segment of the manufacturing or service process this project is focused on. This defines to Management which steps of their process this project will be working with and what is outside the scope of this project. Refer to this often during the project to be sure the project's scope has not "creeped" into new areas.

10. *Process* Scope. What work process or value stream will be impacted by this project? Where does this process begin and end? What work is not addressed by this project?

11. *Project* Scope. **In-scope work**: what project work will be done to achieve the project's objectives? **Out of scope work**: What project work is beyond the scope of this project?

12. Potential Adverse Impacts. What might be affected by this project other than the targeted metrics? What processes that interact with the process changed by this project? What will you monitor for unintended adverse impacts?

13. Potential Barriers. What obstacles do you anticipate? For example, difficulty getting needed data, problems getting a supplier to cooperate, inability to get cooperation from key players such as physicians or specialists.

14. Schedule. The dates you expect to reach major milestones. For example, the milestones might be the completion of each of the PDCA phases. See A3 thinking for examples.

15. Core Team Members and Roles. 4–6 full time members recommended. DACI is
    a way of assigning responsibilities on teams.[4] DACI roles are: **D**river, **A**pprover,
    Contributor, **I**nformed.
    (a) *Driver*. A single driver of the overall project like the person steering a car.
    (b) *Approver*. One or more approvers who make most project decisions and are
        responsible if it fails.
    (c) *Contributors*. Are the worker-bees who are responsible for deliverables and
        with whom there is two-way communication.
    (d) *Informed*. Those who are impacted by the project and are provided status
        and informed of decisions and with whom there is one way communication.

17.4   Project Planning and Scheduling

Projects are comprised of many different tasks performed by many different people.
They take time and consume valuable resources. Usually tasks must be done in a
particular sequence, and often there are dependencies[5] among various tasks. It is
important that the tasks in a project are carefully considered, assigned the resources
they need for successful completion, and are arranged in the proper sequence. This is
all part of *project planning and scheduling*. In this section, we will discuss
identifying the tasks needed to complete the project, who will do each task, what
resources they need, and when each task will begin and end.

Work Breakdown Structure (WBS)

A fundamental idea in project management is that a big project consists of several
smaller, easier to manage, subprojects. It is the simple divide and conquer strategy. A
work breakdown structure is a project management technique for defining and
organizing the final and intermediate products of a project and their relationships.
Defining project tasks is typically accomplished by a series of decompositions
(subdivide bigger tasks into smaller tasks) followed by a series of aggregations
(group the smaller tasks logically). I.e., we will take the project apart and then put the
pieces back together in a certain way.

For example, consider a PDCA project. At the top level, the project phases are
plan, do, check, and act. These tasks can be further divided into subprojects, e.g.,

Plan. Identify your problems and causes.
Do. Identify and select potential countermeasures.

---

[4]Learn more here, including alternatives to DACI http://bit.ly/2w8huTK.
[5]Activity B is dependent on activity A if B cannot begin until A is complete.

Check. Study the results.

Act. Implement the best countermeasures.

    This level of detail is better, but still not good enough. The breakdown continues until the subproject reaches a level called "tiny." A subproject is tiny when the project manager can easily answer two questions: (1) Is the subproject complete? (2) Is the subproject done correctly? If the project has been properly decomposed the answers to these questions should be so easy that they seem trivial. Figure 17.5 illustrates a (partial) WBS for a PDCA project. The illustration traces work breakdown from the "Problem solving project" level to the tiny subprojects of "Locate the VSM, spaghetti diagram and control charts" for the existing process. If the team leader agrees that it will be easy to determine when these tasks are complete, then further work decomposition can cease for this branch of the WBS.

    Aggregation involves linking the tiny subprojects back together to complete the project phase. In this example, when the team has the value stream maps, spaghetti diagrams and control charts the "identify existing data" subproject will be complete. When all PDCA project phases are complete, the problem the project addresses will be solved. (Of course, the Act phase includes tasks that assure that the problem *is* actually solved!)

Project schedule charts (Gantt charts)

In this section, we will describe Gantt Charts, which is a type of bar chart that illustrates a project schedule, as well as present other information about the project.[6] Gantt charts also show the dependency relationships between tasks, i.e., which tasks must be completed before a given task can begin. Gantt charts show current schedule status using percent-complete shadings. Figure 17.6 illustrates these ideas for a hypothetical house building project. Top-level tasks in the WBS are architectural design, interior design, etc. Subprojects under architectural design are create draft of architecture, prepare construction documents, and agreement on architectural design.

    The symbols used in the Gantt chart in Fig. 17.6 are shown in Fig. 17.7. The blue bars indicate the start- and end-dates for each task. Higher level tasks are those WBS tasks that include lower level tasks, e.g., in the PDCA discussed above "current conditions" is a higher level task with sub-tasks of what is happening, identify the value stream, etc.. In the software you identify higher level- and sub-tasks by indenting sub-tasks on a list.[7] The black bars within the blue bars indicate the completed portion of the task. Task dependencies are shown using arrows. The arrow from the end of create draft of architecture and prepare construction document indicates a dependency, i.e., the prepare construction document task cannot begin until the create draft of architecture task is complete. The diamond shapes are

---

[6]The creation of these charts uses the free software available here http://www.ganttproject.biz/.

[7]Be sure to watch the short instructional video by clicking the link on the software download page.

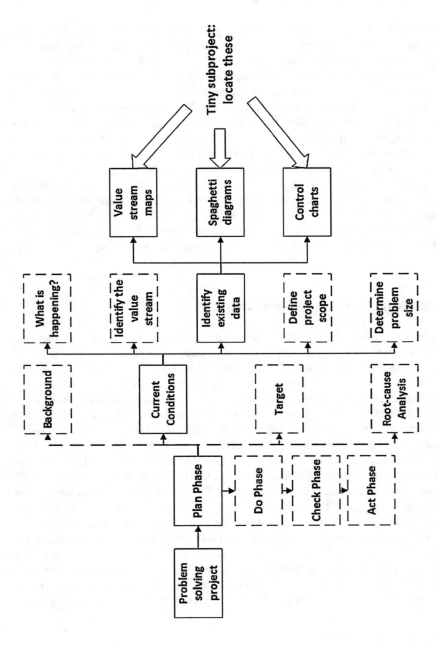

Fig. 17.5 Work breakdown structure for PDCA project

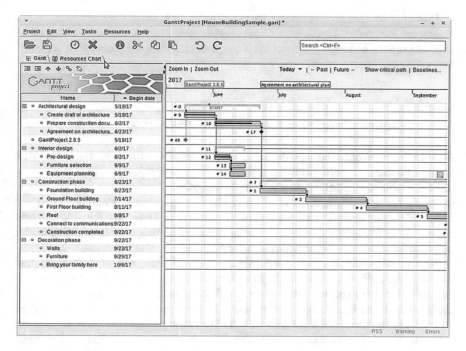

Fig. 17.6 Gantt chart example

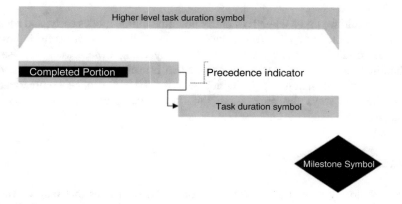

Fig. 17.7 Gantt chart symbols

"milestones." Milestones are used in project management to mark specific points along a project timeline. These points may signal anchors such as a project start and end date, a need for external review or input, and budget checks, among others. In many instances, milestones do not impact project duration. Instead, they focus on major progress points that must be reached to achieve success.

I should note that project management software is not absolutely necessary, it just makes the job easier. I have seen Gantt charts created by hand and by using many general purpose software packages such as spreadsheets, word processors, presentation programs, etc.

17.5   Failure Mode and Effects Analysis (FMEA)

This section will describe a method you can use to assess the risks associated with your project or with the problem addressed by your project, failure modes, and effects analysis, or FMEA. At the completion of this section you will be able to explain what risk management is and why it is important; understand the use of the FMEA risk management process within the context of Lean; use the risk management process to identify risk areas associated with changing a process and prioritize risk areas and develop abatement plans for high priority risk elements.

Risk is the probability that an undesired event will occur and go undetected until found by the customer. An example of an undesired event might be that your project causes something to break that your team had not considered and results in problems that outweigh the benefits of your project. On your project, you must think of the customer as the process owner who will use your new process, the sponsor, or some other stakeholder. Risk management is an effort to eliminate risk, but total elimination is seldom accomplished. Instead, by using a systematic approach you hope to identify most sources of risk and take action to reduce the likelihood of occurrence or the effects.

Why should we do FMEA? To identify potential failure modes early, and because we care about the issues that can make our project fail. FMEA is useful in helping you meet critical customer requirements and by using FMEA you increase the probability that your project will succeed. FMEA is useful in developing risk control plans and in prioritizing risk reduction activity. FMEA can be summarized as identifying the ways the project can fail (i.e., risks) prioritizing the risks, and managing those risks.

Purpose of FMEA

FMEA is closely related to corrective action. FMEA assumes that failures vary in importance and that these differences can be used to classify failure risks. FMEA assumes that the classifications can be useful in allocating resources. Corrective action assumes that failure causes can be identified and classified, that the causes can be controlled, and that identification and control require resources. But resources are limited, which requires that corrective action resources be allocated to the higher payoff problems. The purpose of FMEA is to provide information to help allocate corrective action resources wisely. In this sense, FMEA can be considered a mixture of problem solving and accounting.

FMEA and Project Risks

There are some typical project risks that you will want to consider when performing FMEA on your project. One risk is that your project does not address a metric that drives something on your leadership's high-level dashboard. Hopefully, this was addressed early in the selection of the project, but you have more information now and you should reconsider the question.

Another risk is that your project will cost more than it is worth to your leadership. You now know what the current state looks like, what the goals are for the outputs of the process, and the size of the gap you are trying to close. If, for example, the initial changes made as a result of your audits and your benchmarking efforts have closed the gap considerably, you may want to work with finance to conduct a preliminary cost-benefit analysis before going on. Another very common risk is making a change that comes undone with the passage of time. This will be the topic of its own FMEA at the correct time in the project and is discussed later in this book (see Kaizen Events and A3 thinking).

How to Perform FMEA

FMEA is a rigorous, step-by-step process.

1. *Define.* Define the system to be analyzed. Complete system definition includes internal and interface functions and expected performance at all system levels, system restraints, and failure definitions.
2. *Map the Processes.* Construct process maps that illustrate the operation, interrelationships, and interdependencies of functional entities. Process maps are discussed elsewhere in this book (see process mapping).
3. *Identify Suppliers, Inputs, Process Outline, Outputs, and Customers (SIPOC).* Conduct SIPOC analysis for each process in the system. All processing system interfaces should be indicated.
4. *List Functions.* List the intended function of each step in the process or subprocess.
5. *Identify Failure Modes.* For each process step, identify all potential item and interface failure modes and describe the effect of the immediate function or item on the system and on the mission to be performed for the customer.
6. *Evaluate Consequences.* Evaluate each failure mode in terms of the worst potential consequences which may result and assign a severity classification (SEV) to the consequence (see Table 17.3).
7. *Likelihood.* Determine the likelihood of occurrence for each failure mode and assign an occurrence risk classification (OCC).
8. *Detectability.* Identify failure detection methods and assign a detectability risk classification (DET). This is the risk that the failure will *not* be detected until it reaches the customer.

Table 17.3 FMEA severity, likelihood, detectability rating guidelines

Rating	Severity (SEV)	Occurrence (OCC)	Detectability (DET)
Descriptions → Rating ↓	How significant is this failure's effect to the customer?	How likely is the cause of this failure to occur?	How likely is it that the existing system will detect the cause if it occurs? (Note: p is the estimated probability that the failure will be detected.)
1	Minor. Customer will not notice the effect or will consider it insignificant	Not likely	Nearly certain to detect before reaching the customer (p-100%)
2	Customer will notice the effect	Documented low failure rate	Extremely low probability of reaching customer without detection (p-99%)
3	Customer will become irritated at reduced performance	Undocumented but probably low failure rate	Low probability of reaching customer without detection. (p-95%)
4	Marginal. Customer dissatisfaction due to reduced performance	Failures occur from time-to-time	Likely to be detected before reaching customer. (p-90%)
5	Customer's productivity is reduced	Documented moderate failure rate	Might be detected before reaching customer. (p-85%)
6	Customer will complain. Repair or return likely. Increased internal costs for scrap, rework, etc.	Undocumented moderate failure rate	Unlikely to be detected before reaching customer. (p-80%)
7	Critical. Reduced customer loyalty. Internal operations adversely impacted	Documented high failure rate	Highly unlikely to detect before reaching customer. (p-70%)
8	Complete loss of customer goodwill. Internal operations disrupted	Undocumented high failure rate	Poor chance of detection. (p-60%)
9	Customer or employee safety compromised. Regulatory compliance questionable	Failures common	Extremely poor chance of detection. (p-50%)
10	Catastrophic. Customer or employee endangered without warning. Violation of law or regulation	Failures nearly always occur	Likely that failure won't be detected. ($p < 50\%$)

9. *Risk Priority Number (RPN)*. Calculate the risk priority number (RPN) for the current system using Eq. (16.1). As the name suggests, RPNs are used to prioritize the risks. In general, higher RPNs are given more attention than lower ones.

$$RPN = SEV \times OCC \times DET \tag{16.1}$$

10. *Compensation.* Determine compensating provisions for each failure mode. I.e., how will you deal with the failure mode until you can eliminate it?
11. *Corrective Action.* Identify corrective design or other action required to eliminate failure or control the risk. Assign responsibility and due dates for corrective actions.
12. *Action Effects.* Identify the effects of corrective actions on other system attributes.
13. *After RPNs.* Identify severity, occurrence, and detectability risks after the corrective actions have been implemented. Calculate the RPN after the corrective actions become effective.
14. *Document.* Document the analysis and summarize the problems which could *not* be corrected. Identify the special controls which are necessary to reduce failure risk from these problems.

Many of the teams I have worked with in the past have told me that if they could only use a single continuous improvement tool, the FMEA process described in these 14 steps would be the one they would choose.

SEV, OCC, and DET Category Descriptions and Ratings

Table 17.3 can be used to assist the team in the assignment of SEV, OCC, and DET ratings. It is usually not important to get a precise rating. Close enough is good enough in most cases.

FMEA Workbook

An Excel workbook is available to help you with your FMEA.[8] To enter data copy and paste the bottom row of the table (row 11 for a new workbook) and type over the existing content. When finished select the entire table and use Excel's filters to sort by RPN. Address the highest RPN problem steps first.

17.6   Risk Assessment and Contingency Planning

Despite your best efforts at risk reduction, you may encounter problems as you pursue your improvement project. The use of Failure Mode and Effects Analysis (FMEA) to discover and mitigate these problems was discussed above. However, it

---

[8]You can access an Excel workbook to assist you with FMEA here http://bit.ly/2gL0axf. This is a bare bones document, but there are others available that offer more features. I suggest that you search the Internet for the search term FMEA Workbook.

pays to revisit the issue as you prepare your project management plan. It is also helpful if you can present the risks and actions taken to mitigate the risks in a graphical format.

Process Decision Program Chart (PDPC)

Process decision program charts are a tool to help you prepare contingency plans for dealing with project risks. PDPC helps you identify and mitigate the impact of problems on your schedules and the effects of the failure modes identified during FMEA.

The process decision program chart (PDPC) systematically identifies what might go wrong in a plan under development. Countermeasures are developed to prevent or offset those problems. By using PDPC, you can either revise the plan to avoid the problems or be ready with the best response when a problem occurs.

Creating the PDPC begins with your WBS. Think of the project as a journey and the WBS as a map. If everything goes perfectly, you will reach the end of your journey, your goal, without incident. However, it is possible that some events may occur which could cause problems. The FMEA will have identified many such possibilities. If you have prepared contingency plans for these eventualities, then you will reach your destination with only minor negative consequences. However, if you have failed to adequately plan, the problems might stop you cold.

To draw the PDPC chart begin with your WBS. Create an FMEA with a focus on how the tiny subprojects might fail. Take a look at the New OCC column, which will show the risk of the failure occurring *after* taking the recommended action to mitigate the failure. If the OCC number for a particular failure mode is unacceptably high (a subjective judgment by the team and the sponsor) then create a PDPC for that failure mode.

For example, one of the paths in the WBS shown in Fig. 17.8 leads to the tiny subproject task "locate spaghetti diagram." During team discussions, someone says "I couldn't find that spaghetti diagram when I looked for it last week." The team might come up with the PDPC in Fig. 17.9 to help the task owner.

	A	B	C	D	E	F	G	H	I
10	Process step	Potential failure mode	Potential failure effects	S E V	Potential causes	O C C	Current process controls	D E T	R P N
11	What is the step?	In what ways can the step go wrong?	What is the impact on the customer if the failure mode is not prevented or corrected?	10	What causes the step to go wrong? (i.e., How could the failure mode occur?)	10	What are the existing controls that either prevent the failure mode from occurring or detect	10	1000

	A	J	K	L	M	N	O	P
10	Process step	Actions recommended	Responsibility (target date)	Actions taken	N S e E w V	N O e C w C	N D e E w T	N R e P w N
11	What is the step?	What are the actions for reducing the occurrence of the cause or for improving its detection?	Who is responsible for the recommended action? What date should it be completed	What were the actions implemented? Include completion month/year (then recalculate	10	10	10	1000

Fig. 17.8 FMEA workbook

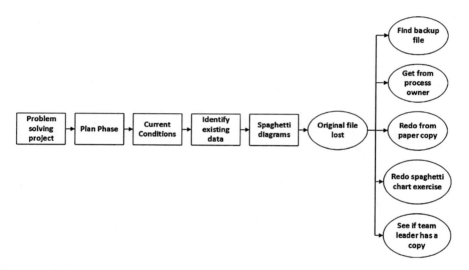

Fig. 17.9 PDPC chart example

Kaizen Events

18

Having performed more than fifty Kaizens in the Healthcare arena, I can confidently say you will have tremendous success with this approach. Kaizen involves taking things apart and putting them back together. You can do that in rapid fashion following the approach described in this chapter. The first step is to determine if the Kaizen Event is right for you. If your project idea is an incremental improvement, small and the goal is process speed, then Kaizen is for you. I put together this handy flowchart to help you decide (Fig. 18.1).

The Kaizen Event is all about getting things done quickly. Because of this, we focus heavily on Lean tools. We know from previous experience that work tends to wait in a process, usually 90–95% of the process time is wait time, so we will focus our Kaizen on moving the work through the process faster. Figure 18.2 shows a chart I created for an actual implementation process for hospital software. We mapped the value add time, non-value add time, business value add time, and wait time. You can plainly see that wait time is the biggest issue. Of course, all this talk about Lean does not mean we forget about reducing variation. We can do that too but we will start by focusing on Lean tools.

18.1 Scheduling

When is the best time to schedule a Kaizen Event? When you have a challenging goal to reach or issue to solve. It could be driven by your business unit strategy, a problem that has stood the test of time, or just a nagging problem where the solution is unknown. You typically have obvious sources of waste and a well-defined scope which leads to minimal project risk. In any event, you must be willing to commit people to identify and resolve the issue. Solutions developed by teams of people

By Larry W. Dyer
    Pyzdek Institute Certified Lean Six Sigma Master Black Belt

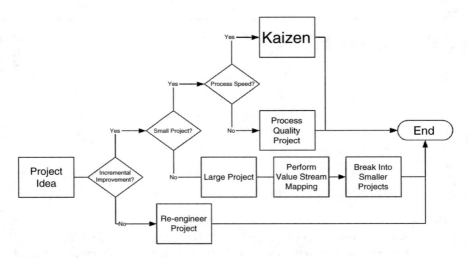

Fig. 18.1 When to use a Kaizen

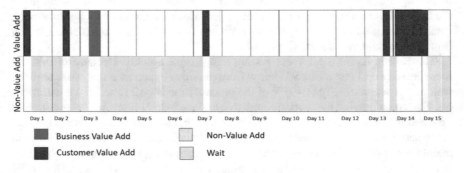

Fig. 18.2 Value add, non-value add and wait time

from the work area tend to be more robust because they are developed by people who work with the process on a daily basis.

Why it is important to complete projects fast? Because you when you do things faster you bring more value to the company. Let us take an example of six projects completed over the course of 20 weeks by dividing effort among all of the projects (Fig. 18.3).

Now let us do two projects at a time, complete them, then start two more (Fig. 18.4). As you can see by comparing the blue area in the two graphs, this strategy brings more value to the company.

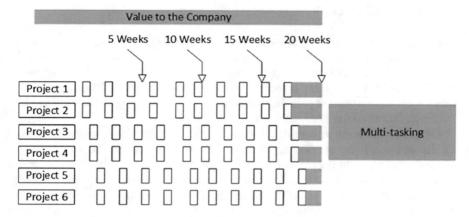

Fig. 18.3 Bringing value to the company multi-tasking version

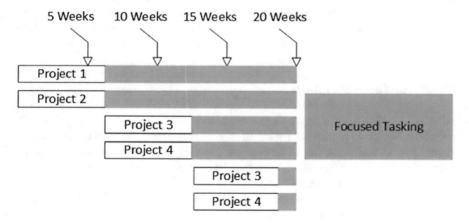

Fig. 18.4 Bringing value to the company focused projects version

18.2 Two Months Before The Event

There are several keys to have a successful Kaizen Event, but one of the most important is to get an early start before the event even happens. If your Kaizen Event team is located at a single facility you may only need to plan 3 or 4 weeks in advance. However, if you have people flying in for the event, you may need additional time to get everyone committed and scheduled.

Finish Your Charter

The first thing you want to get working on is your Project Charter. The key elements of the charter you need are the Problem Statement, Goal Statement, Business Impact, Scope and any metrics information you have. You need to get agreement with your Sponsor and Executive Team before making any additional plans. You are going to spend significant resources planning the event as well as traveling to the event so you need a charter that everyone agrees on.

Other key elements to complete before the event are the Stakeholder Analysis, Communication Plan, and the Failure Mode Effects Analysis (see above). I recently worked a Kaizen with people from eight different groups across six different profit centers. That meant I had six different vice presidents as stakeholders. We decided, using the FMEA, that we should interview all six to ensure they were aligned with the project and its proposed results. In a couple of cases, we had to add items to the project to satisfy them. The scope started with negotiating reimbursement rates with hospitals. This document then went to three different organizations to be entered into three systems. One of the downstream systems processed claims for the Workers' Comp group. This was an extremely complex project to complete. We had three Lean Six Sigma Black Belts working to ensure all deliverables were completed.

Pick Your Team Members

After completing the charter, I like to work with the Sponsor to identify the team members. My go-to phrase is, "I want all of your best people." I want the people you cannot live without. I explain to the Sponsor that the quality of the solution is directly proportional to the quality of the team members. If you want a high-quality solution then give me your high-quality staff.

Sometimes I even include outside customers in my events. We did a project recently where we wanted to remove defects from the Explanation of Benefits document and speed its delivery to the ultimate customer. In this case, we called our customer and asked if they would provide a person as part of the team. They were overjoyed that we were addressing the problem and happy to contribute.

Ensure your team covers all aspects of the process to be improved. You need users of the process as well as customers of the process. You also need people who can help you collect data, so identify the subset of the Kaizen team who you will work with before the Kaizen Event to collect and analyze data. The data collection team may or may not be a part of your Kaizen Event. If I have a team of three helping me collect and analyze data I will usually include one as part of the Kaizen Event.

Schedule the Event

In many of my events, the members of the team were spread across the United States. We had to schedule the event 2 months in advance just to get all of the required attendees committed on their calendar, so the next thing you want to do is to schedule the event 4–8 weeks in the future. You also have to think about the length of the Kaizen Event. Will it be 3 days, 4 days, or 5 full days? If you have people traveling just to be at the event, chances are you will only be able to schedule a 4-day event, starting at noon on Monday and ending at noon on Friday. If your scope for the Kaizen Event is small enough you could even conduct a 3-day Kaizen. Just remember, the shorter the event, the more work you and your team need to do before arriving.

Collect Data

The first thing you do when collecting data is to hold a kickoff meeting for the Sponsor, Executive Team, and data collection team members. Your small team needs to understand the importance of the project to the company and the priority required for data requests. Then you need to determine what type of data you will be using. Perhaps you are collecting voice-of-the-customer (VOC) or data on process cycle time. In any case, you need to determine a sample strategy, collect the data, validate the data, begin the analysis, share results with your Sponsor then make additional data requests. You move back and forth from Define to Measure and back again during this phase.[1] As your analysis continues you need to update the charter accordingly. I have worked on numerous projects where the Project Charter, especially the Problem Statement change during Define and Measure. You may see the same thing.

18.3   Event Planning

As you get closer to the event you need to put together a schedule to share with your team members. Figure 18.5 shows an example of a schedule I did for a 5-day Kaizen Event. You should create something similar to help your team understand what will be required of them. Also, to get a commitment from your Sponsor and Executive Leader to attend the Monday morning kickoff and the Friday afternoon debrief.

This is also the time you want to reserve your conference room and get food ordered for your team lunches. You want to keep them in the conference room and keep them occupied for the full 5 days. Too much time is lost if they go out for lunch.

You also need to develop the ground rules you will use during the event. Some are simple, like:

---

[1] Larry is describing the Six Sigma Define-Measure-Analyze-Improve-Control (DMAIC) framework, rather than the PDCA framework used in this book. These two frameworks overlap in roughly this way: Plan (Define/Measure/Analyze,) Do (Analyze/Improve,) Check (Analyze,) and Act (Improve/Control).—Tom

	Monday	Tuesday	Wednesday	Thursday	Friday
7:00 AM	Event Prep	Prep	Prep	Prep	Prep
8:00 AM	Project Introductions Management Participation		Perform root cause analysis and prioritize results	Develop evaluation criteria and select best solutions	Develop pilot plan for the revised process
9:00 AM	Training (slide presentation on the Kaizen Event)	Develop swim lane process map of the existing process			Update communication plan
10:00 AM	Review the charter, goals for the week and communication plan		Map business requirements to root causes	Map the revised process	Develop project plan to complete the remaining activities
11:00 AM	Perform FMEA		Identify quick improvements		Identify action items and responsible parties
12:00 AM	Lunch	Lunch	Lunch	Lunch	Lunch
1:00 PM 2:00 PM	Review Voice of the Customer data (any	Add value stream components to the	Brainstorm ideas for the new process	Map the revised process (cont.)	Prepare report to management
3:00 PM	Identify Critical Business Requirements	Capture process issues	Prepare a report to management	Identify metrics to measure new process	Report out to Executive Team
4:00 PM	Develop SIPOC		Report out to Executive Team	Update FMEA	Review activities for the following week
5:00 PM 6:00 PM	Meet with Project Sponsor	Consolidate and review daily notes	Consolidate and review daily notes	Consolidate and review daily notes	
	Process Manager	Entire Team			
	Project Sponsor	Executive Team			
	Project Manager				
	Black Belt				

Fig. 18.5 Sample Kaizen event schedule

- Cell phones turned off (not just silenced)
- No laptops
- Bathroom breaks every 2 h
- Do not talk while others are talking

Others may require more explanation, for example,

- Maintain a positive attitude
- Practice mutual respect
- The only stupid questions are the ones not asked
- Ask Why five times to get to root cause
- One person one vote

Day 1 What Is the Problem?

We will spend most of Day 1 trying to understand the problem. We begin by having introductions and going over the ground rules and the schedule for the week. Then we want to hear from our executive leaders to learn why this project is so important to the company. This is really critical. If you cannot get your executives to commit a small amount of time to this event, your team will see that, and maybe they will not be so committed to the project. If your executives are committed your team is more likely to be committed.

You may also need to do some training. If so, you do it at this point. I like to add the training on the eight wastes of Lean. You have probably heard of the seven wastes of Lean but in Healthcare we have eight wastes. They spell DOWNTIME and are[2]:

- **Defects**
- **Over** Production
- **Waiting**
- **Non-utilized Employees**
- **Transportation**
- **Inventory**
- **Motion**
- **Extra Processing**

Now you are ready to review the project Charter. I like to spend plenty of time on the review of the project Charter to ensure everyone has a good understanding of what we want to accomplish. I also like to take the time to do an FMEA, asking the question, "How could this project fail?" It is a worthwhile thing to do and you may uncover some risks that should have a mitigation strategy.

After reviewing the Charter, you are ready to review your data. Use control charts, Pareto charts, spaghetti diagrams, takt time, time studies, and anything else that helps you get the point across. Figure 18.6 shows a few examples of data that might be reviewed.

Now it is time to summarize the actions for Day 1. You want to show your team that they are accomplishing things and remain on schedule. After you release the team for the evening meet with your sponsor to go over the activities for the day and discuss each team member's participation.

Day 2 Map the Process

We start day 2 by mapping the process. There are three views of a process, what you think it is, what it actually is and what it should be. That is because of hidden operations. A person gets a piece of work and they must fix it before they can do their job. When we map the process, we are looking for these hidden operations (Fig. 18.7).

You can use various mapping techniques but my favourite is the swim lane process map or deployment map which you learned about earlier in this book

---

[2]These are slightly different descriptions than the eight types of waste presented earlier in this book. It is okay to have multiple mnemonics to help you identify waste.

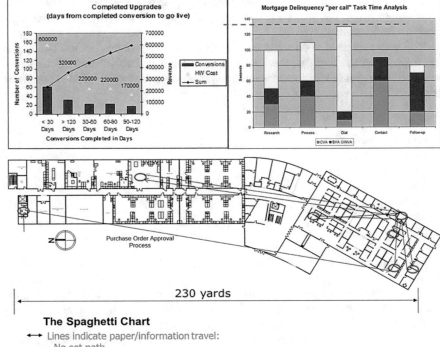

The Spaghetti Chart

↔ Lines indicate paper/information travel:
  - No set path
  - Lots of rework

○ Indicates an in-box or outbox where work
  (forms/information) waits to be worked on or
  transferred

Fig. 18.6 Sample graphics

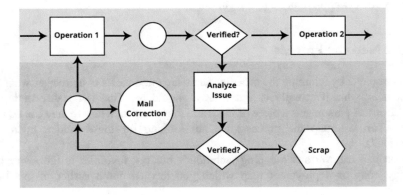

Fig. 18.7 The hidden operation is at the bottom of the process map

(Deployment Maps (Swimlane Maps). I strive to build an L3 process map to start. If additional detail is required we can go to level 4. At this level of detail, you will uncover most, if not all, of your process problem. I sometimes supplement this with the time required for each step, making your process a simple value stream map. You may find the time for each step necessary when the process looks pretty good to start with. I did a project with a group who installed interfaces between our software product and other products within the hospital. When we mapped the process, we did not see any apparent waste, so I had the team go back and put time on each step. Then I asked a question, "Why does this step take 45 days?" The response I got was, "It doesn't, Jeff just has a 45-day backlog." That, it turns out, was something we could improve.

Map the Process by focusing on each step of the process. Sometimes I facilitate by writing all of the Post-It™ notes (with a black medium or large point Sharpie) and putting them on the wall. Other times I allow the team to write their own Post-It™ notes and explain to them while putting them on the wall. You want the team to be able to read the notes from several feet away so the Sharpie is mandatory. You also want the team to describe what they do in detail. They may want to use terms like, "I process it." That could mean a thousand different things so I stop and ask, what does that mean? The point is, if I, an outsider, can understand the process we are putting on the wall, the other team members certainly will be able to understand it as well.

As you are process mapping, you can start identifying areas of potential waste and highlighting these with a different color Post-It™ note. I also like to list these on a separate large sheet of paper next to the process map. Here are a few process mapping ideas:

- If your process creates a work product, then make sure you show this in your process map. For example, I worked with a team to map a process that allowed a nurse to double-check the identity of the person before giving an injection. We asked that an example of the hardware be brought to the Kaizen so the team could understand its functions.
- Include all of the interim deliverables in the process. I like to put these below the process map in the approximate location they are created in the process. I recently worked on a Kaizen reviewing how software was implemented across a hospital. We had several documents that were created during the process. We ended up posting an example of each document on our process map so everyone could keep them straight. You can also just refer to the work product by using a different color Post-It™ note or different color pen.
- Process mapping is absolutely the best way to learn how a process works, as a group.

Process mapping always takes longer to do than you think it will, but it is time well spent. You will spend most, if not all, of Day 2 process mapping, adding additional detail, and identifying potential waste. Your team will be mentally tired but you are not finished yet. After documenting the activities for Day 2 and meeting with the Sponsor you have to put the process map into a tool that can be reviewed by

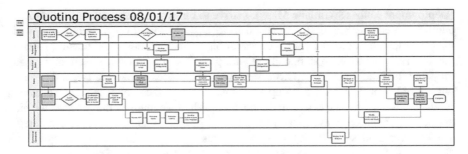

Fig. 18.8   Example swim lane process map

the team first thing on Day 3. You want to use a tool like Visio or Lucidchart[3] to create your process map. Be sure to put a descriptive name and date the chart as shown in Fig. 18.8.[4] You will have several versions of this before the end of Day 3 so dating and recording version numbers is the only way you can tell which is the most recent chart.

Day 3 Root Cause Analysis and Brainstorm Solutions

We begin day three by reviewing the process map created the previous day. Each team member should have a copy of the process map to review and make recommended changes. Once the facilitator captures all of the comments you are ready to move to the Root Cause Analysis above.

When we did the process map we identified areas of waste and posted these on large sheets of paper on the wall. Now we need to take each issue in the process and, using the 5 Whys technique, drill down to the root cause.

Spend some time getting to the root cause. You want to use your 5 Whys for 2–3 h to be sure you get all the root causes. You can have one issue that maps to many root causes or many issues mapping to the same root cause. I did a project a few years ago for our nurse triage organization. We had eight issues that mapped to the same root cause. If we did not fix that one root cause we would not fix any of the eight issues. You may end up with something that looks like Fig. 18.9.[5]

Or perhaps you could end up with a fishbone with only two bones but lots of issues. Either way you need to spend the time needed to get all of your issues to root cause.

---

[3]http://bit.ly/2g0Q1wh.

[4]This figure is a screen capture so the resolution is not very high. All you need to focus on is the information in the heading of the figure.

[5]Cause and effect diagrams, or fishbone diagrams, were discussed earlier in this book. See How to Create Cause and Effect Diagrams.

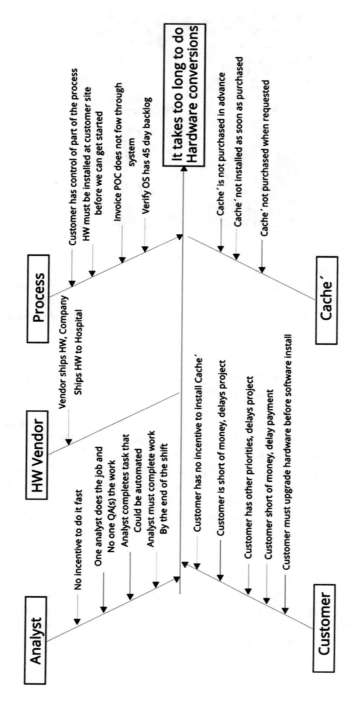

Fig. 18.9 Sample fishbone diagram

At this point, you have probably identified some "just do" items. Typically, "just do" items tend to be things you can stop doing immediately if not sooner. I had one team that was building their process map and at one point the manager stood up and told the team to stop doing that. It was a step that was not necessary due to an improvement put into the system several months earlier (no one ever told them to stop!).

Brainstorming

Now you are ready to start brainstorming solutions to your issues. You have a list of root causes shown on your fishbone diagram. Copy these to a spreadsheet and make copies for every person on the team. There are numerous brainstorming techniques but there are two that I use over and over. The first is just round-robin brainstorming. I go around the room and ask each person to give me an idea. Then I ask the next person. We go around the room until the ideas are exhausted. The other technique I like to use is the Post-It™ note technique. I tell everyone. "You have a list of root causes in front of you. I want you to write five improvements for each root cause. Put one improvement on a Post-It™ note with a Sharpie and put it on the wall." When finished we often have a hundred or more Post-It™ notes on the wall, looking something like Fig. 18.10.

Affinity Analysis

Now we are ready to organize the ideas into categories using a technique called affinity analysis. I tell my team, "I want you to organize the Post-It™ notes into categories and I want you to do it without talking." The reason for not talking is that talking and speech use a different part of the brain to process than the part used for pattern recognition. The team stands in front of the wall of notes reading, thinking, and organizing. It may take an hour or more to get the cards organized into some fashion. The results could look like either example in Fig. 18.11.

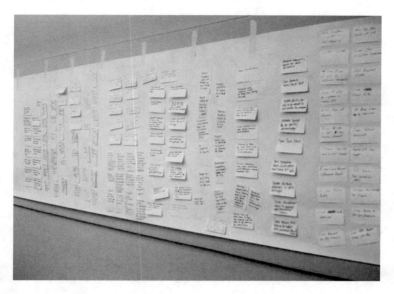

Fig. 18.10   Improvement ideas

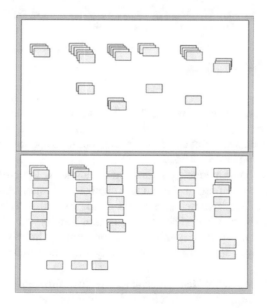

Fig. 18.11   Completed affinity analysis

Now you as the facilitator lead the team in choosing a name for each category. You ask the team to name each category. Let them tell you the category name, then you put the name on a different color Post-It™ and paste it above each category. See Fig. 18.12.

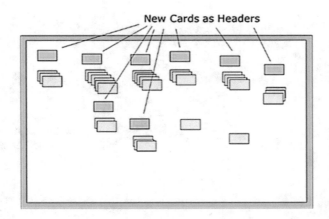

Fig. 18.12 Category names

		Scoring			
		Benefit	Effort	Cost	
		L M H	L M H	L M H	
Category	Improvement Idea	1 3 9	9 3 1	9 3 1	Total
Systems	Flip the Architecture	9	1	1	9
Process	Remove approvals	9	9	9	729

Fig. 18.13 Benefit/effort/cost matrix

As the facilitator, you need to get all of the categories and ideas recorded. You may ask for help from your team or send them on a break and copy all of the ideas to an excel spreadsheet. The point is, when the team comes back you want them to have a list of all of the improvement ideas.

With that list in hand, you tell your team they are going to vote on the ideas that they feel are the most important. I use a technique called multi-voting for this. You take the number of improvement ideas and divide by three. You give each team member that number of votes. Then tell them they can use all of their votes on a single item or use one vote for multiple items or anything in between. The point is you give them only a few votes and the really important ideas start to come to the top.

If you still have too many ideas you can reduce them further using a benefit/effort/cost matrix. This matrix takes each idea and maps it for the benefit to the organization, the amount of effort needed to implement, and any item that must be purchased. For benefit, I use a score of 1, 3, and 9 for low, medium, and high. For negative items such as effort or cost, I use a score of 9, 3, 1 for low, medium, and high. Then I just multiply the three numbers together. That way an idea that is high benefit, low effort, and low cost will score highest. Figure 18.13 is an example of how I set this up in Excel.

After completing the benefit/effort/cost matrix you have a group of solutions that are relatively quick to implement (phase 1) and other solutions that will take longer to implement (phase 2).

Now you want to work with your team to put together a quick presentation for the project sponsor who will visit the team at the end of the day. You want a 15-min or less presentation and you want members of the team to deliver parts of the presentation. Part of the presentation will be to review the improvement ideas with the sponsor to ensure they can be implemented. During one session, I had the team recommend that the company change the bonus structure for vice presidents. It was definitely something they needed to do long term but not something they could do in the middle of the year as it would affect everyone's bonus.

Day 4 Build the New Process

Now you are ready to start building your new process. I usually start by reviewing the Lean techniques we talked about earlier in the week so the team can be sure to implement them when building the process. Then we start mapping the new process. As the facilitator, I usually write the Post-It™ notes for this part of the Kaizen. I make sure each team member checks off the improvements as we put them into the process. As we identify actions to be completed we document those on an action item list with the owner and estimated completion date.

As we build the new process we make an outline of training scenarios that must be developed. By the time we finish mapping the new process, we will have a long list of action items.

We now need to determine the additional requirements needed to run a pilot. Usually you run a pilot for a single customer or for a small portion of the total workload. You do this to ensure you find any unintended consequences before you go into full production.

At the end of Day 4, I like to do one more thing. I complete an FMEA by asking the team, "What could go wrong during the rollout of this solution?" If you do this right, you will have several new additions to your action item list as the group thinks about the new process operating in the organization.

Day 5 Launch

To start Day 5 I ask the question, "what else do we need to do to launch the pilot?" We will focus on these issues first. Then we will review the action items to determine if there are other items already documented that we need to complete, prior to the pilot.

For some processes, you may be able to start the pilot right away. For other processes, you need to complete some of your action items first. If your pilot requires additional action items be complete, focus on getting estimated completion dates for these in the next week or two.

Process Step	Measurement	Spec Limits	Response
	Turn around time for the Front End Process	8 hours	Contact management
Describe the process	List measurement that monitors this step	List the limit at which action is taken	Describe the actions to be taken

Fig. 18.14 Sample process control plan

Your next step is to identify the company policies and procedures that need to be updated and assign these as action items. Then review the metrics used for the old process and determine if new metrics should be added to keep the gains in the new process. I document this in a process control plan. This plan explains to the process owner how to manage the new process by explaining:

- What measurements should be taken?
- Where in the process the measurements should be taken?
- What are the triggers that indicate an action is required? and.
- What action should be taken?

I use Excel for this activity as Fig. 18.14 shows.

Now the team is ready to develop a presentation for the executive leadership team to describe the activities for the entire Kaizen Event. Once again, I let the team members build the presentation and present it to their management, making sure they include a Lessons Learned slide at the end. Once that is complete, be sure to get agreement from the team to meet weekly (or more if needed) until you have this new process in production.

After the presentation, there is one more thing I want the team to do. I pass out an evaluation form to gather their feedback on the Kaizen Event, the materials used, and the facilitator. Once that is complete, the team is ready to fly home or just leave for the weekend, but as the facilitator, you have more to do. Schedule follow up meetings to address all action items to completion and schedule meetings with the executive team to keep them appraised.

Once the new and improved process goes into production it is time to celebrate. Have the team meet for a fun event. Pass out tee shirts or prizes so that each person has something to remember the event by.

Feedback

Just as with everything else, Kaizen Events should also be continuously improved. I use the form shown in Fig. 18.15 to get feedback from all of the participants in the Kaizen Event. I use the feedback to help myself do better in the future, and I share my findings with others who are organizing Kaizen Events.

Kaizen Event Evaluation Form

Date: Kaizen Name: Name:	Black Belt: Project Sponsors:

1. What was your overall impression of the event?

2. Describe the best or most useful part of the event.

3. What would you change about the event to make it more useful?

4. Would you like to participate in another event, yes or no, and tell why?

5. Did the event accomplish all that it could, or was there more that could have been done?

6. How were you treated? Could you give your opinions freely?

	Poor	Great
7. Please rate the instructor:	1 2 3 4 5 6 7 8 9 10	
8. Please rate the team leader:	1 2 3 4 5 6 7 8 9 10	
9. Quality of training material:	1 2 3 4 5 6 7 8 9 10	
10. Usefulness to the University:	1 2 3 4 5 6 7 8 9 10	

11. Additional comments please

Fig. 18.15 Kaizen event evaluation form

18.4   Sustain

After the process has been in production for 3–6 months, there is one more thing you need to do, validate the proposed benefits. Schedule a meeting with the executive team, finance team, and project team. Get finance to review the metrics and financial gains to ensure we keep the gains.

Now, as the facilitator, you are ready for your next project, and your team may be ready for another project too. Each one has improved skills and improved understanding of the organization, its customers, and its business. What can they fix now?

A3 Thinking

19

This chapter will introduce a tool and process to greatly enhance the adoption, practice, and benefits from Lean. Few elements of Lean are as powerful as the A3 for leading and delivering Lean to build and reinforce principles, behaviors, and skills, however many organizations find effective usage of A3 an elusive goal. This chapter will help you achieve this goal.

19.1   What Is the A3 and A3 Thinking?

Most simplistically the A3 is the size of a sheet of paper exactly double the size of the A4 page.[1] The A3 size was created in a time in history when facsimile (fax) machines were the standard business communication technology and the A3 sheet of paper was the largest paper sheet able to be shared across sites via fax machine. The actual size is not important, the process and approach is. As a template, the A3 provides a tool for using the PDCA scientific method described earlier in this book (see PDCA). One of W. Edwards Deming's most popular statements perfectly sets the scene as to why the A3 is such a potent element of Lean Thinking, "If you can't explain it simply you don't understand it well enough." With only limited real estate available on the page, to explain things, the A3 and A3 Thinking support developing a culture of continuous improvement underpinned by deep understanding. Figure 19.1 illustrates a basic A3.

Figure 19.1 is but one possible layout and uses for an A3. The actual layout selected is far less important than the thinking applied. A3 Thinking is about grasping the actual situation by first-hand observation and knowledge to link problems to the process causes driving them.

By Kevin Ryan
    Pyzdek Institute Certified Lean Six Sigma Master Black Belt

---

[1]The A3 size is roughly $11'' \times 17''$, double the standard A4 8.5" $\times$ 11" letter sized page.

T. Pyzdek, *The Lean Healthcare Handbook*, Management for Professionals,
https://doi.org/10.1007/978-3-030-69901-7_19

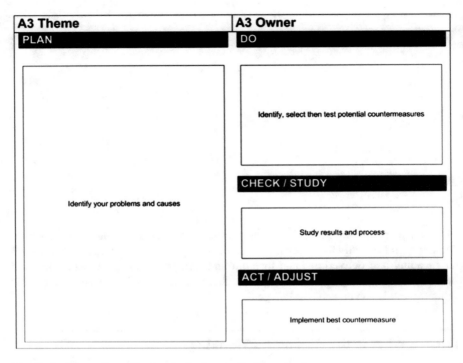

Fig. 19.1   A3 template with plan-do-check act scientific method

Table 19.1   Types of A3s

A3 Type	Description of use
Problem solving	Plan-Do-Check-Act problem solving typically executed using breakdown called Practical Problem Solving
Strategy deployment	Hoshin Kanri, Policy Deployment or Hoshin strategy management applies a cascading set of A3 templates and process, often summarized by a unique X-Matrix A3
Project status	Part of visual management aimed at surfacing problems or opportunities in plans, programs, projects, etc.
Business proposal	Proposes an investment or course of action for others to decide such as budget approval
Information sharing	Focused documents aimed at sharing information or standards without a scientific method component

Types of A3

A3s are not the exclusive domain of continuous improvement. A3s are most commonly used for the five general applications shown in Table 19.1. Note that all five types are related to PDCA in whole or in part.[2]

This chapter is focused on problem solving. However, a Lean strategy team or group should at least evaluate where and how A3 Thinking may also fit in strategy, being mindful that while A3 is very flexible, it should not be used everywhere or for everything.

Properties of Good A3s

Good A3s typically come from good managers. This is easy to understand when you connect the purpose and content of A3s to the work of managers, for example,

- Deep knowledge of the work
- Capability for problem solving (kaizen)
- Plan and execute improvement, and
- Communicate, present, collaborate, and influence

The most effective managers have these capabilities and tend to excel at A3s. For managers trying to become more effective the A3 provides a tremendously effective development tool and process for coaching and developing their subordinates.

Figure 19.2 illustrates some of the factors which explain why the A3 is held in such high regard and is so widely used in Lean.

While not a complete list of benefits, consider the following reasons for using A3 Thinking in a Lean program.

Standardized Problem Solving

The A3 is a simple visual tool that allows a manager or coach to quickly size up how well the process owner is using the scientific method to improve their process. Like 5S, the A3 provides a flexible roadmap that reinforces the sequential nature of problem solving and process improvement. The limited real estate on an A3 sheet forces the user to communicate simply and clearly using visual tools.

Develop Scientific Method

Practical Problem Solving sequenced in the PDCA cycle along with a rough spatial balance of time and/or effort for each step supports having A3 owners rigorously practice effective problem solving. Coaching people to solve real problems with A3 develops leadership skills and is a key benefit of A3.

---

[2]Some of the uses described in Table 19.1 are for upper management and are not covered in this book. The A3 Types of most interest for Continuous Improvement as discussed in this book are problem solving and project status.

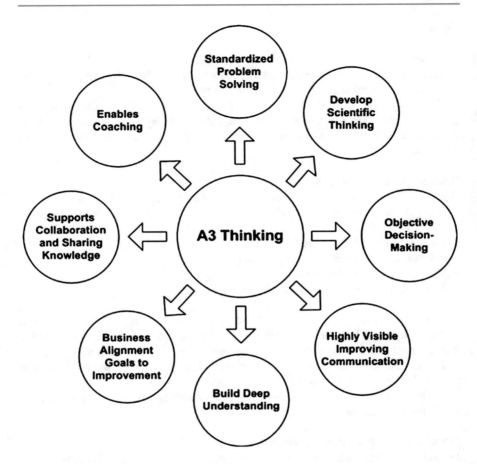

Fig. 19.2 Many facetted features of A3 thinking

Objective Decision-Making

The A3 combined with Lean or Lean Six Sigma tools and techniques, supported by an experienced coach, and with ongoing collaboration and scrutiny by process participants strongly encourages problem solving based on objective information collected at the Gemba. This data-driven approach avoids many of the biases inherent in human nature and greatly improves decision-making.

Visual Communication

The A3 is a Swiss army knife of value. They are easy to carry about, straightforward for two or more people to engage in discussions of, add to, revise, agree on, present, and share. The great advantage of the A3 is its brevity, but it is hard work to achieve, and the quote by Blaise Pascal comes to mind "I would have written a shorter letter, but I did not have the time."

Deep Understanding of Problems
Following the scientific method, employing visual techniques built with knowledge and facts collected from the Gemba and driven from a limitation of real estate, an A3 author is forced to demonstrate clear and deep understanding of a problem. Other elements of the Lean enterprise such as daily management will benefit tremendously from this deep dive into how processes really work.

Alignment Between Key Process Indicators (KPIs) and Projects
The sequence of problem solving provided by A3 thinking provides a mechanism to clearly establish a cause and effect linkage between a problem and its relative importance to organizational goals and metrics. The downstream benefit of this is in collaboration and consensus building through two mechanisms; first, as the executive team has set priorities for the organization, improvements that align to these goals are implicitly endorsed and sponsored by senior management. Second, other managers, work areas, and teams more readily see the connection to business goals and targets which encourages participation and agreement.

Collaboration
The A3 is a compelling and accessible communication enabler. Contrast a good A3 with a conventional text-heavy multi-page report filled with unsubstantiated assertions and opinions. The A3 is a clear winner over conventional approaches in its ability to engage and enlist the support of stakeholders important in transforming the design of work.

Coaching
Coaching is a challenge for many and this is where the humble and unassuming A3 really shines. Not only will an A3 allow a coach to quickly size up the effectiveness and quality of the PDCA cycle in real time, but within moments the coach will be able to assess how the A3 owner is approaching problem solving, the strengths and weaknesses of their thinking process, evidence of having been (or not been) to the Gemba and having gained deep understanding is what makes the A3 so valuable to the expert or novice coach. A3 thinking process combined with a coach produces incremental improvement and, sometimes, breakthrough improvement. At the very least A3 produces better results in terms of practical, implementable countermeasures that address the actual root-cause.

19.2   A3 Content and the A3 Thinking Process

It is common to see the A3 of the 7 or 8-step PDCA variety referred to as Practical Problem Solving (PPS), and for good reason. The PPS sequence of PDCA translates the Plan-Do-Check-Act cycle into more readily understandable chunks.

Figure 19.3 illustrates the 7-step PPS in the A3 layout. This approach devotes 40–60% of improvement time to the Plan stage, gaining deep understanding before

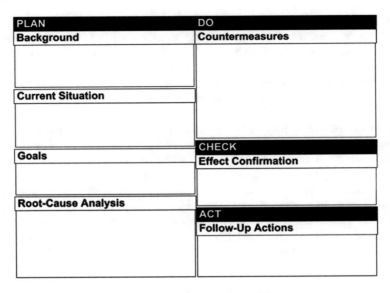

Fig. 19.3 Example of an A3 with 7-step practical problem solving

making changes. While individuals and the organization's culture may favor jumping to action immediately, the A3 template combined with the reasoning and guidance of a coach will promote spending sufficient time on the left side of the A3. This effort will pay dividends in the long run.

Figure 19.3 is a good visual representation of how the A3 can be thought of as simply a tool or a template for standardizing problem solving. This usage of A3 will be covered in more detail later. Lean Thinking is incorporated in that the A3s left side contains the problem solving and coaching steps necessary to gain the deep understanding of how things currently are and how we would like them to be. The A3's right side shows the actions and cooperative work needed to get where we would like to be. This standardized sequence is a real gem, a point-of-use visual system which through a simple design provides a Lean deployment with numerous benefits provided by few other Lean tools.

Figure 19.3 is a typical layout for an A3, especially in a fledgling Lean program where both the A3 author and the A3 coach may be new to the PDCA cycle of problem solving. The flow and proportion of space devoted to each PDCA topic help reinforce what is done and the relative time spent on each topic over the cycle.

Creating an A3

Here are the steps for creating an A3 using PPS.

1. **Document Identification**—Identifying the A3 including title or topic, A3 author/ owner, sponsor, team members, and document version and/or revision date.
2. **Problem Background** is the first of four steps of the Plan phase. It describes the problem to be solved. Avoid setting goals or solutions, and avoid allocating blame. Describe how the effort to address the problem aligns with organizational goals.
3. **Current Conditions** contains knowledge and facts gathered from the Gemba of the current process or situation. Often illustrated with visuals such as process or value stream maps, diagrams, charts or tables of metrics, even photos.
4. **Target Condition** provides either a visual of the desired state or a table or summary of measurable targets to be used to determine if the improvement has been successful. The target must be objectively measurable and it will serve as the basis of comparison between current state and future state.
5. **Root-Cause Analysis** shows tools and techniques used to answer the question "why is there a gap between the current state and the future state?" Analysis applies a range of visual and statistical approaches described in this book such as Cause and Effect (fishbone) diagram, Check sheets, Pareto analysis, 5-Whys, Scatter plots, etc. Insights from this step should lead to action in the next step.
6. **Develop Countermeasures** is moving to the Do part of PDCA cycle. It involves looking at potential countermeasures and then narrowing these down to the most practical and effective based on the root-cause or causes identified in step 5. When root-cause analysis has been effective this is often obvious, but at times techniques such as brainstorming and Affinity analysis are needed. **Implementation Plan** is also part of the Do phase of the PDCA cycle. The focus here is on developing an action plan consisting of the countermeasures for each root cause, and a plan describing who, when, and where each countermeasure will be delivered. You may utilize traditional project management, Just-Do-it, or initiate kaizen events. The key is to see the countermeasures through in a timely manner.
7. **Effect Confirmation** is the Check phase of the PDCA cycle which looks at results and the problem solving process itself. This step verifies the results of actions taken. It compares actual results to intended results. This step also involves reflection as to whether the outcome was due to actions taken, or just good luck.
8. **Follow-Up Actions.** The Act phase of the PDCA cycle has three components: first, planning and implementing any further actions to close any gaps that remain. Second, to standardize the improvement so that gains are maintained. The third is sharing insight and knowledge of success to other parts of the organization who can benefit from the learning gained on the journey.

Figure 19.4 illustrates the conceptual layout and flow of this 8-step PPS adaption of Plan-Do-Check Act cycle.

The A3 thinking systematic approach to problem solving is summarized in Fig. 19.5.

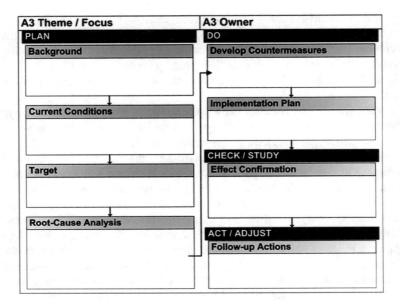

Fig. 19.4   A3 using 8-step practical problem solving

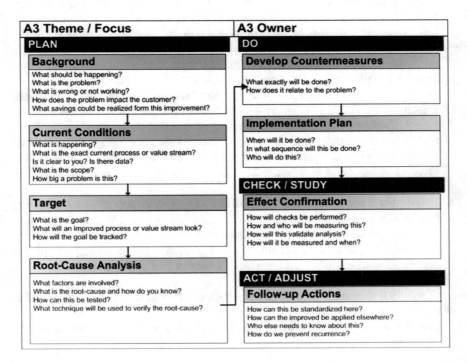

Fig. 19.5   A3 thinking across the A3 tool

Example

Let us look at the 8 steps used to create the A3 shown in Fig. 19.6 in detail.

Document Identification

The A3 theme or title serves as an introduction to the A3 content as a brief and objective statement the problem A3 addresses. The theme should be effective at helping your audience quickly understand the essence. Like the problem background, the theme should be problem focused and avoid solutions or judgment. For the example shown in Fig. 19.6 this is "Reducing Clinic Admission Delays." At least one other important piece of information often found in the document header is the A3 project sponsor and also the A3 owner, which will typically be the process owner but may also be a project leader. (This information is shown in the status bar at the very bottom left of Fig. 19.6).

Problem Background

The first step of the Plan phase is aimed at establishing the problem as substantive enough to necessitate more than a Just-Do-It action, and demonstrating the importance through the alignment of the problem with goals of the organization. This is discussed in the section of the book entitled True North Projects.

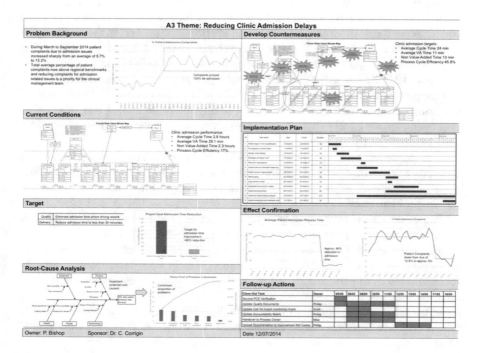

Fig. 19.6 Example of an A3

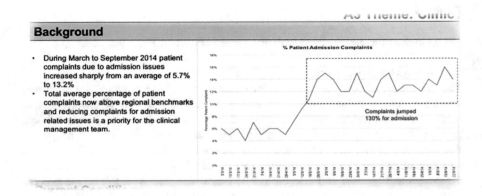

Fig. 19.7 The problem background step example

The problem background is best presented as a combination of key points or concise problem statement and charted time series data describing the context of why it is a problem now and its significance in the mix of problems forming the gap in organizational goals. Time series data is excellent in providing background to a problem, providing both scale and trend as well as information about special causes of variation. Other presentations of data in highly visual formats help communicate the gap and the trend, for example, the problem is substantial and getting worse. Of course, other forms of visuals may be useful in setting the context of the problem, for example, column charts, pie charts or Pareto charts are useful supporting information to time series to help communicate a problem relative to targets and trends.

Figure 19.7 illustrates the description of the problem using a statement describing and supporting a time series chart. It also links the problem to the clinic's high-level performance metric and target. In terms of selling the problem in a mix of possible improvements we clearly show how it is related to organizational KPIsand provides clear evidence of the problem.

It is important to avoid including a solution in the problem background. For example, a problem statement recommending or suggesting cost reduction describes a symptom rather than the problem; cost is a symptom of the underlying problem, not the problem itself.

The goal of making the problem statement clear is to show that the problem is worth solving and to provide senior management with sufficient information to select improvement priorities effectively. As with problem statements in project charters, well-crafted problem statements in A3s help keep improvement activity focused through to completion, and help sustain support for the improvement long after the kick-off.

While this first step appears simple enough, being able to succinctly state why is this a problem answers "why do we need to work on this and why now?" Quantifying the problem is not always easy to do. However, doing so sells the importance of the problem.

Current Conditions

The second Plan phase step in the 8-step PPS approach (Fig. 19.4) is moving from how the problem affects organizational goals to getting specific about what is currently less than ideal. Visual descriptions of the current state are useful here and options include as-is value stream or process maps, Spaghetti diagrams, tables of metrics such as cycle time, queue/wait times, rework rate, etc. to simplify the communication of the extent of the problem in the context of the process.

Figure 19.8 captures, for our example A3, a great deal of information about the problem in a value stream map. However, having complete value stream maps is the exception rather than the norm. Defining the current condition is most often achieved using metrics, a process map or process illustrations. Depending on the problem being solved, other diagram types, charts, photos, tables, and few bullet points may also be helpful ways to demonstrate the current state of the problem.

For the A3 novice, a rule of thumb for deciding what information to put here versus into the problem background section of the A3 is to include in the background only that information required to make the A3 compelling. The rest of the knowledge of the problem can be put in the current condition section to provide the deep understanding of the problem situation.

The aim of this step is to establish what is *not* ideal about the current situation. I. e., to show the extent of the problem with facts and ensure it represents how work is really done.

Understanding the current state will come from going to the Gemba, following the flow of work, engaging process participants and supervisors and/or managers, recording observations, and mapping or notations of the sequence of the real work. While at the Gemba, take out your smartphone, take a picture, record video, etc. Avoid discussing solutions. This is not the place for that.

It is acceptable to merge current condition section information with target section information, especially when summary data is used extensively in defining the current condition.

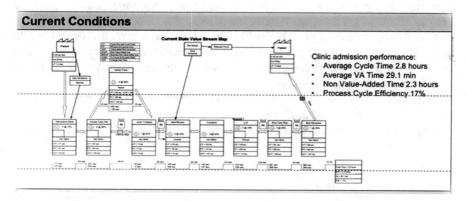

Fig. 19.8 Current condition example

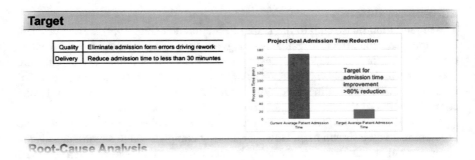

Fig. 19.9 Target condition example

Target Condition (Future State)

The third step of the Plan phase is to set a clear measurable goal as a basis for comparison for the improvements success. The metric must be cost effective and practical to measure. The purpose of the target is to provide an unambiguous means by which you know if the problem has been solved. Therefore it must be specific to the problem being solved. Commonly used metrics for targets include defect/error/ mistake rate, rework rate, lead time, or cycle times. Metric selection will depend on the nature of the problem, the maturity of process measurement and analysis, and experience with more advanced Lean methods such as Value Streams.

The target condition is an element of problem solving best presented using summary information in the form of charts and tables. Avoid the trap of describing solutions or symptoms using blocks of text. It is common to merge the goal or target condition with the previous step current conditions, but this is not necessary.[3]

The A3 element shown in Fig. 19.9 includes the key organizational goal to show the alignment of the A3 to business-level goals. This also helps ensure that targets in the future state value stream map are connected to the True North goal. Again, the arrangement is not as important as the thinking and rigor and an A3 can go from current condition to root cause to target, or from target to root cause. Do whatever is needed to clearly describe the current state, the desired future state, and the path you need to follow to get from one state to the other.

Concise clear visual content in the form of before-and-after charts or tables with as-is against to-be metric targets is the language of management and will cut through the lack of specific process and problem knowledge more effectively. If you can add cost information, so much the better.

When using metrics to define a target state, ideally two to three metrics is best, and not more than five is highly recommended. If the problem was well described and the current condition aptly defined then the A3 owner should not need to use a

---

[3]Demonstrating the flexibility of the A3, specifics of the target state may also be presented in the Develop Countermeasures step shown below.

Table 19.2 Root-cause analysis tools and techniques

Direct observation	Capture know-how	Collect & analyze data
Go See	Talk to team members	Check sheet
Ask Why	5 Whys	Pareto analysis
Notes and drawings	Fishbone (C&E) diagram	Time value map
Basic process diagram	Problem analysis tree	Scatterplot
Value stream map	Brainstorming	X chart
Photo or video	Affinity diagram	

large number of success metrics. Besides, many performance metrics are correlated with one another, and using highly correlated metrics is redundant.

When target setting is difficult it is wise to review the problem background, and think ahead to when you will need to confirm the new level of performance. The target itself may be a single end point figure, or multiple improvement milestones with incremental points of measurement. Ensure the target is measurable and not merely a statement of what will be done.[4] A final element of an effective target is that it sets a challenging stretch goal that may or may not be realized rather than a less ambitious goal that would be easy to achieve. It is better to try to climb to the mountain top and fail than to be content to sit comfortably in camp at the base of the mountain. Encouraging teams to pursue stretch goals requires a leadership attitude that tolerates failure and inspires the team to undertake another PDCA cycle if the target is not achieved on the first attempt.

Root-Cause Analysis

The fourth and last step in Practical Problem Solving's Plan phase is moving from a good understanding of the business *problem* to narrowing down all potential *causes* to the most likely root-cause or root-causes. It is testing assumptions to confirm a hypothesis using a range of simple to complex analytical tools and techniques. It is important to rigorously apply the scientific method to understand the causes before going from the Plan phase to the Develop Countermeasures phase.

Root-cause analysis is where the A3 owner must possess a range of skills including visual and statistical analysis, communication and facilitation, and Lean Thinking concepts. Root cause analysis approaches range from direct observation to engaging process operators and experts to data collection and analysis (see Table 19.2). Direct observation includes Go See, Ask Why, and basic drawing[5] and note taking. Capture know-how tools include talking to team members who perform the process work and capturing, sorting, and ranking knowledge from the Gemba. Hard to observe processes such as the movement of patients or equipment may require more data intensive techniques.

---

[4]For example, say "Average emergency department time per patient will be less than 30 min," not "We will simplify the registration form used by the emergency department."

[5]Personally, I find drawing a stick-man challenging so I try to find someone with drawing skills to accompany me when I go to the workplace.

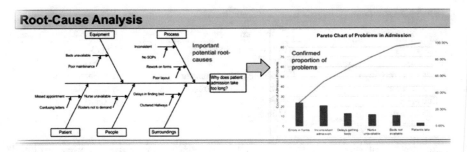

Fig. 19.10   Root-cause analysis A3 example

It is common that root-cause analysis tools are applied in a sequence so broad ideas of the root-cause can be distilled into the most likely causes. For example, the sequence might progress from a Fishbone diagram to a data collection plan to a check sheet, and finally to a Pareto analysis. Figure 19.10 illustrates an example where a Fishbone diagram leads to data collection and a Pareto analysis to separate to most significant causes of admissions problems.

Effective root-cause analysis ensures that cause and effect is established. Do not settle for opinions or superficial work that misidentifies a symptom of the problem as a cause. High costs for repeated x-rays are a symptom of some other problem, not a cause. Another common failure in root-cause analysis is confusing cause with effect. For example, data show that people who exercise more are healthier and most people assume that this means that exercise causes better health. Maybe so, maybe not. Could it instead mean that sick people exercise less because they are sick? Who feels like jogging when they have arthritis? Questions of cause and effect are often challenging and they can only be explored by thinking deeply about the problem and its causes.

Good root-cause analysis will pay off in countermeasures that close performance gaps. When the true root-cause is identified, countermeasures are often very simple to identify so spending adequate time for root-cause analysis has a large payoff for both the A3 owner and the organization.

Develop Countermeasures
Having determined the root-cause or root-causes, the A3 next moves to identifying and selecting countermeasures. Developing countermeasures is a significant shift in focus as we move from Plan to Do. It involves actually making a change by conducting an experiment. The experiment will be based on the deep understanding gained in previous steps.

Again, the A3 format provides cues as to how much time is spent in the countermeasures phase. The space allocated for this task on the A3 diagram provides a clue as to the complexity of countermeasure development. When the Plan phase has been effective, countermeasures tend to be obvious and emerge logically, especially early in a Lean deployment. However, as improvement programs mature

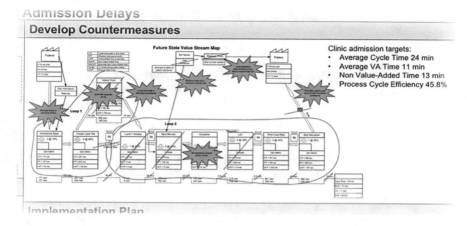

Fig. 19.11   Countermeasures developed with a future state Value Stream map

Table 19.3   Broad categories of countermeasures for the Lean enterprise

Stabilize	Create flow	Inventive
5S	Set-up reduction	Brainstorming
Visual management	Work cells	Affinity Diagramming
Standard work	Co-location	Impact-Effort Matrix
Error proofing	Cross-skilling	PACE Matrix
	Kanban and Pull systems	SCAMPER
	Demand leveling	ASIT/TRIZ

and low hanging fruit is picked, solving more challenging problems requires ongoing skill development.

Figure 19.11 uses Kaizen Burst symbols (see Kaizen and Continuous Improvement) and project loops (see Selecting Subprojects) on a value stream map to show where countermeasures are needed to address problems. Countermeasures may involve basic process stability and standardization, actions to improve flow, or coming up with novel solutions to specific technical problems with the processes in the value stream. Table 19.3 summarizes the broad categories of countermeasures commonly used for A3.

Where countermeasures are not obvious, various approaches to identifying and prioritizing countermeasures may be helpful. Tools such as Failure Mode and Effects Analysis (FMEA) will help you identify and prioritize countermeasures. Preference should be given to methods that are simple, accessible, and easy to visualize on the A3. Like root-cause analysis, developing countermeasures often uses a sequential approach. For example,

1. Brainstorm countermeasure ideas
2. Sort the brainstorming ideas into categories
3. Prioritize options

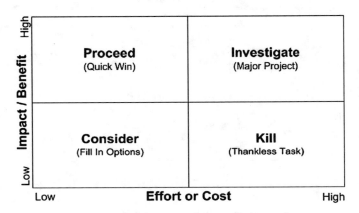

Fig. 19.12   Cost/benefit matrix

Root-Cause	Countermeasure	Effectiveness	Specific Actions	Feasibility
		☐ Low ☐ Medium ☐ High		☐ Low ☐ Medium ☐ High
		☐ Low ☐ Medium ☐ High		☐ Low ☐ Medium ☐ High
		☐ Low ☐ Medium ☐ High		☐ Low ☐ Medium ☐ High
		☐ Low ☐ Medium ☐ High		☐ Low ☐ Medium ☐ High

Fig. 19.13   Example countermeasure table

4. List options in order of priority
5. Perform cost/benefit analysis to help choose the best option(s). See Fig. 19.12

Regardless of how obvious the countermeasure identification is, the A3 owner is advised to work through and visualize a simple evaluation. The example shown in Fig. 19.13 serves many purposes. It is a very straightforward technique that summarizes multiple tools such as brainstorming, affinity diagramming, and prioritization matrices into a single table while maintaining the linkage between root-cause and countermeasure. Apart from being a simple and powerful aid to decision-making, such organization of thinking makes communication far easier, which in turn makes consensus building much simpler.

Implementation Plan

Part two of the Do phase (or step 6 of PPS) is implementation. This is a switch from investigation to the management of actions. Here the A3 owner is translating selected countermeasures into a specific action plan of the what, whom, where, and when. If improvement activities cross-functional boundaries in an organization, the A3 serves as a communication tool that is useful for building consensus. The A3 owner can use the A3 to communicate to all functional area managers the linkage from the top-level metrics to the improvement activities in their areas. Even better, when you see that improvement activities are likely to involve others who are not part of the A3 team, bring people from these areas into the planning process. Once all implementation activities and responsible parties are identified, the project management activities described in the chapter on Project Management should be used to create a sub-project for implementing improvements. Project Schedule Charts (Gantt Charts) developed as part of the project management effort can be shown on the A3 to graphically summarize improvement activities, responsibilities, and the timeline. See Fig. 19.14.

Effect Confirmation

Effect confirmation asks a simple question, how do we know we have hit our target condition? This step sees the A3 owner move into the Check phase and focus moves to measuring whether the countermeasures achieved what was intended. We are testing whether the actions closed the gap to the target determined in the Plan phase. Additionally, there is reflection on the problem solving process itself which improves the learning cycle of PDCA. In the Toyota Production System this is termed Hansei and it forms an important pillar within Toyota's system. The purpose of this self-reflection is to recognize mistakes and take appropriate action to avoid re-occurrence.

ID	Task Name	Start	Finish	Duration
1	Patient Sign-in Form simplification	6/10/2014	8/10/2014	3d
2	Re-sequence consent steps	7/10/2014	7/10/2014	1d
3	Design cross-training	8/10/2014	10/10/2014	3d
4	Redesign admission form	9/10/2014	13/10/2014	3d
5	Pilot form improvement	14/10/2014	14/10/2014	1d
6	Kaizen event for admission balancing	13/10/2014	17/10/2014	5d
7	Kaizen account prep process	16/10/2014	20/10/2014	3d
8	Pilot leveling	20/10/2014	22/10/2014	3d
9	Improvement review	20/10/2014	21/10/2014	1d
10	Implement hour-by-hour review	22/10/2014	27/10/2014	4d
11	Implement bed kanban	20/10/2014	29/10/2014	8d
12	Implement cross-training program	13/10/2014	10/11/2014	21d
13	Update procedures and standard work	3/11/2014	5/11/2014	3d

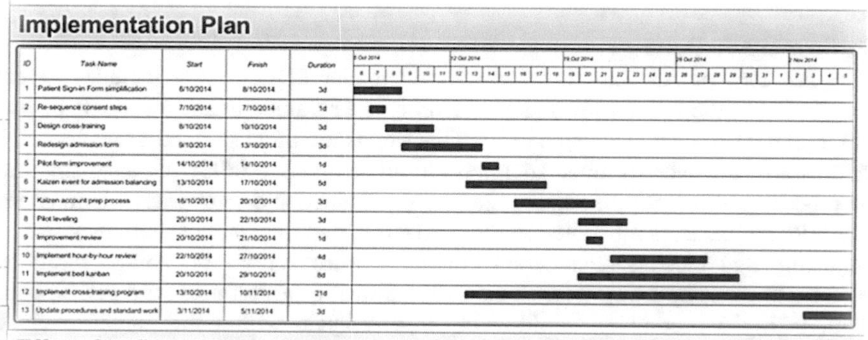

Fig. 19.14 A3 implementation plan

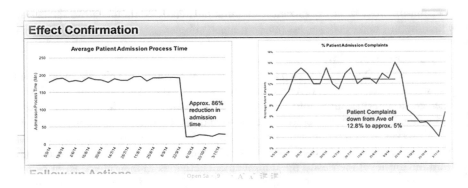

Fig. 19.15   Example of effect confirmation

If the measurement of these performance indicators was not well defined in the target setting step the A3 owner will need to identify how, where, and who will collect the data. Once the data is collected the A3 owner performs the analysis or adds data to an existing KPI chart as illustrated in Fig. 19.15. This graphical before versus after comparison is powerful evidence of improvement or of the lack of a substantial improvement. Ideally, the improvement will be so dramatic that statistical methods are not needed to confirm that the change is not due to chance. However, the control charts discussed in Chap. 13 can be used if statistical evidence is needed.

It is important for the A3 owner to plan and follow-up on another one or two medium-term checks post improvement to assure that gains have been maintained.

Due to the many challenges of this step, the effect confirmation measurement can and should be considered a child-level activity or sub-plan of the main A3 plan. A good plan for effect confirmation requires a Work Breakdown Structure (WBS) that defines specific actions for measurement, who is responsible, how and where measurement is to be undertaken, and when the measurement is to be taken and completed. Where the organization has well-defined process ownership, measurement of process performance hits fewer problems.

Follow-Up Actions

The last step of A3 Thinking and of the broader PDCA cycle includes several activities for the A3 owner and/or the process or value stream owner. It bears a resemblance to the Sustain step in 5S. This step is too often skipped or inadequately addressed. However, as much attention should be given to follow-up as to any prior step because this is where ongoing gains are sustained and sometimes where targets are fully realized. As illustrated in Fig. 19.16 this step may include activities such as adjusting and closing outstanding countermeasure actions (as things rarely go exactly to plan) updating work standards and quality procedures, and perhaps also undertaking a secondary "child-level" PDCA cycle within the parent-level A3 improvement to close a remaining gap to an improvement target.

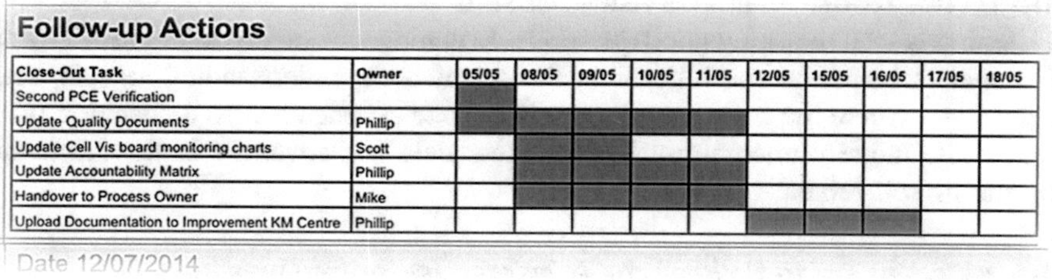

Close-Out Task	Owner	05/05	08/05	09/05	10/05	11/05	12/05	15/05	16/05	17/05	18/05
Second PCE Verification											
Update Quality Documents	Phillip										
Update Cell Vis board monitoring charts	Scott										
Update Accountability Matrix	Phillip										
Handover to Process Owner	Mike										
Upload Documentation to Improvement KM Centre	Phillip										

Follow-up Actions

Date 12/07/2014

Fig. 19.16 A visual follow-up plan

Ongoing follow-up may be substantial if the improvement requires scaling up from a pilot improvement into full scale across related value streams, different teams, or even other physical locations. The A3 owner may be coordinating a significant range of activities at a time when interest is waning for this improvement. Substantial tasks such as hiring and training people in the new process, standardization of the activities through procedures, establishing or revising visual standards, visual layout such as wayfinding,[6] storage locations, inventory layout and procedures, changes to metrics and targets, and visual boards and daily management sequences designed. The A3 plays a key role at this stage in maintaining focus and momentum, and effectively using what limited space remains at the end of the A3 must be carefully planned to clearly signal what remains to be done, who is doing it, when it is due, and whether it is on track for completion.

Ongoing verification of improvement is a common activity planned and undertaken in this follow-up phase especially where measures are infrequent or throughput in the process is low. Like the implementation plan step, follow-up should be well planned, responsibilities clearly defined, dates set, communicated, and monitored.

Another purpose of follow-up is to identify where countermeasures can be leveraged to address similar problems. This depends heavily on collaboration across the organization. Organizational leaders or Lean support teams should consider visual systems, events, or programs where improvements are shared systematically and in a highly accessible way. Consider improvements to the A3 itself. Modified versions of A3 have proven very effective in reinforcing Lean Thinking.

Tips for Coaches

A3 coaches have experienced Lean Senseis who work with multiple A3 owners. Following are six tips the A3 coach should consider as part of their coaching routine.

---

[6]Wayfinding simply means finding ones' way. Hospitals and medical centers are complex environments. The task of catering for the wayfinding needs of the different groups of users (blind, elderly, children, newcomers, foreign visitors, wheelchair users etc.) who visit hospitals needs careful consideration. (While consulting for a vast medical center I once encountered an armed S.W.A.T. team member engaged in an anti-gang exercise. He whispered "How do I get to the emergency department?"—Thomas Pyzdek).

Tip 1: Listen More Than You Ask Questions

Listening is vital in asking good questions. Listening and silence after the A3 owner has spoken helps the coach consider the A3 owner's understanding, development needs, and where the improvement needs to head. Silence is also a coaching tactic that while initially uncomfortable can often yield big advances in the A3 owner becoming self-reliant.

Tip 2: Do Not Try to Have all the Answers, Use Better Questions

As a coach, you do not need to have all the answers, so do not sweat it, feeling you need full technical knowledge of a process or full system of work. Often the A3 owner's understanding of the real problem will far surpass that of the coach, and attempting to provide answers undermines the development of the A3 owner.

Tip 3: Avoid Answering the "What Do You Think?" Question

This question is often tempting to answer, nevertheless, it is a trap that you should try to avoid. Like the previous tip, answering this question cheats the A3 owner of development and the coach is often speculating anyway. The better way to handle this situation is with a clarifying question, for example, "What decision or next step are you trying to take here?"

Wait for the A3 owner's response, be patient and comfortable with silence, if the "coachee" has asked for your answer they will also often wait for you to step back in and answer the question.

Tip 4: Mistakes Are Learning Moments

When missteps are taken through the problem solving process the coach should be tuned in and recognize these as opportunities for powerful coaching moments. But these fortuitous missteps are not the only means of creating coaching moments. With time and practice, the coach can at opportune and safe times deliberately make mistakes to create coaching moments. An example of such a tactic is to allow the A3 owner to go down a path that leads to a known dead end. With good coaching, they will gain insights from the failure.

Tip 5: Make Time for Short but Frequent Coaching Interactions

Letting the A3 owner progress through large sections of A3 Thinking without coaching is worse than providing no coaching at all. Frequent coaching interactions are demanding on time and schedule so planning is required. The cost is justified if the development of people is a priority, as it is in Lean.

Tip 6: Begin with Questions and Selectively Shift to Mentoring When Required

Regardless of the A3 owner's technical competence the A3 coach should attempt to always start in coaching mode and switch to mentoring or instructing when appropriate. Mentoring too often or too willingly may encourage a dependency on the coach, especially since the manager/coach's real work is developing talent in the organization.

Being a good A3 coach does not mean always being in coaching mode. Highly effective A3 coaches balance the needs of the organization, process, customer, and coachee. Organizational priorities such as time or cost, customer, value and risk, and the growth and development for the coachee are continuously weighed by the coach. The coaching approach is dynamic rather than programmed. Just as A3 Thinking for the A3 owner is learnt and improved through practice, so is coaching. Start with simple questions, use a cue card if it helps. Listen, really listen. Give your A3 owner time to think. Explore beyond technical know-how and test understanding of the Lean principles and scientific method.

Appendix

Lean Six Sigma Lexicon

Term	Explanation
Available Time	The time per day that the value stream can operate if there is product to work on. Excludes shutdowns for breaks, lunches, special meetings, etc. Does not include the time when the process continues to operate while part of the workforce is relieved. Does not include setup time, unplanned downtime, etc. We do not want these types of unavailable time to be lost by having them accounted for in available time; instead, we want to keep them highly visible targets for improvement.
Batch Size	The quantity of product worked on and moved at one time.
Buffer Stock	Finished goods produced to protect the customer from fluctuations in the production rate.
Capacity	The maximum output for a given process.
Cycle Time (CT)	A measure of how often a flow object is completed by a process. This is a *rate* measure, not an elapsed-time measure. Cycle time can be calculated for a given process by dividing processing time by the number of people or machines doing the work, e.g., insurance claims processed/customer service agent.
Defect	An occurrence of an event or feature that does not meet customer requirements. Examples: a cracked pane of glass, a stain on a garment, a long wait.
Defect Rate	The number of occurrences of defects divided by the number of opportunities for defects. Examples: long waits per customer served, missing buttons per 100 shirts.
Defective Rate	The proportion of product that does not meet customer requirements.
Finished Goods (FG)	The product that has been completed but not yet shipped.
Flow Object	One piece or unit as defined for the value stream map. Examples: insurance claim, widget, credit card transaction, sales order, etc.
Inventory Turns	A measure of how quickly materials are moving through the value stream. Calculated as the total cost of goods/average inventory on hand.
Lead Time (LT)	The time required for a flow object to move through the entire value stream.

(continued)

Term	Explanation
Number of workers	For each process, the number of full-time-equivalent (FTE) employees. This number can be fractional, e.g., a process with three full-time and one half-time employees would have 3.5 workers.
Pack Size, pack out quantity	The quantity of product required by the customer for shipment or movement.
Process	A place in the value stream where material flows without significant waiting time. Examples: assembly, welding, claims processing, talking to a customer about your product, etc.
Processing Time (PT)	The elapsed time from a flow object entering a process until it leaves the process.
Product Mix	The number of different products, types, or models being produced. Sometimes called product variation.
Production Rate	The rate at which the product completes the value stream.
Raw Material (RM)	Material or work that has not yet been processed.
Rework Rate	The proportion of product that does not meet customer requirements and can be economically made to meet requirements by performing additional work. Rework usually requires a branch in the regular process.
Safety Stock	Product held within the value stream to protect downstream processes from fluctuations in the production rate upstream.
Scrap Rate	The proportion of product that does not meet customer requirements and cannot be made to do so by rework.
Setup Time (SU)	The elapsed time from the production of the last good batch of flow objects until reaching normal production of the next flow object. Includes activities such as tooling changes, adjusting, first article inspection, trial runs, etc.
Shipping Stock	Finished goods at the end of the value stream being accumulated for the next shipment.
Takt Time	The time between completion of flow objects through the value stream is required to meet customer demand. E.g., if the customer demand is 100 items/day and the production process has 480 min/day available time, then Takt Time = 480 min/100 items = 4.8 min per item. Thus, the value stream should complete 1 item every 4.8 min.
Uptime (UT)	The proportion or percent of the time the process actually operates compared to the planned operation time, assuming the product is available for processing.
Value Stream	Value streams are the whole set of activities, resources, and information required to provide a product or service to a customer.
Work-in-process (WIP)	The product that has entered the value stream but is not yet finished.

Index

Printed in the United States
by Baker & Taylor Publisher Services